ART IN SEATTLE'S PUBLIC SPACES

ART IN SEATTLE'S PUBLIC SPACES

FROM SODO
TO SOUTH
LAKE UNION

JAMES RUPP AND
MIGUEL EDWARDS

A MICHAEL J. REPASS BOOK

UNIVERSITY OF WASHINGTON PRESS
SEATTLE

Art in Seattle's Public Spaces was published with the assistance of a grant from the Michael J. Repass Book Fund, which supports publications about the history and culture of Washington, Oregon, and Idaho.

Printed and bound in China
Design by Heidi Smets
Composed in Scala, typeface designed by Martin Majoor
22 21 20 19 18   5 4 3 2 1

UNIVERSITY OF WASHINGTON PRESS
www.washington.edu/uwpress

LIBRARY OF CONGRESS CATALOGING-IN-PUBLICATION DATA

Names: Rupp, James M., author. | Edwards, Miguel, photographer (expression)
Title: Art in Seattle's public spaces : from SoDo to South Lake Union / James M. Rupp and Miguel Edwards.
Description: Seattle : University of Washington Press, 2018. | Update of the 1992 title but focusing only on the downtown core. | Includes bibliographical references and index.
Identifiers: LCCN 2018010435 | ISBN 9780295744087 (pbk. : alk. paper)
Subjects: LCSH : Public art—Washington (State)—Seattle—Guidebooks. | Seattle (Wash.)—Guidebooks.
Classification: LCC N8845.S43 R872 2018 | DDC 700.9797/772—dc23
LC record available at https://lccn.loc.gov/2018010435

Frontispiece: 3.4 *Wake* (detail), Richard Serra
Page 6 photograph: 1.10 *Gordon Hirabayashi, American Patriot*, Roger Shimomura (Photo by Spike Mafford)

TO SUSAN AND CORINNA

CONTENTS

OLYMPIC
SCULPTURE
PARK

FOREWORD

PUBLIC ART IS ART THAT exists in or is expressly created for civic space. In a public location, rather than private museum or home, art finds a diverse, shifting, and distracted audience. I like the word *engagement*, as applied to our experience of art in public places, as it is a gentle word that suggests cordial interactions between art and observer. *Webster*'s definition of *engage* is to "occupy or involve (as in someone's interest or attention)" and to *engage in* is "to participate or become involved in." Both terms nicely describe, I think, the first step in an aesthetic experience, whether public or private.

Seattle has a lively history of public art that stretches back to the city's early years. James Rupp captures the ebb and flow of private and public patronage that brought art to city streets and urban spaces as the city grew from frontier town to aerospace industrial hub to high-tech innovation center. James Rupp traces the history and primary players in the accretion of Seattle's public art, while providing a wealth of information and historical detail. This book is intended as a user's guide for exploration of historical and contemporary art in the city and is accompanied by detailed artwork location maps.

Rupp is to be congratulated for taking on the challenge of chronicling and documenting Seattle's eclectic collection of public art. This guide will be of interest to a citizen of the city seeking information about a work of art they pass by daily or for those curious about works in other neighborhoods. A tourist or casual visitor to Seattle might find reasons for side trips based on the images and maps included here. Historians will appreciate the detail and behind-the-scenes stories. And, of course, artists, collectors, and curators will find this guide to be indispensable in their search for particular works. *Art in Seattle's Public Spaces* will serve as a source of inspiration to anyone interested in the inclusion of works of art into the formal and informal places that constitute our public realm.

Richard Andrews is an independent curator and board president of the Skystone Foundation. He was the director of the University of Washington's Henry Art Gallery from 1987 to 2008.

3.18 *Echo*, Jaume Plensa (Photo by Richard J. Birmingham)

A HISTORICAL OVERVIEW

THIS IS A BOOK ABOUT THE ART that is all around us in downtown Seattle, which stands out among American cities for the abundance of art in its public spaces. No city of comparable size can match the collection on view here. Artworks run the gamut of artistic mediums and styles. Many stand in prominent places; others are somewhat hidden. Many are praised, much is criticized, and a lot goes unnoticed. In some cases they will teach you about local history and culture. You deserve to know what it is, where to find it, who created it and why.

In this guide, *public spaces* includes public and private building lobbies, plazas, parks, and other spaces readily accessible to the public. *Art in public spaces* is not limited to publicly funded creations, works designed to relate to their specific environment, or socially engaged interactive art with a message—all distinctions made in some circles. Thus, the art included within encompasses a vast and varied collection of expressions, including paintings and murals; metal, stone, glass, and ceramic art; and electronic, lighting, and video installations.

Many building developers have included art in or near their buildings. In three cases—the Washington State Convention Center (6.1), the Sheraton Hotel (6.3), and the US Bank Centre building (6.4)—viewers are within easy walking distance of museum-quality art collections of twentieth- and twenty-first-century Pacific Northwest art. Another impressive collection is on display in the Four Seasons Hotel on First Avenue (6.18).

A grand array of art can be seen at the Seattle Art Museum's Olympic Sculpture Park (chapter 3), which provides for free viewing of a large and impressive collection of contemporary art in an unsurpassed setting of expansive views.

Most of the artists represented in the collection of art displayed in Seattle's public places live or have lived in the Pacific Northwest, but a good number of artists outside of the region are represented and many have international reputations. Seattle is known worldwide as a principal center for studio glass art, a status made possible by Dale Chihuly's early efforts, both as a distinguished master of that art form and as a cofounder of the renowned Pilchuck Glass School in Stanwood, Washington. The numbers of glass artists who have achieved wide acclaim are too many to list, but their works in Seattle's downtown public places are included here. An impressive collection can be seen at the US Bank Centre building (6.4).

3.28 *Snoqual/Moon the Transformer*, Roger Fernandes

Seattle also has an unusually large number of fountains in its public places, most of which are abstract designs rather than the formal European-style fountains prevalent elsewhere in the country and in Europe. This is, in part, the result of Seattle's comparative youth. At the time that fountains in older cities, such as New York, Chicago, and Kansas City, were being commissioned by an established wealthy class, Seattle was young and less sophisticated and large fortunes were not as common. By the time Seattle began spending money for public art in the late 1950s, traditional fountain design was passé. At the same time local artists George Tsutakawa and James FitzGerald were available to build their welded bronze fountains, which achieved national recognition for their unique and innovative designs. Downtown Seattle is home to five Tsutakawa fountains, and several others appear throughout the city. Only two of FitzGerald's fountains remain (2.3; 8.26); a third is now a waterless sculpture at the IBM Building (5.25).

Most of what we see today has been installed within the past fifty years, and much credit is due to an effective group of art supporters who laid a vital foundation for support of the arts, including art in public places, in the 1950s. Before then the accumulation of art in Seattle's public spaces was a slow, evolutionary process. During the nineteenth and through the first half of the twentieth century, urban art in this country was created for special events and special people. The Civil War was a major event that fostered monuments and memorials throughout the East. Washington State was a territory far removed from that conflagration, and no Civil War generals or battles

are immortalized here. Soldiers who fought in the Spanish-American War and other military endeavors at the turn of the last century are honored with *The Hiker*, an Allen Newman sculpture located in Woodland Park.

It was a peacetime event that first fostered any significant amount of public art in Seattle. In 1909 the city held its first world's fair, the Alaska-Yukon-Pacific Exposition, on the campus of the University of Washington. In relative terms, it was a banner year for public art, and sculptures were placed throughout the grounds. Works that remain on the campus are the commissioned bronze sculpture of George Washington and large busts of Edvard Grieg and James J. Hill. The statue of William H. Seward in Volunteer Park stood in front of the expo's New York Pavilion, which was a replica of Seward's New York home. A bust of Chief Seattle was also placed in Pioneer Square (1.3) for the 1909 exposition; it was a study for part of the better known 1912 statue of Seattle's namesake (7.18).

In 1910, after the death of John Harte McGraw, the state's second governor and a Seattle civic leader, Seattle citizens commissioned New York sculptor Richard Brooks to create a statue of McGraw (6.24), which was dedicated in downtown Seattle in 1913.

The First World War was the impetus for the commissioning of many public statues and memorials throughout the country. Alonzo Victor Lewis's *American Doughboy Bringing Home Victory* at Evergreen Washelli Cemetery honors Washingtonians who fell in that catastrophe. It was completed in 1932, after years of delay due to controversies related to its design and cost.

A lesser known historical event inspired a large, now forgotten memorial in the city. On July 27, 1923, President Warren G. Harding stopped in Seattle on his return from a visit to Alaska and British Columbia. At an annual Elk's picnic in Woodland Park that celebrated boys, Harding gave a speech and led attendees—including a large contingent of Boy Scouts—in the Pledge of Allegiance, and later that day he spoke at the University of Washington stadium. It was his last public speech. The president was ill, and his condition worsened after leaving Seattle. He died in San Francisco on August 2, 1923. Harding's Seattle visit was commemorated by a large memorial erected in Woodland Park in 1925. It was constructed of concrete with a bas relief depiction of the president addressing the crowd; Harding is flanked by two bronze Boy Scouts giving the Scout salute. More than fifty years later it became the only memorial sculpture erected in Seattle intended to be permanent that no longer stands. It was demolished to make room for zoo expansion. Although most of Harding's memorial is reportedly debris under the central knoll of the zoo's African Savannah exhibit, the two Boy Scout sculptures, created by Alice Robertson Carr, were given to the Seattle Boy Scouts organization.

In 1925 the death of Judge Thomas Burke, one of Seattle's most prominent citizens, resulted in the construction of a now little-known monument to his memory in Volunteer Park. It was commissioned with funds donated by the many admirers of that extraordinary man.

On the national level government support for the arts received a substantial jolt during the Great Depression. In 1933 Franklin Roosevelt's New Deal created the Federal Art Project of the Works Progress Administration (WPA) and the lesser known Section of Fine Arts of the US Treasury Department. For the next ten years the federal government paid over one thousand artists, craftsmen, and teachers to create artworks for public buildings and teach art. The WPA enabled many of the Northwest's most prominent artists in the twentieth century, such as Mark Tobey, Morris Graves, Kenneth Callahan, Guy Anderson, Carl Morris, and William Cumming, to pursue their artistic careers and create public art. One of the rare WPA projects that can still be seen in Seattle, although only in parts, is Kenneth Callahan's 1936 *Men Who Work the Ships*. Of its eleven paintings, seven are on view at Pacific Tower, 1200 Twelfth Avenue on Beacon Hill, and another is prominently displayed at the Museum of History & Industry (MOHAI) in South Lake Union Park.

The WPA planted seeds for further growth when it implemented an art-in-architecture program in which a half of 1 percent of total construction costs of a federal building project would be used to purchase contemporary art for the structure. But WPA programs were a historical aberration. Local government and industry support for the arts remained comparatively rare, and the first half of the century was fairly unproductive in terms of public art. As both pursued their traditional roles, the philosophic outlook of the times was not conducive to the commissioning of public art. One must remember that until the 1960s the role of federal, state, and local government in America was far less extensive than it is today. In almost every case the artworks erected in Seattle from 1899 through the 1950s were privately commissioned by nonprofit corporations or citizen groups. Supporting the arts was simply not considered a proper government function.

The late 1950s and early 1960s saw a gradual change in Seattle and the country. Seattle's awareness of art's place in an economically and spiritually healthy community was heightened through the efforts of Allied Arts of Seattle. For a detailed history of Allied Arts and its impact on Seattle, see R. M. Campbell's *Stirring Up Seattle: Allied Arts in the Civic Landscape* (Seattle: University of Washington Press, 2015). Founded in 1954, the energetic group of arts advocates and cultural organizations pledged to bring the arts to a position of prime importance in Seattle, thereby ensuring that the city would increase in beauty as it increased in size. One of its major goals was the creation of a Municipal Art Commission to champion public art and other civic improvements to enhance the quality of urban life.

The time was ripe to lobby for such a commission. On the federal level President Eisenhower had already urged the creation of an advisory commission to encourage the arts and other cultural activities. The debate over the extent to which governments could spend public money for civic beautification ended in 1954 when the US Supreme Court ruled that it was permissible to do so. Regardless, the concept of active government support was still radical. Eisenhower was recommending an advisory body, not a budgeted commission. The New Deal's WPA projects were still criticized by some as boondoggles, and the postwar era was a conservative period of recovery, not one of innovative approaches to cultural support. Although some citizens were becoming more receptive to the concept of local government support for the arts, it was not a belief held by a majority, and local governments were not going to lead the way.

In 1955 the Seattle City Council agreed to create the Municipal Art Commission. Unlike today's arts commissions, its role was to advise the mayor on cultural issues. It had no budget, and its power was limited to the persuasive talents of its members and supporters, principally those in Allied Arts. The commission lobbied for city beautification projects such as planting trees and burying utility lines. Other prominent issues of the commission included historic preservation, the creation of ballet and opera companies, and improved facilities for the city's performing arts. And it recommended that a "reasonable percentage" of the project cost for major public buildings be budgeted for "interior design, painting, sculpture, landscape, architecture and other arts." That recommendation was not accepted.

But this is not to say that public art in Seattle was unheard of in the 1950s. In 1958 Seattle took its first major step in acquiring art for art's sake when the Seattle Public Library Board of Trustees commissioned artworks for the new Seattle Public Library downtown, which included George Tsutakawa's *Fountain of Wisdom* (5.20) and a decorative screen by James FitzGerald (5.21). The following year the city installed at its new Municipal Building a sculptural screen by Everett DuPen (5.14) and a now demolished fountain by Glen Alps. The expenditures for these commissions were more than the government had allocated for

4.2   *Restless Bird*, Philip McCracken

public art up to that point, having previously limited itself to partial funding of statues honoring prominent citizens.

In 1959 the Norton Building—developed by Norton Clapp family interests—was the first large office building constructed since the art deco Exchange Building in 1930. It was also the first building project in Seattle to use corporate profits to commission non-architectural art for its public places. Two sculptures were installed: Philip McCracken's *Restless Bird* (4.2) and Harold Balazs's *Totem* (removed after remodeling in 1984). The Logan Building, also completed in 1959, displayed Archie Graber's sculpture *Morning Flight* (since removed) in its lobby. The placement of art in Seattle's public places was limited to the efforts of those venturesome few.

During the same period, the Municipal Art Commission and Allied Arts also began promoting cultural expansion to encourage Seattle's economic growth because it was becoming more widely believed that the arts and a city's prosperity were related. Cities perceived as cultural backwaters would not attract enlightened businesses and investment. One way to show the world that Seattle was robust and sophisticated was to have some sort of exposition, something to show that in addition to the natural beauty of its region, a strong economy and an active cultural environment were prominent features of Seattle. Since the mid-1950s, Allied Arts had as one of its goals Seattle's hosting a world's fair. The 1962 Century 21 Exposition, held at what is now the Seattle Center, was energetically supported by citizens and the business community and it became a milestone in the history of public art in Seattle.

Two years before the world's fair, the General Donation and Gift Trust Fund was created to allow the city to receive private gifts of art and money to purchase art. The world's fair became the focal point for gifts of art by artists with regional and international reputations. Fountains, paintings, murals, and sculptures were commissioned and funded through donations of over $750,000 from private citizens, businesses, the World's Fair Corporation, and local and federal government sources. Several other works were loaned for the event. Three major commissioned works remain at the Seattle Center: Paul Horiuchi's glass mosaic mural (8.9), Everett DuPen's *Fountain of Creation* (8.19), and James FitzGerald's *Fountain of the Northwest* (8.26).

The Century 21 Exposition was a great success and, like its 1909 predecessor, it closed in the black. More important, it increased awareness in Seattle that artworks can create inspirational settings and break the standard urban monotony of bare walls and concrete as it ushered in a new age of public and private art support. In his book, *The Eighth Lively Art*, artist and historian Wesley Wehr notes that support of artists in Seattle in the 1950s and early 1960s was limited to funding provided by Dr. Richard Fuller, the founder and director of the Seattle Art Museum, and a few other patrons and collectors. Before then, he said, "there wasn't much money around. There were scarcely any foundation grants, and not much public art. Most of the artists here held the idea that a 'career' was something people had in Hollywood. . . . The day the Seattle World's Fair opened in 1962 marked a turning point. . . . Seattle on that day stopped being a big town and became a small city in the nationwide scheme of things. . . . There was no turning back."

In the larger scheme of things, increased support for the arts in Seattle was part of a national trend. The Kennedy administration, spurred by the president's personal interest in culture, recognized the value of government support for the arts and attempted to broaden the federal government's involvement. In 1962 the US General Services Administration followed earlier actions by the WPA and instituted a program that required allocation of a half of 1 percent of federal building renovation and construction budgets for artworks. Although the program lasted only a few years, the principle would later become typical of local and federal programs.

In 1966 the federal government created the National Endowment for the Arts, which has since provided assistance to programs and projects throughout the country in all areas of the arts. Its public art program provided partial funding for artworks across the US, although the purchase or commissioning of monumental public works of art didn't become common until the 1970s and 1980s. That period saw the acquisition of a few of Seattle's most important sculptures, including Isamu Noguchi's *Black Sun* in Volunteer Park, Tony Smith's *Moses* (8.5), Michael Heizer's *Adjacent, Against, Upon* (3.22), and Ronald Bladen's *Black Lightning* (8.3). All were made possible with partial funding by the National Endowment for the Arts.

Washington State became an early leader in government support for the arts with the creation of the Washington State Arts Commission in 1961. Like the Seattle commission before it, the state entity was merely advisory and was a far cry from the budgeted, influential body of today. Nevertheless, it was part of the groundwork laid for the next decade of activity in the arts.

A new, vibrant era for public art gathered speed in the 1960s in urban centers throughout the nation. Charitable institutions, such as the Rockefeller and Ford Foundations, had been increasing their support of the arts in general. However, it was a growing recognition by American corporations that art was a worthwhile investment that made a major difference. Some businesses also believed that they should actively support the arts because they could afford to do so in a manner that could measurably improve the quality of urban life.

As the Medici family financed the artistic growth in the city-state of Florence, major corporations became the Medicis of the modern age, supporting the arts and collecting artworks on a grand scale. Seattle's most prominent corporate collector throughout the 1960s and 1970s was Seattle-First National Bank (acquired by Bank of America in 1983). When Seafirst's office building—Seattle's first modern skyscraper—was completed in 1968, its Fourth Avenue plaza and lobby had more public art per square foot than those of any other building in the city. It included new works by regional artists such as George Tsutakawa, Guy Anderson, and James Washington Jr., as well as Henry Moore's bronze *Three Piece Sculpture: Vertebrae* (5.18) and a unique lighting sculpture by Harry Bertoia (removed in 2017). Seafirst was joined by other corporate collectors, notably Rainier Bank (now US Bank), Pacific Northwest Bell (now CenturyLink), and Safeco

Insurance Company (now part of Liberty Mutual Insurance). By the 1990s, collecting art for public spaces was no longer a popular corporate goal. Corporate support for the arts was being accomplished with donations and grants through corporate foundations.

The local government's outlook, like that of the business community, came full circle by the early 1970s. Public art for purposes other than commemorating people and events was deemed necessary to a city and therefore worthy of government support. However, no bold steps to provide government support of the arts were taken until after citizen groups had pushed and prodded for more than a decade. Continuous lobbying and a gradual change in philosophical outlook brought an enlightened approach that was able to survive even the local economic recession in the 1970s known as the "Boeing Bust."

In 1967 King County created its arts commission (now known as 4Culture, a tax-exempt public development authority), the nation's first publicly funded county arts agency. Seattle's earlier unfunded Municipal Art Commission died quietly in 1969 and was replaced in 1971 with a budgeted entity, the Seattle Arts Commission (now the Office of Arts and Culture). That same year the Seattle Arts Commission began working with the Seattle Water Department in a process that eventually selected Ted Jonsson's fountain design for the department's Operations Control Center at 2700 Airport Way South. Although the city did not have a 1 Percent for Art program at that time, funds for the fountain were set aside from the building's construction budget, and the commission

directed a statewide competition to select a suitable design. A jury of artists and art supporters selected design finalists, and the commission, the water department, and the building's architect selected Jonsson's design. That selection process became the model for future Seattle Arts Commission projects.

Commissioned artworks became the norm after Seattle's 1 Percent for Art ordinance was enacted on June 30, 1973. The Seattle City Council recognized that the "development of the visual and aesthetic environment is a fundamental responsibility of civic government." It provided that 1 percent of funds appropriated for municipal construction projects in the city's Capital Improvement Program be set aside for the "selection, acquisition and installation of artworks in public places." The law was also one of the first in the nation to include its public utility—the largest developer of capital improvement projects—in the 1 Percent program. The ordinance describes the city's lofty goals: "The City accepts a responsibility for expanding public experience with visual art. Such art has enabled people in all societies better to understand their communities and individual lives. Artists capable of creating art for public places must be encouraged and Seattle's standing as a regional leader in public art enhanced. A policy is therefore established to direct the inclusion of works of art in public works in the City."

The passage of Seattle's law in a troubled economic climate came about primarily because the city had a fortunate alignment of enlightened citizens and groups, primarily working together as Allied Arts, and newly elected public officials who changed the political culture of

Seattle. John Stewart Detlie, the first president of Allied Arts, who had moved to Los Angeles in 1960, said in a 1965 visit to Seattle, "You don't appreciate what great strides have been made here . . . until you have lived somewhere else for a time. . . .When you recognize the lethargy and disinterest that paralyzes other American cities you are doubly impressed with what Seattle has done." Early Allied Arts members included Paul Schell, who, as president of the organization in 1974, said that "those of us who cared about urban living and felt the decay and helplessness of Eastern and Midwestern cities look on Seattle as a possibility, a newer city without a crusty establishment controlling everything. There was an opportunity to get involved in a meaningful fashion."

In the political arena, the Seattle City Council had traditionally been an insular collection of controlling white businessmen whose outlook was not concerned with the arts. In the mid-1960s the *Seattle Post-Intelligencer* described the body as "musty" and "crusty." Times changed rather quickly. In 1969 Wes Uhlman, a young progressive, was elected mayor and served two terms (1969–78). He believed that art was part of the fabric of any great city and supporting the arts was an essential city service. He was followed by other progressive mayors who supported the arts, notably Charles Royer (1978–90), Norm Rice (1990–98), and Paul Schell (1998–2002). On the city council, progressives Phyllis Lamphere and Sam Smith were elected in 1967. They were joined in 1970 by young progressives Tim Hill and Bruce Chapman and in 1972 by John Miller. Chapman and Miller introduced the 1 Percent for Art ordinance to the city council

in 1973. Its approval was one of many changes made during the period because, as Phyllis Lamphere succinctly put it, "We had the votes."

Seattle wasn't the first US city to pass such legislation. Philadelphia was the first, having passed its law in 1959. Baltimore and San Francisco passed similar ordinances in 1964 and 1967. Seattle, tucked away in its little corner of the country, was a comparatively young city far removed and uninspired by processes in older cities. It implemented an energetic public art program and became a national leader in the field. King County had enacted its 1 Percent for Art ordinance in February 1973. A year later the state legislature enacted a half of 1 percent for art law that established the Art in Public Places Program of the Washington State Arts Commission. It was the second state to establish such a law, and its approach remains unusual because public schools are allowed to participate in the program. All of these programs provide vital sources of support for the arts in the city, county, and state and have resulted in the installation of a wide variety of public art.

Under the city's new law, the Seattle Arts Commission was given the responsibility of administering the public art program by working with city departments whose budgets contain 1 Percent funds, selecting artworks, and maintaining the city's art collection. Once a city department had a construction project, it worked with the arts commission to select interior and exterior artworks. Eventually those tasks and long-range planning were undertaken by the commission's Art in Public Places committee. In 2002 the commission became an advisory board of volunteers appointed by the mayor, and managing the public art program was assigned to a new city department, the Office of Arts and Culture. If a capital project is small, the city department can have its funds set aside in a Municipal Arts Fund until additional department funds are accumulated to permit purchase of an artwork. Seattle City Light, Seattle Public Utilities, the Department of Parks and Recreation, and the Building Department have the largest construction budgets and have been major sources for public art acquisitions since the law was enacted. In 2004 the city's 1 Percent funding program was under serious attack in a lawsuit brought by citizens who argued that the resources of a public utility such as City Light, funded by rate-paying citizens specifically for utility operations, could not be used to fund the city's overall arts program. In 2005 an appellate court approved the use of utility funds for public art, but City Light funds could be used only for art that has a close connection to the business of the utility, not for other civic purposes or facilities.

According to Richard Andrews, coordinator of the public art program from 1978 to 1984, at the outset committee members included artists. This was a different approach from that taken in East Coast commissions, which were composed entirely of art connoisseurs and patrons. The inclusion of artists had a major impact. They were young, socially inspired, passionate, and energetic advocates who wanted to make public art available. "It was," he said, "a yeasty environment committed to expanding the local art experience rather than support local artists." That environment also included arts patrons who were committed to the same goals, but those patrons were not a controlling force.

An early Seattle Arts Commission milestone was the installation in 1976 of minimalist artist Michael Heizer's commissioned sculpture, *Adjacent, Against, Upon* (3.22) at Myrtle Edwards Park. It was widely criticized and maligned as a meaningless collection of rocks and concrete, but it stands with Henry Moore's Three-Piece Sculpture: *Vertebrae* (5.18) and, to a lesser degree, Jonathan Borofsky's *Hammering Man* (6.15), as an example of how modern art can be widely accepted by a public that first rejects it. In his 1981 article in Artforum, John Beardsley referred to this phenomenon of rejected art becoming city icons: "A pattern can be detected in the response to many works that suggests that a growing familiarity produces feelings of appreciation and support. Such was the case with Michael Heizer's *Adjacent, Against, Upon* in Seattle. . . . Scorn has given way to praise for the work, despite its lack of recognizable content or function. A segment of a recent TV news program broadcast in Seattle, sharply critical of a newly completed, publicly funded artwork, concluded with the query: 'Why couldn't they have done something interesting, like the Heizer?'"

As noted earlier, Heizer's sculpture was partially funded by the National Endowment for the Arts and by private funding. For the most part, 1 Percent for Art funds are either the sole or the principal source of funds for acquisition of art in Seattle's public places and the funds available are more than many may realize. A major impact on the city's public art expenditures has been the passage of bond measures for capital improvements. For instance, in 1994 Seattle voters approved a $290.7 million Libraries for All Bond that resulted in construction of the Central Branch in downtown Seattle,

6.23 Untitled mural, Fay Jones

6.23 Untitled mural, Gene Gentry McMahon

new branch libraries, and facility and technology upgrades affecting twenty-two branch libraries. Community center renovations were made possible by a 1999 levy that provided $36 million for nine community centers and two neighborhood projects. Similarly, in 2000, Seattle voters approved a $198 million Pro Parks levy to finance the acquisition of property for new city parks, upgrade existing ones, and preserve greenbelts. The 2008 Parks and Green Spaces levy had similar goals. In 2003 voters approved a $196 million levy to fund, among other things, the upgrade, renovation, or replacement of thirty-two neighborhood fire stations. The capital projects made possible by the passage of these measures resulted in not only new and improved city facilities but also in a large number of commissioned artworks to add vitality and interest to libraries, parks, community centers, and fire stations throughout the city.

Since its inception, the 1 Percent for Art program has helped improve the urban environment by placing artworks throughout the city. Selecting the art is a challenge that requires balancing the need for some degree of public acceptance with the goal of installing works of artistic merit. For many years the process involved design competitions in which the choices of a selection jury were subject to confirmation by the arts commission. Artists and artworks were chosen only after a building or capital improvement project was designed, nearly finished, or completed. Art was not included in the overall design, other than designating a spot for its possible placement. The selection of the art was a totally separate process.

An artist-architect design team approach became the favored route because many public art supporters objected to treating art as an unrelated attachment or afterthought to projects. They argued that by allowing artists to participate in the initial project design, a wide range of artistic possibilities would be considered and implemented. Seattle first included artists as members of construction project design teams in the mid-1970s, and it was quickly realized that artists working with architects and engineers often stimulated their colleagues into departing from the customary restraints of their disciplines. What were initially considered impractical ideas of an artist became well-received parts of a larger whole.

The first design team artists—Buster Simpson, Andrew Keating, and Sherry Markovitz—worked on Seattle City Light's Viewland-Hoffman Electrical Substation in north Seattle and integrated Emil Gehrke's folk art windmills and colorful geometric shapes into what would otherwise have been a dreary gray electrical complex. Since the dedication of that award-winning substation design in 1979, the creations of many successful design teams in the Seattle area have been widely acclaimed. The Metro Downtown Seattle Transit Project, which opened in September 1990, was a well-regarded success. Five artists worked with project architects and incorporated their artworks and those of sixteen other artists into both functional and decorative elements for underground transit stations and street improvements. Seattle's design team concept was soon used as a model for cities throughout the United States.

There have been many successes, but it is widely recognized that over the past thirty years the design team approach has evolved into one in which the requirement for practical design and function often displaces the range of creativity that fosters inspired, thought-provoking work. To improve efficiency and in an attempt to control quality, rosters were created that list artists who are deemed qualified to work on public art projects. Some artists now define themselves as "public artists" and their works are often derived from conversations with community members and incorporate local interest, history, and culture. The difficulty with such an approach is the inherent limitation of ideas from a group (whether creating and/or managing the process) that understands the importance of political sensitivities and the need for consensus when spending public funds. The approach limits the ability of many artists who join such teams. A newcomer who stirs things up may create better art, but governments are fearful of controversy.

Local and national controversies over public art in the 1980s created a looming shadow of concern in the minds of arts administrators and supporters of art in public places. Vitriolic debate in Olympia in the early 1980s over the installation of contemporary works in the state legislature's Beaux-Arts buildings resulted in the removal of major commissioned works by Michael Spafford and Alden Mason. Both were highly regarded by the art world but considered by a majority of legislators to be too abstract for the traditional architecture. To add insult to injury, some thought Spafford's *Twelve Labors of Hercules*, by which the artist intended to refer to the struggles inherent in the legislative process, was sexually suggestive with its abstract, seemingly naked, wrestlers. National controversies made matters worse.

Public displeasure in 1981 with the installation of Richard Serra's 120-foot-long steel *Tilted Arc*, which bisected a federal building plaza in New York, resulted in its removal after an eight-year legal dispute. A prolonged attack against the National Endowment for the Arts by conservative politicians was inspired by the fact that NEA funds were used to exhibit Andres Serrano's *Piss Christ*, a greatly enlarged photograph showing a small crucifix submerged in a glass containing Serrano's urine. It was a relatively minor expenditure for toxic subject matter that blew up in the press and created an outcry in many circles. Artistic and free speech arguments failed to triumph over politics and perceived religious insult. The resulting threat of lost government support for the arts inspired a conservative and more cautious approach to selecting public artworks.

Caution and the resulting desire for consensus was discussed in a 2008 article by *Seattle Post-Intelligencer* art critic Regina Hackett in which she reviewed the record of public art installations in Seattle: "For every hit . . . there are dozens of misses. . . . Artists afraid to offend anyone won't move anyone either." To some, the results bring to mind the query in a Rudyard Kipling poem, "The Conundrum of the Workshops": "It's pretty, but is it art?" Others may refer to the language of the 1 Percent for Art Ordinance, which recognizes that public art "has enabled people . . . to better understand their communities and individual lives." Many works that focus on culture and history may not be artistically significant, but they may elicit an emotional response about one's background or at least be educational about a neighborhood and its residents.

The placement of art in privately owned lobbies and building plazas is, for the most part, unhindered by political consensus and team approaches and has resulted in an important collection of sculptures in Seattle. Major downtown real estate developers, having recognized that public art added interest to their buildings and set them apart from others, were early investors beginning in the 1980s. In the 1980s and 1990s, Wright Runstad & Company placed works by Beverly Pepper (4.6), Tom Wesselmann (4.7), and Anne and Patrick Poirier (4.11) in and around its office buildings and, more recently, installed a sculpture by Manuel Neri (4.10). During that same period Martin Selig was very active in funding public art installations for his office buildings until business conditions slowed his efforts and several sculptures were sold and moved out of town, including the first Alexander Calder sculpture in a Seattle public place. Part of his earlier collection remains (3.29), and his acquisitions in the twenty-first century have reached new levels (3.31, 4.8, 4.9). Richard Hedreen has placed major artworks at downtown hotels he has developed (6.26, 6.27). The first, James Rosati's *Loo Wit*, was later donated to Seattle University and now stands on the university's campus.

In the twenty-first century it has become common for lesser-known developers to include art in the public places of their office and residential buildings. While works have not typically been created by important artists with significant reputations, the reasons for including art in these projects are the same.

The most extraordinary turn of events affecting the collection of art in Seattle's public spaces is the involvement of Microsoft cofounder Paul Allen. His purchase of the Seattle Seahawks and the resulting construction of CenturyLink Field resulted in five commissioned artworks outside that facility and many others inside that were made possible by Allen's substantial donation of funds. Subsequent construction of nearby Allen-owned buildings brought additional art to the area. But in the history of art in Seattle's public places, nothing surpasses Allen's efforts in the South Lake Union neighborhood.

When the first edition of this book was published in 1992, the chapter covering the district that is now called South Lake Union included that area, the Denny Triangle and Belltown. There were five artworks in that chapter. Chapter 9 of this new guide covers only South Lake Union and includes over thirty sculptures, most of which were placed there by Allen's interests. This came to be because in 1992 Paul Allen supported a proposal to create Seattle Commons, an immense park in the district, and loaned the funds used by the Commons measure to acquire 11.5 acres of property for the project. That loan was to be forgiven if the measure passed. When voters defeated the proposed park plan, the property reverted to Allen, and he subsequently purchased additional parcels to increase his holdings to nearly 60 acres. He later began developing his properties through Vulcan Real Estate.

Vulcan's philosophy is that art in public places is essential to creating dynamic spaces and thriving pedestrian environments. Many Vulcan-developed buildings (in some cases developed in conjunction with a major tenant such as Amazon) include a sculpture in their public spaces. Allen named his company after the Roman god of fire, and company literature

5.13 *Sargasso Stir*, Lois Graham

describes Vulcan as a smith and a craftsman "who forged works that no one imagined were possible." Twenty-six years ago the transformation of the neighborhood and the plethora of artworks installed by a single owner would have been deemed unlikely, to say the least.

The Vulcan collection joins hundreds of other works of art in this book that are as varied as their creators and elicit a wide range of emotional reaction from viewers. Whatever the responses, the art in our public places can teach us many things and help counteract the mundane concrete, steel, and glass repetition that often surrounds it and add a level of energy and intellectual challenge to the urban environment. It is my hope that this book will inspire many to admire and investigate the artworks around them, wherever they may be. The enjoyment of your surroundings, whether familiar or foreign, is always enhanced by learning about it and observing more than the immediate, ground-level scene. A hike through the terrain without noticing the richness of the surroundings results in a plethora of missed experiences.

In Norton Juster's fantasy, *The Phantom Tollbooth*, we learn that urban dwellers understood that "the most important reason for going from one place to another is to see what's in between. . . . Then one day someone discovered that if you walked as fast as possible and looked at nothing but your shoes you would arrive at your destination much more quickly." The citizens all followed that quicker approach, and the city ultimately disappeared because no one cared to look at it. If you don't look, it won't get as bad as all that, dear reader, but your life will be richer if you know about the art around you.

HOW TO USE THIS BOOK

SEATTLE PRIDES ITSELF ON having a fine collection of art in its public spaces; but where is it? What is it? Who created it and why? It is frustrating for the culturally curious to be faced with so many works of art and not have readily obtainable and reliable answers to those questions. The earlier edition of this book provided a plethora of information about artworks throughout Seattle. Since then, so many more have been installed that this volume covers art only in downtown Seattle, stretching from SoDo to South Lake Union and including the entire waterfront. A future volume will cover the rest of the city.

In the case of some artworks, readers may find another source, perhaps on the internet, that provides a different name or date for the art. Research for this book has been thorough. The artists themselves (in some instances now deceased) have been relied upon for the titles of their artworks. In some cases, an owner may misspell a title or provide their own. Titles selected by the artists are used here and if there is none, it is listed as untitled.

Most quotations in this book have come from the author's interviews or correspondence with over ninety artists, comments by the artists on their websites, and written descriptions provided by the artists to the owners of the pieces, including government entities. If an artist's comments are from a book or a newspaper, a source is referred to.

Although Seattle has many fine examples of art at places of worship, they are not included here because the collection throughout the city is so vast that covering it would require a separate volume. Painted wall murals are also excluded because they are often marred by graffiti, maintained poorly, or destroyed when the buildings succumb to development. The one exception is the Hing Hay Park mural, an International District icon that remains well maintained after more than forty years (1.20).

Art in Seattle's Public Spaces is organized into nine chapters. The boundaries of each were drawn to create the easiest areas to tour—or envision if one is reading in the comfort of home. The artworks are numbered on splendid maps in a manner that attempts to create an orderly progression, but readers can design their own routes, perhaps starting from a favorite bistro or convenient parking place.

Included with the title of each artwork is the name of the artist(s) who created it, the medium used and its measurements, the source of that artwork, and its location. Measurements are listed by height (H), length (L), width (W), and diameter (Dia). The use of length and width varies in

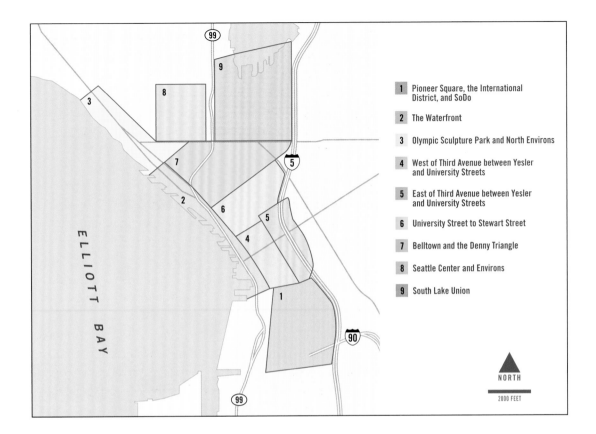

1　Pioneer Square, the International District, and SoDo

2　The Waterfront

3　Olympic Sculpture Park and North Environs

4　West of Third Avenue between Yesler and University Streets

5　East of Third Avenue between Yesler and University Streets

6　University Street to Stewart Street

7　Belltown and the Denny Triangle

8　Seattle Center and Environs

9　South Lake Union

ELLIOTT BAY

NORTH

2000 FEET

different art texts. Here, length is a measurement of the artwork's face or in some cases the longer surface. Width measures the distance perpendicular to the length. No dimensions are provided in the few cases where measuring was impractical.

Short, up-to-date biographies of most of the artists mentioned can be found in the back of the book. More details are usually available on the internet, but in a few cases the internet has no information about the artist.

Whether touring or engaged in scholarly study or both, do not forget the index, which lists not only artists and titles of artworks but also various topics of interest. The index is a very useful tool if you wish to compare a particular artwork with the artist's creations elsewhere in the book.

Enjoyment derived from viewing art may arise from the beauty of a piece, its artistic statement, or its spiritual message—or perhaps all three. But that enjoyment can never be the same as that experienced when a viewer is provided with background facts or the creator's insight. Whatever is experienced, it is hoped that the material supplied by this book will increase manyfold the pleasures of learning about the art that surrounds us in downtown Seattle.

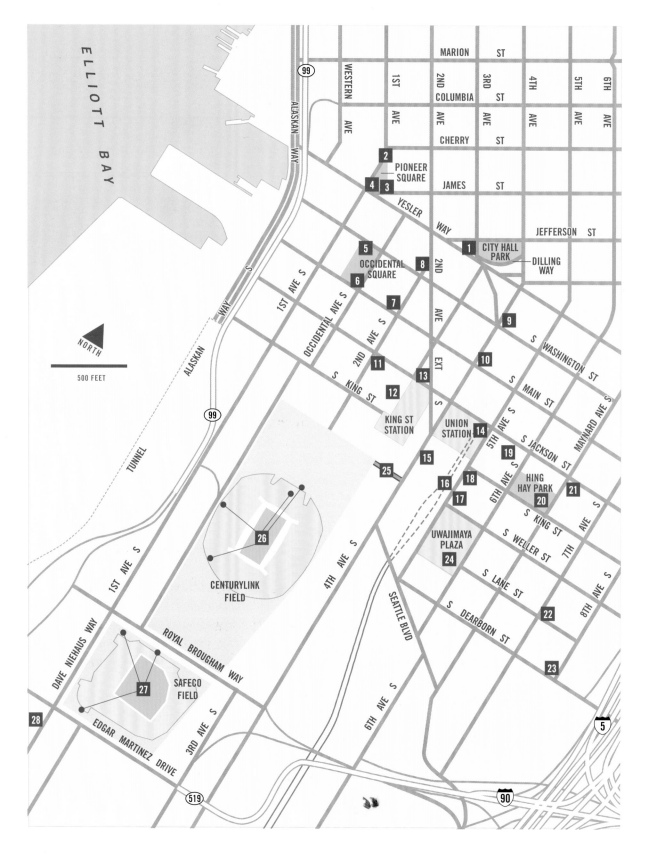

ELLIOTT BAY

NORTH

500 FEET

MARION ST

WESTERN AVE

1ST AVE

2ND AVE

3RD AVE

4TH AVE

5TH AVE

6TH AVE

99

ALASKAN WAY

COLUMBIA ST

CHERRY ST

2

PIONEER SQUARE

4 **3**

JAMES ST

YESLER WAY

JEFFERSON ST

1 CITY HALL PARK

DILLING WAY

5

OCCIDENTAL SQUARE

6

8

2ND AVE

7

9

S WASHINGTON ST

1ST AVE S

OCCIDENTAL AVE S

S KING ST

2ND AVE S

11

10

2ND AVE EXT S

S MAIN ST

13

12

KING ST STATION

UNION STATION

14

5TH AVE S

S JACKSON ST

MAYNARD AVE S

19

HING HAY PARK

15

16

18

6TH AVE S

20

21

17

25

26

CENTURYLINK FIELD

ALASKAN WAY

99

TUNNEL

UWAJIMAYA PLAZA

24

S KING ST

S WELLER ST

7TH AVE S

8TH AVE S

S LANE ST

SEATTLE BLVD

4TH AVE S

S DEARBORN ST

22

23

1ST AVE S

ROYAL BROUGHAM WAY

27

SAFECO FIELD

DAVE NIEHAUS WAY

EDGAR MARTINEZ DRIVE

3RD AVE S

6TH AVE S

28

519

5

90

1 PIONEER SQUARE, THE INTERNATIONAL DISTRICT, AND SODO

Art arises when the secret vision of the artist and the manifestation of nature
agree to find new shapes.

—Kahlil Gibran (1883–1931)

PIONEER SQUARE AND THE INTERNATIONAL DISTRICT are areas rich with

Seattle history, ranging from the first shipment of gold from the Klondike gold rush in 1897,

the installation of Seattle's Pioneer Square totem pole—its first work of art in a public

place—in 1899, and the continual influence of Asian immigrants that started in the late

nineteenth century. Asian history and culture is referred to in many of the artworks in this

neighborhood's public places. And since 1979 the SoDo neighborhood has been the site of

professional sports venues, each of which has been graced with a variety of commissioned

public artworks.

1.1 PIONEER SQUARE METRO STATION ARTWORKS, 1990

Garth Edwards, Jim Garrett, Laura Sindell, Kate Ericson, and Mel Ziegler

Mixed media
King County Metro commission
Pioneer Square Station, Third Avenue at Jefferson Street

The Pioneer Square Station at Prefontaine Place is graced with six sections of steel grillwork by Garth Edwards. Each section has a group of four cartoon-like figures similar to those on Edwards's cast-iron hatch covers at various locations downtown. The design was inspired by figures of patrons and saints on the gates of European cathedrals and a bus driver's comment to Edwards that the figures reminded him of people lined up waiting for his bus. The entrance gates at the station were designed and created by Seattle metal designer Jim Garrett.

The major artwork at the foot of the stairs at the station's entrance is *Sounding Wall*, an eight-by-fifty-foot ceramic tile mural by Laura Sindell. It combines a landscape and a soundscape with two technical drawings of a Native American dugout canoe, the artist's reference to a past mode of travel in the modern transit station.

Two unique clocks by Kate Ericson and Mel Ziegler stand at each end of the station's tunnel level. The face of the south clock is made of masonry remnants dug up during tunnel

1.1 *Sounding Wall,* Laura Sindell

construction, and the face of the north clock is made of leftover construction materials from the tunnel project. The numbers on the clocks are fashioned by tools donated by the tunnel workers.

Surface artworks at this and other Metro stations include unique cast-iron grates for the bases of the five tree species planted on Third Avenue and along Pine Street. Norway maple leaf shapes make up Maren Hassinger's maple tree grate design. The linden leaf is included in Garth Edwards's design for linden tree grates, and Dyan Rey incorporated ginkgo leaves in her grate design for those trees. Birds, acorns, and oak leaves are in Susan Point's classical design for the oak tree grates. Virginia Paquette's linear art deco–inspired design incorporates serrated zelkova leaves, Z shapes, and references to a high-heeled shoe, water, and people—all of which might come in contact with the grate.

> Next to the Third Avenue side of the tunnel entrance is *Prefontaine Fountain*, Seattle's first fountain. It was made possible by Father F. X. Prefontaine, a prominent Jesuit priest in Seattle who built the city's first Catholic church in 1870. When Father Prefontaine died in 1911, he left the city the then princely sum of $5,000 for a fountain "sparkling with clear water to beautify the city." In 1926 his wishes were fulfilled. The park and *Prefontaine Fountain* were designed by Carl F. Gould, one of Seattle's leading architects at the time. The now worn concrete tortoises were sculpted by James Wehn.

1.2 TOTEM POLE, 1940

Charles Brown and William H. Brown, with James Starfish, William Andrews, James Andrews, and Robert Harris

Carved cedar; H 50 ft.
Gift to the city from the US government
Near Pioneer Square at intersection of First Avenue S
    and Yesler Way

The first work of art in a public place in Seattle was a fifty-foot-high totem pole placed in 1899 at Pioneer Square. The pole originally stood in the Tlingit village of Tongass, Alaska, but was removed in 1899 by a group of touring Seattle businessmen who decided to take it home as a souvenir. The "donors" were fined for their theft, but the stolen property was never returned and $500 was reportedly paid as a settlement with the tribe. "Seattle's" totem pole became a city landmark. In 1938 the pole was damaged by an arsonist and the fire damage plus extensive dry rot necessitated its removal. The original pole was replaced with this 1940 near replica, which was carved near Ketchikan, Alaska, primarily by Tlingit carver Charles Brown with the help of his father, William H. Brown. They were assisted by Tlingit craftsmen James Starfish, William Andrews, James Andrews, and Robert Harris.

The tree for the new totem pole came from US Forest Service land, and the federal government paid the carvers under a government program promoting the restoration of Native poles. As a result, a special act of Congress transferred ownership of the pole from the US government to the City of Seattle.

Totem poles are a three-dimensional art form generally associated with the Tlingit of

1.2   Totem pole, Charles Brown and William H. Brown

stood alone and in other cases served as memorials or grave posts or as architectural supports. The designs were varied and most often consisted of figures representing myths and legends of the Native people, clan lineages, or historical events. Native tribes in the Seattle area carved wood, but none practiced this particular art form. The design of Seattle's pole was created to honor the Chief-of-all-Women, a Tlingit noblewoman who had drowned in the Nass River.

Totem pole symbolism is read from the top down, and the top figure identifies the pole's owner, which in this case was a Tlingit lineage of the Raven clan. The figures on this pole depict, from the top, Raven, holding a crescent moon in his beak; Woman, holding her frog child; Woman's frog husband; Mink; Raven; Whale, with a seal in its mouth; and Grandfather of Raven, a major mythical being also called Raven-at-the-Head-of-Nass. The pole represents the legend of how Raven stole the sun and moon from Raven-at-the-Head-of-Nass and brought light to the world. A similar story is illustrated in Duane Pasco's nearby *Sun and Raven* totem pole (1.5).

1.3 BUST OF CHIEF SEATTLE, 1909

James Wehn

Bronze; H 2 ft.
City of Seattle collection
Pioneer Square, 100 Yesler Way

southeastern Alaska, the Haida of Haida Gwaii, formerly known as the Queen Charlotte Islands, and the Tsimshian and Kwakw<u>aka</u>'wakw of western British Columbia. Totem poles often

In 1908 Seattle was sprucing itself up for its first world's fair, the Alaska-Yukon-Pacific Exposition, which was set to open in 1909. One desired improvement was an ornamental watering fountain for animals in Pioneer

1.3 and 1.4   Bust of Chief Seattle, James Wehn; *Day/Night*, Edgar Heap of Birds

Square. At that time, Seattle sculptor James Wehn was working on the clay model for his large statue of Chief Seattle for Tilikum Place (7.18). The head of the city's Street and Sewer Department asked him to make a bronze bust of Seattle for the new watering fountain. Completed in 1909, this is the first sculpture of the city's namesake to be placed in Seattle.

1.4 DAY/NIGHT, 1991

Edgar Heap of Birds (Hock E Aye Vi)

Enamel on steel; H 8 ft. × L 3 ft. 6 in.
Seattle 1 Percent for Art Program and private donors
Pioneer Square, 100 Yesler Way

Behind the bust of Chief Seattle are two double-sided panels of porcelain enamel on steel by Native American artist Edgar Heap of Birds, whose Southern Cheyenne birth name is Hock E Aye Vi (Heap of Birds confirms that although some sources use "Hachivi" in his Native name, that is incorrect). The statements on the front of each panel are in Lushootseed, the native language of the Salish people and the language Chief Seattle spoke, while those on the reverse are the English translations. The panel on the right reads, "Far away brothers and sisters, we still remember you." The left panel, decorated with crosses and dollar signs, reads, "Chief Seattle, now the streets are our home." The artist says that this sculpture refers to the fact that although Seattle is full of references to Indigenous people—from the city's name, to totem poles, to Seahawk helmets—there is no institutionalized evidence of those people in the city, and that the Native people who live on streets are held "in close and high regard" by Native peoples in rural communities.

The title, *Day/Night*, comes from a version of a speech Chief Seattle gave in 1854 in which he reportedly said, "Day and night cannot dwell together. The red man has ever fled the approach of the white man, as the changing mists on the mountainside flee before the blazing morning sun."

1.5 NORTHWEST COAST INDIAN CARVINGS

Duane Pasco

Carved cedar; *Sun and Raven*, 1973, H 32 ft.; *Man Riding on Tail of Whale*, 1971, H 20 ft.; *Bear*, 1974, H 12 ft.; *Tsonoqua*, 1973, H 12 ft.
Private collection
Occidental Square

Duane Pasco's four sculptures in Occidental Square are some of the city's finest examples of carving in the Northwest Coast Indian style. *Sun and Raven* was carved for the 1974 world's fair in Spokane, Washington, and refers in part to the Indian legend about Raven's bringing light to the world. At the pole's base the sun is held above the box in which it was stored before Raven stole it. At the top Raven holds the moon. Part of the same legend is depicted in Seattle's Pioneer Square totem pole (1.2).

The nearby human figure with arms outstretched depicts Tsonoqua, a mythical giant of the deep forest. She is usually shown with lips pursed to utter a cry. In some stories her cry could bring supernatural power, good luck, or great wealth. In others she is a terrifying figure, threatening to eat children and referred to by parents to frighten children into obedience. In some versions of the Tsonoqua myth she is called "the nightmare bringer."

Pasco's sculptures were given to the Pioneer Square Association by Richard White, a prominent art gallery owner and leading Pioneer Square supporter.

1.5 *Sun and Raven* and *Man Riding on Tail of Whale*   1.5 *Tsonoqua*, Duane Pasco

1.6 FALLEN FIREFIGHTERS MEMORIAL, 1998

Jason (Hai Ying) Wu

Bronze and granite; life-size
City of Seattle Collection, private and city funding
Occidental Avenue S and S Main Street

The event that inspired Seattle's *Fallen Firefighters Memorial* was a tragic 1995 warehouse fire in the International District. Four firefighters were killed, but the four bronze figures represent all members of the Seattle Fire Department who have died in the line of duty, beginning with the first death in 1891. Artist Jason Wu says that their placement "is intended to symbolize the firefighters' strength with unity, forging their individual energies into a powerful team effort." Wu placed the granite stones to "create a pyramidal composition reinforcing this sense of strength and unity," but they are also intended to suggest a building collapsed around the firefighters, representing the dangers they face in the pursuit of their service. The memorial was created with students at the University of Washington School of Art in a project managed by UW art professor Norman Taylor.

1.6 *Fallen Firefighters Memorial,* Jason Wu

Another tribute to firefighters adorns the corners of the fire department's headquarters at the corner of Second Avenue S and S Main Street. The three heroic silhouettes of firefighters were created by Spokane artist Tom Askman in 1988. Made of bronze-covered zinc panels, each is accentuated with lighting for dramatic emphasis at night.

1.7 WATERFALL GARDEN, 1977

Masao Kinoshita

Private commission

Second Avenue S and S Main Street, just east of Occidental Park and across Main Street from the fire department headquarters

This corner park was constructed on the site where United Parcel Service was founded in 1907. Seventy years later that company's

1.8   *Anawog,* Jan Evans

founder, James Casey, had this park built for the enjoyment of Seattle citizens. It is owned and maintained by the Annie E. Casey Foundation, a private entity named for his mother. The park was designed by Masao Kinoshita of Sasaki Associates, Inc., of Watertown, Massachusetts. The natural-looking waterfall was constructed in an ancient Japanese fashion. Granite slabs stand at each end of the upper walkway, and water passes between them in a granite streambed. Drinking fountains and trash receptacles are outlined in polished brass. Per square foot, this park is said to have been the most expensive in the country to create.

1.8 ANAWOG, 1978

Jan Evans

Painted steel; H 7 ft. 7 in. × L 9 ft. 6 in.
Gift to the City
Second Avenue S and S Washington Street

This abstract red painted steel squiggle is admired by many, but little is known about it or its creator, Jan Evans—except that the artist may have been inspired by the works of Joan Miró. Anawog was given to the city by the Seattle Foundation after an anonymous donor gave funds to the foundation for that expressed purpose.

1.9 FIRE STATION 10, EMERGENCY OPERATIONS CENTER AND FIRE ALARM CENTER WORKS, 2008

Stuart Nakamura, Gloria Bornstein, Nancy Chew, Jacqueline Metz

Seattle 1 Percent for Art Program
400 S Washington Street

Three sculptures at Fire Station 10 and the adjoining Emergency Operations Center and Fire Alarm Center illustrate the role of those who work in the centers and the cultural diversity of the International District and the other neighborhoods they serve. Stuart Nakamura created *Call and Response,* which stands outside of the fire station entrance, to pay tribute to the service and valor of the firefighters of Fire Station 10 and its historic tradition of responding to emergency calls and protecting the downtown and International District communities. A focal point is a sheet of stainless steel in the shape of an arc of water, with the profile of a firefighter wielding a hose and battling a smoking blaze. The form refers to Tom Askman's designs on the upper corners of the original Fire Station 10 (at 301 Second Avenue S) that this new building replaced. Nakamura points out that Fire Station 10 is known in the Seattle Fire Department as "the Rock," and closer to the entrance is a large granite boulder etched with lines that evoke water ripples. The third element of Nakamura's creation is the inlaid arcs of stone in the surrounding concrete that refer to the fact that stone was used to construct new buildings after the central

1.9 *Call and Response*, Stuart Nakamura

1.9 *bamboo, luminous*, Nancy Chew and Jacqueline Metz

1.9 *Sentinels*, Gloria Bornstein

business district was destroyed in the Great Seattle Fire of 1889.

Up the hill, on the south side of the brick-faced operations center building, is Gloria Bornstein's *Sentinels*, a collection of eight red steel sculptures that diminish in size as they progress up S Washington Street. Bornstein explains that they stand as guardians of the city representing both the staff of the fire station and members of the Asian community who stand watch over the interests of the neighborhood. These forms were inspired by the artist's study of protective gear used by fire departments in different cultures and by Asian art, architecture, and folk craft. The latter is represented by the shapes that refer to Japanese kokeshi dolls.

The bright green, luminescent bamboo stems standing at the entrance of the Emergency Operations Center on Fifth Avenue is *bamboo, luminous* by Vancouver, British Columbia, artists Nancy Chew and Jacqueline Metz. The artists selected bamboo not only because it is important to many Asian cultures represented in Seattle's International District but also to serve as a symbol of the resilience, strength, endurance, and ability to adapt that has enabled many Asian immigrants to survive and prosper in the region. Morihei Ueshiba (1883–1969), the founder of the Japanese martial art of aikido, advised his students to "study the teaching of the bamboo. . . . The bamboo is strong, resilient and unbreakable." Chew and Metz point out that those qualities are also evident in many of those within the adjacent buildings who provide essential services to the community.

1.10 GORDON HIRABAYASHI, AMERICAN PATRIOT, 2015

Roger Shimomura

Acrylic on canvas; H 10 ft. × L 8 ft.
Private commission
Hirabayashi Place, 442 S Main Street

The painted mural in the front window of Hirabayashi Place is Roger Shimomura's tribute to the life and achievements of Gordon Hirabayashi (1918–2012), a brave American who fought to overturn President Franklin D. Roosevelt's Executive Order 9066 (signed in 1942) that imprisoned well over a hundred thousand Japanese Americans during World War II. Hirabayashi was a student at the University of Washington and refused to comply with the government-imposed curfew for Japanese Americans on the West Coast and the requirement that Japanese Americans register, which would enable the government to send them to internment camps. He was convicted of violating the impositions and was imprisoned. Hirabayashi was later also convicted and imprisoned for refusing induction into the US Army because he would not sign a statement renouncing allegiance to the Japanese emperor, a requirement that he considered racially discriminatory because no other citizens were required to renounce a foreign leader.

Hirabayashi appealed his conviction for violating the curfew to the US Supreme Court and, in 1943 the court ruled in *Hirabayashi v. United States* that the president had the authority during wartime to impose such restrictions because military assessments of risks justified the imprisonment of all Japanese Americans. In 1985 Hirabayashi told the *New York Times* that he fought the government actions not only for personal vindication but for all others who were affected by Executive Order 9066. "My citizenship did not protect me one bit," he said. "Our Constitution was reduced to a scrap of paper."

In the 1980s it was discovered that Gen. John L. DeWitt, who implemented the curfew

1.10   *Gordon Hirabayashi, American Patriot,*
Roger Shimomura (Photo by Spike Mafford)

and evacuations, based his actions not on a military assessment of imminent danger to the country but on his racist views. That evidence was hidden from the Supreme Court in 1942. A US federal district court judge in Seattle ruled that Hirabayashi's conviction was improper and granted a writ of *coran nobis* that overturned the conviction on the grounds that Hirabayashi would not have been convicted had the evidence of racial prejudice been before the court. A 1987 decision of the Ninth Circuit Court of Appeals, written by Judge Mary Murphy Schroeder, found that none of Hirabayashi's convictions were valid.

Shimomura's painting includes these facts and more. He explains that "central in the mural is the arm holding the scale of justice that weighs the egregious actions" of Roosevelt and DeWitt "and the courageous decision of Judge Mary Murphy Schroeder." In the mural's upper left quadrant Shimomura painted a young Hirabayashi and his parents, who emigrated from the Mount Hotaka area of Japan. In the lower left are references to Hirabayashi's college years, the outbreak of war, the prison camp, and his two jail sentences. In the upper right portion are references to Hirabayashi's teaching in Canada and living and teaching in Egypt and Lebanon. Finally, in the lower right portion are references to the years waiting for justice and President Barack Obama's posthumous award of the Presidential Medal of Freedom to Hirabayashi in 2012. Hirabayashi is also shown standing with Minoru Yasui and Fred Korematsu, two other Japanese Americans who fought Executive Order 9066.

Other subjects in the mural are what Shimomura describes as "incidents, objects, logos, structures, and other details that tell a more complete story of this American patriot," including the fact that the Catalina Federal Honor Camp near Tucson, Arizona, where Hirabayashi was imprisoned and which is now part of the Coronado National Forest, was renamed Gordon Hirabayashi Recreation Site.

The mural was commissioned by Interim Community Development Association through a project called the Gordon Hirabayashi Legacy of Justice Committee. That committee convened community members and partner organizations to raise funds and administer public art and interpretive elements at Hirabayashi Place to honor Gordon Hirabayashi's story and legacy.

1.11 KING STREET CENTER BUILDING

Jean Whitesavage, Nick Lyle, Maya Radoczy, Dale Chihuly

King County 1 Percent for Art Program
201 S Jackson Street

Jean Whitesavage and Nick Lyle have created many hand-forged steel sculptures in Seattle's public places, but their 1999 *Rainforest Gates* at the northwest corner of King Street Center is their tour de force. It consists of a main gate that is twenty-two feet high and twenty-two feet wide, two sets of bifold side gates, two large decorative brackets, and, at the top of the building, an "eyebrow" with a decorative band beneath it. Each section is decorated with hand forged and painted steel depictions of native plants and creatures in the Pacific Northwest ecosystem that are woven together in what has been described as "visual poetry." Sword ferns and alder leaves can be seen in the eyebrow above. Subjects below include ferns growing

1.11 *Rainforest Gates,* Jean Whitesavage and Nick Lyle

amid vanilla leaves and branches of big leaf maple, a flicker, a pileated woodpecker, and a cedar waxwing with an unusually long bill (an example of the artists' desire not to be too literal). Lyle explains that an important aspect of their work is the manipulation of the metal surfaces to reflect light and create shadows and to have a sense of movement.

The lobby of the King Street Center includes sculptures by Maya Radoczy and Dale Chihuly. Radoczy's three-part installation, created in 1999, consists of glass depictions of earth, wind, and water. The chandelier above the entryway is *Wind,* a swirling form constructed of curved metal tubes that impale descending groups of irregularly curved metal and glass shapes. *Water* is a small grouping of back-lit glass panels that are somewhat lost in the extended ceiling framework. The surface of each is a collection of low-relief ripples. Adorning the wall at the end of the lobby are ten rectangular glass panels attached to a sheet of stainless steel. This is *Earth,* and its panels look like sheets of ice with protruding ice crystals randomly placed with no two groupings alike, haphazard and complicated as natural forms often are.

In the middle of the lobby is Dale Chihuly's *Sunny Yellow Macchia with Peacock Lip Wrap,* a blown glass vessel with a bright yellow interior, a skin of mottled green with red and orange hues, and a thin line of peacock blue around the lip. It is a grand example of his Macchia series in which speckled colors (*macchia* is Italian for "spot") are created by rolling molten glass in small shards of colored glass during the blowing process. The interior and exterior layers of color are separated by adding a white layer, known as a cloud, that keeps the layers of colors from blending together.

1.12 THE PLAZA, 1999

Jack Mackie

Concrete, steel, landscaping
King County 1 Percent for Art Program
King Street Center, 201 S Jackson Street, exterior plaza at
    southeast corner off of S King Street

Across from the King Street Station's lower entrance on King Street is a massive curved concrete wall with a textured surface designed

to be reminiscent of a bluff extending above a beach. It is topped by railings of yellow curved steel lines of different sizes that refer to windblown seagrass. Behind that wall is a grand staircase that leads up to the rest of Jack Mackie's intriguing installation called *The Plaza*. It sits on land in a seismically active region that was once shoreline before early Seattleites filled it in. In collaboration with NBBJ and Hewett Architects and the building's developer, Wright Runstad & Company, Mackie created a plaza with a central area that appears to have been affected by a massive earthquake that lifted the ground and the trees and left them askew. The plaza floor has large red-, green-, and yellow-colored pavement and concrete bands that represent urban gridlines. Those walking through will notice that the grid reassembles itself and returns to normal at the base of the building. *The Plaza* is also accessible off of S Jackson Street at the northeast corner of the King Street Center building.

1.13 4 (WHERE SHALL I GO AHEAD?), 2001

Bill Will

Granite
Seattle 1 Percent for Art Program
Union Station Square, S Jackson Street between
    Third Avenue S and Second Avenue Ext. S

Transportation is the central theme of Bill Will's sculpture *4 (Where shall I go ahead?)*, which consists of twenty-three granite blocks in the triangular space north of the King Street Amtrak Station. The tops of these blocks are engraved with railroad references, including the

1.12   *The Plaza*, Jack Mackie

1.13   *4 (Where shall I go ahead?)*, Bill Will

1.14 INTERNATIONAL DISTRICT METRO STATION ARTWORKS, 1990

Sonya Ishii, Alice Adams, and Laureen Mar, with architect Gary Hartnett

Mixed media

King County Metro commission

International District Metro Station, S Jackson Street,
    between Fourth and Fifth Avenues S

The southern terminus of Metro's transit tunnel includes artworks above and below ground by local artist Sonya Ishii and New York sculptor Alice Adams, some of which reflect the Asian character of the district. Both artists collaborated on the twelve colored-brick figures of the Chinese calendar in the station's street-level plaza. Each figure is approximately seven feet, six inches square. Adams and Ishii also worked with station architect Gary Hartnett on designs for steel trellises on the station's plaza level. Etched on stainless steel on the overhead beams of the trellis walkway is poetry by Laureen Mar. At the Jackson Street entrance, visitors are welcomed by two

logo of the Northern Pacific Railway (which was served by the King Street Station), rail designs, hobo and railroad slang, and a patent drawing of the famous Pullman sleeping car. Other blocks reference travel and the surrounding neighborhood, including a comment by Ray Charles, who lived in Seattle from 1948 to 1950 that "Travelling the world opened up my ears." The title of this sculpture is derived from a lesser-known aspect of the Morse code, which uses numbers as abbreviations for statements. In this case Bill Will elected to use 4, which refers to the question, "Where shall I go ahead?"

1.14   Untitled sculpture, Sonya Ishii

1.15　*Ship Painting*, Whiting Tennis

hundred tiles designed by students of Gatzert and Beacon Hill elementary schools.

Prominent features on the east wall of the station tunnel are Sonya Ishii's nine sixteen-by-sixteen-foot stainless steel sculptures showing different stages in the creation of two origami designs. Origami is the ancient art of Japanese paper folding, and the figures here are male and female guardians that Ishii found in a book of origami designs dating back to the seventeenth century.

1.15　SHIP PAINTING, 1998

Whiting Tennis

Acrylic on paper mounted on canvas; H 9 ft. 6 in. × L 14 ft.
Private collection
505 Union Station lobby, 505 Fifth Avenue S

Ship Painting is an early work by Seattle artist Whiting Tennis and refers to the first sighting by Native Americans of English settlers arriving on the *Mayflower* off of Cape Cod in 1620. Tennis read that the Native Americans were sitting on the dunes at Cape Cod when they first saw the ship's sails in the distance. He went to Cape Cod and hiked across the white sand dunes, trying to imagine the scene. The result is this energetic painting/collage of clouds, ocean swells, and dunes, and in the center are the sails of a tiny vessel on the horizon.

1.16　CASCADIA, 2000

John Hoge

Columnar basalt
Private commission
505 Union Station plaza, 505 Fifth Avenue S

Cascadia is a multipart sculpture in which Seattle stone artist John Hoge refers to a flood that scoured the landscape of central and southeastern Washington, leaving formations of basalt, the stone used in each element here. The portion of *Cascadia* in the center of the plaza is *Garden of Vessels,* a thirty-four-foot-wide collection of columns (the tallest is twelve feet) that have water bubbling out of concave tops and flowing down over their unfinished sides. These are surrounded by a ring of hexagonal basalt blocks, with two large concave boulders that also have water bubbling out of their tops. To the south is *Sentries of the Palisades*, a twenty-eight-foot-wide design containing four columns with rounded tops (the tallest is sixteen feet) that are bordered by low basalt blocks, some rough and others partially sculpted. Behind them in a bed of ivy is a checkerboard arrangement of low basalt stones.

Near the building's entrance is a two-part entry sculpture with a fifteen-foot-tall sculpted column and a smaller boulder at its base. To the right is *Water Table*, two horizontal sections of carved and polished basalt with water flowing

quietly out of holes on their flat polished surfaces, creating a mirror-like effect. The final element of Hoge's *Cascadia* is a three-part sculpted bench. Note the finely polished ends of the separated elements—which almost fit together—create what Hoge calls "ball-and-socket joints." The ball-and-socket design is also apparent in the tops of the *Garden of Vessels* columns in the plaza. Hoge's work was commissioned by Vulcan Real Estate, the property developer.

The stonework surrounding the plantings in the 505 Union Station plaza was created by the Seattle landscape design firm Murase Associates. Murase also created the assemblage of stone elements on the building's north side, which is designed to collect and redirect water that drains down the building's curved north wall.

1.17 PUBLIX STREET SIDE MURAL, 2017

Laura Brodax

Ceramic tile; H 2 ft. × L 45 ft.
Private commission
Publix Hotel, at 504 Fifth Avenue S

At the south end of the Publix Hotel is *Publix Street Side Mural*, a long ceramic tile mural by Laura Brodax. Created in 2017, her design is an homage to the historic Publix Hotel, which opened in 1928 and housed immigrant workers from Asia. The mural depicts Japanese-inspired plant arrangements and in the background are signatures from the hotel's registry from 1928 to 1945. The flower arrangements refer to the rooftop garden maintained

1.16　*Cascadia*, John Hoge

1.17 *Publix Street Side Mural,* Laura Brodax

by the grandmother of the family that managed the hotel after World War II. The Publix Hotel was converted to apartments and commercial space in 2017.

1.18 SEATTLE CHINATOWN GATE, 2008

Paul Wu and MulvaneyG2 Architecture

Steel and ceramic tile; H approx. 43 ft.
Gift to the city
Fifth Avenue S and S King Street

The *Seattle Chinatown Gate* not only marks the west entrance to Chinatown, it also stands as a symbol of the long presence and contributions of Chinese people and culture in Seattle. Completed in 2008, it is a traditional Chinese design. It is painted red, gold, blue, and green—all auspicious colors in Chinese culture—with upturned rooflines supported by interlocking roof bracket supports and decorated with ceramic tiles. The curve of the roof is said to ward off evil spirits, which move only in straight lines, or at least soften the force of

shooting energy. The roof is full of symbolism. At the top is a fireball from heaven that symbolizes good luck. Figures include a phoenix, both a harbinger of peace and prosperity and symbol of the sun and plentiful harvest; a lion, symbolic of energy and valor; and a dragon, a creature whose many symbolic references include protection and vigilance. The gold vertical Chinese calligraphy in the center of each side says "Chinese Gate."

Although *Seattle Chinatown Gate* looks like a traditional wood structure, it is actually made of steel. Paul Wu was the principal architect, and the MulvanneyG2 architecture firm assisted with the preliminary design, which required pilings extending eighty-five feet down so the four posts could rest on hard ground. The Kaiping Design Institute in China helped with the ornamentation. Most of the gate's elements were created in China, and an expert in Chinese gate construction came from China to help construct it. Seattle's Chinese community spearheaded fund-raising efforts for gate design and construction. Contributors include individuals and businesses as well as city and county neighborhood matching and development funds.

1.19 DRAGONS, 2002

Heather Presler, Martin Brunt, Meng Huang, Jerry Caldwell, and Kevin Lorentzen

Painted fiberglass; L 12 ft. to 20 ft.
Private commission
International District, along Fifth Avenue S, S Dearborn, and S Jackson Streets

The red dragon coiled around the light pole on South Jackson Street between Fifth and Sixth Avenue South is one of ten installed in 2002 along the perimeter of the International District. They were commissioned by the Chinatown/International District Business Improvement Area. The dragon is one of the most important, powerful, and complex creatures in Chinese mythology. Its species inhabit the mountains, sky, and oceans; its magical powers are abundant; and it is the vigilant guardian of treasures. All in all, it is the perfect guardian of the International District. These dragon sculptures range in length from twelve to twenty feet and the design and color of each is unique. Lead artist Heather Presler started her creation process by working with Martin Brunt's designs. She created each head and the claws and devised the color schemes for the dragons. The bodies were constructed by Brunt and Jerry Caldwell, and the painting was done by Kevin Lorentzen.

An important adviser was the late Chinese artist Meng Huang, who ensured that design elements, such as the claws and horns, would be authentic. Each of the dragons has five

1.19   *Dragon,* Heather Presler, Martin Brundt, Meng Huang, Jerry Caldwell, and Kevin Lorentzen

claws, which is common today, but for centuries the five-clawed dragon was a symbol of imperial power reserved only for the emperor. Another advisor for this project was Shan Tung Hsu, a feng shui expert who provided advice about the proper placement of the sculptures.

1.20 UNTITLED MURAL, 1977

John Woo

Painted mural
Seattle Walls Project, funded by the city and private sources
Overlooking Hing Hay Park, Maynard Avenue S and S King Street

1.20   Untitled mural, John Woo

John Woo's dragon mural on the south side of the Bush Hotel depicts the struggle of Asian Americans after their arrival here as laborers in the nineteenth century. The figures shown include Chinese railroad workers, Filipinos working in local canneries and farms, and Japanese Americans in World War II internment camps. Also pictured are local residents taking part in Asian festival celebrations and a view of the International District with the Kingdome (Seattle's first, now demolished, multipurpose stadium) in the background. The mural's central dragon figure is a symbol of good luck.

Woo's mural was the result of the Seattle Walls Project in which the Downtown Seattle Development Association and the Seattle Arts Commission sponsored the creation of painted murals on the walls of select downtown buildings. Most have disappeared, but Woo's mural has become a neighborhood icon that has been well maintained over the years. It looks down on a traditional Chinese pavilion that was constructed in Taipei, Taiwan, and erected in Seattle in 1975. It was gift of the city of Taipei and the government of Taiwan.

In 2017 Hing Hay Park was renovated and expanded west and is now twice its original size. The bright red painted steel plate seats and steps are supplemented with laser-cut patterns from the Chinese zodiac and other patterns, all backlit with LED lights. They were designed by Amanda Bruot and Jeff Hudak of Seattle's Studio Fifty50, who also designed the red gateway at the park's southwest corner, which is also made of laser-cut steel. Its shape was inspired by Japanese origami designs, and nearby terraces in the park were inspired by Asian rice paddies. The expanded park was designed by landscape architecture teams from MIG/SvR Design Company in Seattle and Turenscape in Beijing.

1.21   Untitled street sculpture, George Tsutakawa

1.21 UNTITLED STREET SCULPTURE, 1978

George Tsutakawa

Silicon bronze; H 12 ft. 2 in. × L 2 ft. 9 in.
Seattle 1 Percent for Art Program and private sources
Corner of S Jackson Street and Maynard Avenue S, one block
    north of Hing Hay Park

George Tsutakawa, a master of sculptural fountains, explained that this vertical bronze sculpture is closely related to other themes he used in his works, such as totemic designs and obos (the piled rock memorials placed on mountain trails in Tibet), "but without the use

of water I had to be more careful with proportion and concentrate on the scene from different angles. Sculpture, not water, became the most important aspect." Tsutakawa included in this sculpture an unusual aspect: three stylized characters of Chinese calligraphy for Heaven, Man, and Earth.

> Half a block up the hill from the Tsutakawa sculpture is an interesting collection of photos transferred onto ceramic tile. They line the tops of semicircular sidewalk planters in front of Nihonmachi (Japantown) Terrace. Ceramic signage describes the theme of each group of photos, which relate to Japanese American heritage and the history of the Japantown neighborhood. This artwork was created by Laura Brodax.

1.22 DONNIE CHIN INTERNATIONAL CHILDREN'S PARK SCULPTURES

Gerard Tsutakawa and Stuart Nakamura

Seattle 1 Percent for Art Program and private sources
Donnie Chin International Children's Park, Seventh Avenue S
    and S Lane Street

In the center of the rear portion of this small park is *Dragon Play Sculpture*, created in 1981 by Seattle sculptor Gerard Tsutakawa (his first public commission). This creature's undulating silicon bronze form culminates with the contrasting brightness of stainless steel eyes. Tsutakawa was careful to make his dragon as safe as possible to play on. Edges are rounded

1.22 *Dragon Play Sculpture*, Gerard K. Tsutakawa

1.22 *Spin,* Stuart Nakamura

1.22 *Bounce*, Stuart Nakamura

and it is filled with sand to absorb heat from the metal on hot days.

When the park was to be renovated, Stuart Nakamura was commissioned to create *Roll, Spin, Bounce*, three 2011 sculptures whose designs are based on toys from the Pacific Rim. He chose the designs to reflect the diversity of cultures found in the International District. *Roll*, which stands in the upper portion of the park to the left of *Dragon Play Sculpture*, is a thirty-two-inch-diameter stainless steel coin standing on its edge. This sculpture began as a depiction of a toy hoop that children roll with a stick. There was a concern that children could get hurt if they climbed through it, so Nakamura closed the space and created an Asian coin design. On the opposite side is *Spin*, a thirty-two-inch-tall stainless steel top that appears to be delicately balanced as it spins along a thin stainless steel line in the concrete. The third piece is *Bounce*, a bronze thirty-inch-diameter depiction of the woven rattan ball used in the Southeast Asian sport of *sepak takraw*. It is located on the edge of the low wall next to the curved brick plaza.

1.23 WELLSPRING, 2005

Rene Yung

Teacups and miscellaneous materials
Seattle 1 Percent for Art Program
Seattle Public Library, International District Branch,
    713 Eighth Avenue S

Wellspring is Rene Yung's innovative celebration of tea and teacups that she created as a "symbol of sustenance and hospitality to unite a community with internal cultural schisms." It consists of three separate elements, each

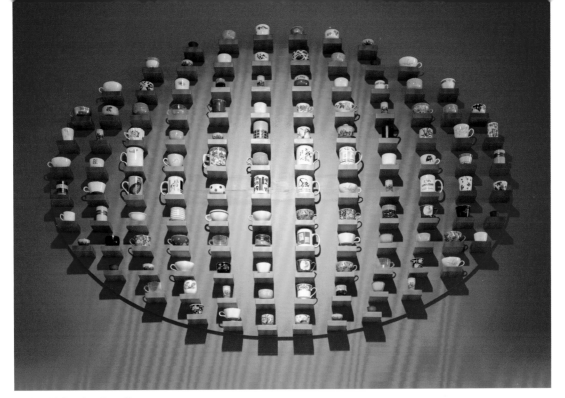

1.23   *Wellspring,* Rene Yung

with the teacup as the central figure. The principal element—a collection of 120 traditional and contemporary teacups that the artist gathered from the community—is arranged in the shape of a globe. Each teacup stands on a small wooden shelf mounted against the red interior north wall of the library. For her second element, Yung placed additional single cups "floating" in internally lit resin cubes that have been placed on the shelves among the library books.

The artist calls her third element *Story Teacups.* She placed cups in an interior casework with etched glass narratives that she says "impart the personal amidst the symbolic." One of the etched statements reads, "Making and drinking a bowl of tea—a simple, open, and honest meeting—the oneness—of guest—and host." Yung says that the cups in *Wellspring* represent "an individual well of nourishment and jointly a gathering of goodwill and vitality."

1.24 DRAGON TOWER, 2002

Aki Sogabe

Cut copper sheets
Private commission
Uwajimaya, 600 Fifth Avenue S

The dragon design, cut from copper sheets, wrapped around the twenty-one-foot-tall steel tower at the entrance to Uwajimaya is the kiri-e design of Bellevue artist Aki Sogabe. Japanese kiri-e (paper cutting) is an ancient form of art in which a very sharp blade is used to create intricate artworks out of paper. Sogabe is a master of that craft. *Song of the Earth,* another Sogabe paper-cut design, rendered in porcelain enamel, can be seen at the Pike Place Market (6.20). *Dragon Tower* was commissioned by Uwajimaya.

1.25 BRIDGE BETWEEN CULTURES, 1999

Fernanda D'Agostino and Valerie Otani

Cut steel

King County Metro commission

Weller Street pedestrian bridge, S Weller Street and
  Fourth Avenue S

The metal grillwork on the sides of the Weller Street pedestrian bridge, which crosses over the railroad tracks and passenger loading zones of King Street Station, have laser-cut designs created by Oregon artists Fernanda D'Agostino and Valerie Otani. The images refer to the culture and history of the area. Included are Chinese workers who were instrumental in building the railroads, a modern Amtrak train, a poster for the Sleeping Car Porters' Union and posters promoting travel to Southeast Asia, travelers disembarking from a 1950s-era plane, an antique box of imported Japanese tea, wheat destined for export, gambling cards and jazz musicians, a graph showing rising and falling numbers of immigrants to the area, and images of balls used in different sports played in nearby stadiums.

1.25 *Bridge Between Cultures* (details), Fernanda D'Agostino and Valerie Otani

1.26 CENTURYLINK FIELD ARTWORKS, 2002

Robert Haozous, Susan Point, Beliz Brother, Claudia Fitch, Peter Shelton

Private commissions
800 Occidental Avenue S

When state voters approved the construction of what is now CenturyLink Field, First and Goal, Inc., a Paul Allen enterprise, which is the private partner of this public facility, contributed $1.75 million for artworks. After a juried selection process, twelve works were commissioned, five of which are outside and readily available for public viewing. Those works, created in 2002, have nothing to do with sports. Rather, the selection process was focused on commissioning unique, thought-provoking art by regional and national artists that would represent a diverse range of culture and artistic perspectives.

On the stadium's imposing north tower entrance is *Earth Dialogue*, four twenty-four-foot-diameter painted steel disks by Native American artist Robert Haozous. Haozous notes that each disk has symbols that relate to his Warm Springs–Chiricahua Apache heritage, but they also have universal meaning and refer to our deep connection to the earth. The lowest disk features skyscrapers and refers to the urban world that supplants nature. Above it is a green disk that symbolizes life and growth, but in its upper half human figures are drifting away, referring to the loss of human ties to nature. The yellow disk represents the sun, which the artist uses to remind us of the "dependence on the natural world and the redemptive powers of nature." With the white disk at the

1.26   *Earth Dialogue*, Robert Haozous

1.26   *Written into the Earth*, Susan Point

1.26 *Colossal Heads (The Girl Next Door)* and *Colossal Heads (Ivory Coast Mask)*, Claudia Fitch

top Haozous depicts clouds to suggest "the immensity of the natural environment."

Susan Point, a master of Coast Salish Native art, installed two sets of works at CenturyLink that are collectively called *Written into the Earth*. In an arc at the bottom of the stairs in front of the Haozous tower are cast bronze bas-relief sculptures in four designs that represent world cultures. Point also designed the cast-iron tree grates that lie at the base of the trees throughout the stadium and Exhibition Center grounds. Their designs are related to those of native spindle whorls. Spindle whorls are handheld poles with flywheel-like disks traditionally used by Natives to spin wool into yarn. Those disks were often embellished with carved designs.

Embedded in the concrete at the northwest portion of the plaza outside of the stadium is a series of white and purple lights that are best seen at night. This is *Lumen*, a commissioned artwork by Beliz Brother.

Two other commissioned sculptures are on the west side of CenturyLink Field. On the columns along the Stadium Arcade entrance on Occidental Avenue are the six massive (H 6 ft. × L 4 ft. × Dia 3 ft.) *Colossal Heads* by Claudia Fitch. Fitch says that during her graduate studies in Rome she was not only inspired by the monumental statuary in the ancient stadiums but also by "the power of good urban/streetscape design and its intentional enfolding of sculpture as a counterpoint to architectural rhythms, visually setting the stage for a rich social drama." She applied those inspirations to this grand concrete setting. Bold street signage, corporate logos, and festival masks were also inspirations, including masks seen at Rio de Janeiro's Carnival, sculptural signs from Coney Island, and traditional African and Asian theatrical masks. Fitch also had in mind iconic photographs of twentieth-century movie stars. Each head is made of fiberglass

1.26 *ROCKshadow*, Peter Shelton

over polystyrene foam and painted with auto-
mobile epoxy. Their individual titles, starting
at the north end, are *Sleeping Spectator, Ivory
Coast Mask, Lauren Bacall, The Girl Next Door,
Dutch Elvis*, and *Roman Spectator*.

The last of the five CenturyLink artworks is
Peter Shelton's two-part *ROCKshadow*, located
in the pocket park between the stadium and the
convention center. *ROCK* is a ninety-thousand-
pound, thirteen-foot-tall by eight-foot-diameter
white granite boulder retrieved from a glacial
moraine near Kent, Washington. The boulder
was used both as a pattern to form a wax skin
that covered a chalk-drawn map describing
the contour of the boulder's surface. Once the
wax skin was removed and cast in bronze, the
black patinated adjacent partner, *shadow*, was
created. The concept of this two-part sculpture
arose from the artist's interests in "seemingly
opposite values like inside and outside, big and
small, heavy and light" and his fascination with

the idea of using the boulder as a dressmaker
would use a manikin or "dummy" to create
a coat. Shelton was interested in how these
two elements would relate to one another and
how they would be perceived. Would viewers
recognize that the boulder is the pattern for
the darker shape? Would they ask which came
first? Might the real boulder appear lighter
than its shadow?

1.27 SAFECO FIELD ARTWORKS

**Gerard Tsutakawa, Ries Niemi, Lou Cella, Stuart
Keeler, Michael Machnic, Linda Beaumont**

Public commissions
1250 First Avenue S

Safeco Field was built and is owned by the
Washington State Major League Baseball
Stadium Public Facilities District, an entity
created in 1995 by the Washington State
Legislature and the King County Council. The
budget for the stadium included $1.31 million
for public art, which amounted to 0.5 percent
of the hard construction costs of the ballpark
and the adjacent garage. The owner engaged in
an extensive public process and review to select
artists and art for the facility, including a number of exterior works that are readily available
for public viewing.

Standing at the north entrance of Safeco
Field is Gerard Tsutakawa's welded bronze
sculpture, *The Mitt*. This nine-foot-tall, twelve-
foot-long iconic and much photographed symbol of the baseball stadium includes an example
of the artist's sense of humor—a circular hole
where a fastball might have burned through.
This is one of two works created in 1998 for

1.27 *The Mitt,* Gerard Tsutakawa

1.27 *Ken Griffey Jr.,* Lou Cella

1.27 *The Tempest,* Stuart Keeler, Michael Machnic and Linda Beaumont

the new facility. The second is a collection of Ries Niemi's twenty-four larger-than-life baseball players cut out of stainless steel. The piece above the entrance is called *Game in Progress*; Niemi created an entire team and an opposing batter and placed them under an eighty-foot-long arc of baseballs flying through the air. Also on the north side of the stadium is Niemi's *Batting Fence*, showing a batter hitting a variety of well-known pitches, and each ball is labeled with its nickname, such as "Can of Corn," and "Pop Fly." Niemi's figures on the south side of the stadium, along Royal Brougham Way, are pitchers and catchers.

Outside of Safeco Field's south entrance, at the corner of First Avenue S and Edgar Martinez Drive S is Chicago sculptor Lou Cella's bronze statue of former Mariner star Ken Griffey Jr. This seven-foot-tall likeness, dedicated in 2017, shows the Baseball Hall of Fame inductee executing the home-run swing for which he was so well-known during his career. He was a thirteen-time All-Star who racked up 630 home runs and drove in 1,836 runs during his twenty-two big-league seasons, thirteen with the Mariners and subsequent stints with the Cincinnati Reds and (for a short while) the Chicago White Sox.

Hanging just inside the south entrance gates, behind *Ken Griffey Jr.*, is *The Tempest*, a swirling collection of fifteen hundred translucent resin baseball bats on a brushed aluminum frame that spirals up above the rotunda floor. It suggests the whirl of a batter's swing and is made more dramatic by a system of strobe and incandescent lighting. This sculpture was inspired by a portion of Prospero's lines in act 4, scene 1

of Shakespeare's play, *The Tempest*, beginning with,

Our revels now are ended. These our actors,
As I foretold you, were all spirits and
Are melted into air, into thin air

The Tempest was created in 2000 by the team of Stuart Keeler, Michael Machnic, and Linda Beaumont. They also created the steel entrance gates, which have patterns evoking the rigging of tall ships and the lines of a baseball diamond; plaques with quotations pertaining to baseball; a colored concrete floor that suggests a churning sea; and a twenty-two-foot-diameter terrazzo compass rose at the top of the grand staircase. The theme of those four elements is "Through the portals across the swirling sea, the Tempest rages above."

1.28 RED STIX, 2012

Konstantin Dimopoulos

Composites, steel, and concrete; H 33 ft.
Private commission
Home Plate Center, 1501 First Avenue S

In the plaza of Home Plate Center are three groups of bright red vertical rods that sculptor Konstantin Dimopoulos uses to refer to the primordial past and plant life that once grew on this developed site of filled-in tidelands. Surrounded by granite water features and lush plantings, the rods gently sway in the breeze and present what the artist describes as an organic aspect to the built environment.

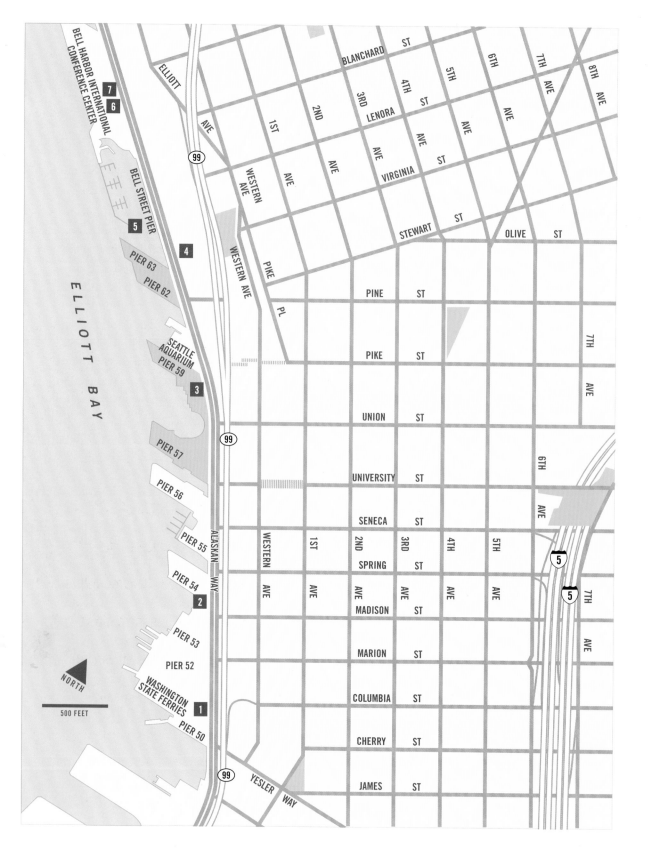

ELLIOTT BAY

BELL HARBOR INTERNATIONAL
CONFERENCE CENTER

7
6

BELL STREET PIER

5

PIER 63

4

PIER 62

ELLIOTT AVE

99

SEATTLE
AQUARIUM
PIER 59

3

PIER 57

WESTERN AVE

99

PIER 56

PIER 55

ALASKAN WAY

PIER 54

2

PIER 53

PIER 52

NORTH

500 FEET

WASHINGTON
STATE FERRIES

1

PIER 50

99

YESLER WAY

BLANCHARD ST

6TH AVE

5TH AVE

7TH AVE

8TH AVE

4TH ST

3RD AVE

LENORA

1ST AVE

2ND AVE

WESTERN AVE

VIRGINIA ST

STEWART ST

OLIVE ST

PIKE PL

PINE ST

7TH AVE

PIKE ST

UNION ST

6TH AVE

UNIVERSITY ST

SENECA ST

WESTERN AVE

1ST AVE

2ND AVE

3RD AVE

4TH AVE

5TH AVE

SPRING ST

MADISON ST

5

5

7TH AVE

MARION ST

COLUMBIA ST

CHERRY ST

JAMES ST

2 THE WATERFRONT

Objective painting is not good painting unless it is good in the abstract sense. A hill or tree cannot make a good painting just because it is a hill or tree. It is lines and colors put together so that they may say something.

—Georgia O'Keeffe (1887–1986)

SEATTLE'S WATERFRONT HAS ALWAYS BEEN A HUB of activity for visitors and residents alike. With the removal of the Alaskan Way viaduct and renovations and construction under the Waterfront Seattle Program to be completed in 2023, the area will be a hive of activity with twenty acres of new and improved public space and more direct connections to the Pike Place Market and downtown. Seven artworks were installed before waterfront renovations began. Thanks to state and local 1 percent for art programs, at least six more will be added for the enjoyment of all.

2.1 JOSHUA GREEN FOUNTAIN, 1966

George Tsutakawa

Silicon bronze; H 6 ft. × W 7 ft. × L 9 ft.
Gift to the city
Across the promenade from the Washington State Ferry
    Terminal at the foot of Columbia Street

This bronze fountain is a gift to the city from the late Joshua Green, an early Seattle shipping magnate and banker. One commentator has suggested that Tsutakawa's design for this early work has a flower or nature theme, perhaps inspired by his Japanese heritage. Tsutakawa suggested otherwise: "I suppose you could see a flower theme, but there was a lot of abstract work in the 1960s and I think I was probably working with abstract design when I made this fountain." The fountain was originally placed in front of the Washington State Ferry Terminal. It has been removed for terminal remodeling, and after completion of the Seattle waterfront redevelopment project it will be placed east of its original location, on the edge of the pedestrian promenade.

2.2 IVAR FEEDING THE GULLS, 1988

Richard Beyer

Cast bronze and aluminum; H 5 ft. 8 in. × W 5 ft.
Gift to the city
Foot of Madison Street in front of Ivar's Acres of Clams
    restaurant

This memorial to Ivar Haglund (1905–85) is the first statue of a Seattle citizen to be placed in a public location in Seattle since the statues of Chief Seattle (7.18) and John Harte McGraw (6.24) were installed in 1912. Haglund was a successful restaurant owner and entrepreneur who was admired for his good humor and unassuming devotion to the city and its people. After his death, a group of his friends (whose names are listed on the bronze captain's chair) donated money to create this memorial. Ivar is shown wearing a seaman's coat and captain's hat and is engaged in one of his favorite pastimes at his Acres of Clams restaurant, feeding french fries to the local gulls. Sculptor Richard Beyer was known as a good-humored lover of children, and he made the gulls here oversized to allow children to sit on them, and one of those birds is reaching beneath the chair to catch a bronze clam running away.

2.2   *Ivar Feeding the Gulls*, Richard Beyer

2.3　*Waterfront Fountain*, James FitzGerald and Margaret Tomkins

2.4　*Welcoming Spirits*, Melvin Schuler

2.3　WATERFRONT FOUNTAIN, 1974

James FitzGerald and Margaret Tomkins

Bronze; H 16 ft.6 in. × W 18 ft. × L 21 ft.
Gift to the city
Waterfront Park

Waterfront Fountain is the last fountain that James FitzGerald created for Seattle's public places. Made of cast and welded bronze, he designed it only a few months before his death in October 1973. His wife, noted Northwest painter Margaret Tomkins, executed the commission from her husband's bronze scale model. She was assisted by sculptor Terry Copple and welder Art Sjodin, both of whom had worked with FitzGerald on past commissions. This work does not have the craggy, eroded shapes of the artist's earlier fountains at the IBM Building (5.25) and the Cornish Playhouse (8.26). It is a combination of cubical structures with comparatively little surface treatment. *Waterfront Fountain* was given to Seattle by Helen Harrington Schiff in memory of her parents, Edward M. and Margaret J. Harrington. The Harringtons came to Seattle from Delaware in 1921 after Edward's retirement from the DuPont Company, and they maintained an undying love for Seattle. Edward died in 1931, and Margaret was an active philanthropist in this area until her death in 1966.

Note: This fountain may be moved to another location during a later phase of waterfront development. Whether that will occur and its ultimate location were unknown when this guide went to print.

2.4　WELCOMING SPIRITS, 1997

Melvin Schuler

Redwood with copper cladding; H 8 ft. × W 7 ft. 6 in.
Private collection
1950 Alaskan Way

Welcoming Spirits is an example of the signature style that the late California sculptor Melvin Schuler began pursuing in the 1970s. He carved abstract forms out of redwood and then covered

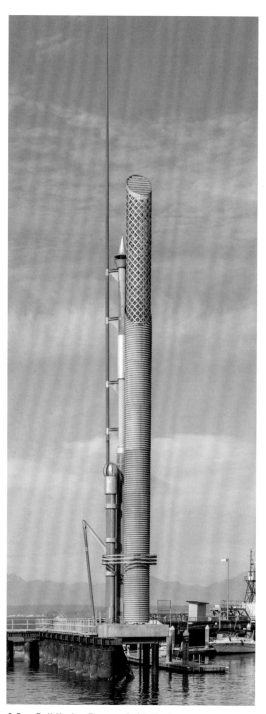

2.5 *Bell Harbor Beacon*, R. M. Fischer

all of their surfaces with overlapping sheets of copper fastened with bronze nails. As is evident here, their armor-like skins acquired a rich green copper patina, and the pieces may bring to mind artifacts from an ancient civilization.

2.5 BELL HARBOR BEACON, 1996

R. M. Fischer

Painted steel and light; H 130 ft.
Port of Seattle commission
Bell Harbor Marina, Bell Street Pier/Pier 66, 2203 Alaskan Way

Bell Harbor Beacon is the lighted, silver spire that rises above Bell Harbor Marina. It harkens back to ancient beacons that directed seafarers into port, and to some it may seem like a futuristic landmark. Both are consistent with New York artist R. M. Fischer's reputation for creating public artworks that inspire descriptions such as "Buck Rogers sci-fi aesthetic" and a "Flash Gordon feel." Art critics have referred to his sculptures in public places as "neofuturistic." That term seems to fit with his comment to the *Philadelphia Inquirer* that his monumental sculptures refer to the "remembered future" that engages people, who may see something familiar in his work "but can't quite figure out why."

2.6 DANZA DEL CERCHIO, 1996

Ann Gardner

Mosaic; L 48 ft.
Port of Seattle collection
Bell Harbor International Conference Center,
  2203 Alaskan Way

2.6   *Danza del Cerchio,* Ann Gardner

Seattle artist Ann Gardner is known for her skill in creating glass mosaics using ancient Byzantine techniques (see 9.17). The same technique was used to create *Danza del Cerchio* (Italian for "Dance of the Circle"), the mosaic at the bottom of the outside stairs leading up to the Bell Harbor International Conference Center. This forty-eight-foot-long mural has multicolored disks with color tones ranging from the greens of spring to the more subdued orange and yellow tones of fall and winter. The images arose from her earlier ink on paper works, and she transferred them to durable mosaic tile to add a playful, colorful piece to brighten up darker Seattle days.

2.7 OUSHI ZOKEI-MADOKA, 1992

Keizo Ushio

Granite; H 6 ft. 6 in. × W 3 ft. 8 in. × L 9 ft. 6 in.
Gift to the City
Bell Harbor International Conference Center,
   2203 Alaskan Way

The carved granite sculpture on the second-floor landing of the outside stairs at the Bell Harbor International Conference Center is one of many examples of complex sculptures in which Japanese sculptor Keizo Ushio uses a Möbius band. A Möbius band can be created out of a paper strip by giving it a half twist and joining the ends together. A full-twist band is created by turning the strip 360 degrees before joining the ends. Tracing one's finger along the band's surface leads to the conclusion that the finger travels along only one surface. There is no front or back.

Creating such shapes is easy with paper; carved granite is another matter. In the case of *Oushi Zokei-Madoka*, the artist created a full twist band from one piece of black granite and then split the piece into two loops after drilling numerous, carefully placed holes along its center line. He then slid the sections apart to create two interlocking elements.

Oushi Zokei is a generic name that Ushio has applied to his Möbius band sculptures. The

2.7   *Oushi Zokei-Madoka*, Keizo Ushio

Japanese word *Oushi* means "deep truth" but also "bull" and the shape of a bull's curved back or tail. *Zo* means "to form or create," while *kei* refers to a "shape" or "form." *Madoka*, which means "round" or "tranquil," is the name of Ushio's third daughter, who was born in 1987, the year he began working with these complicated sculpture forms. The artist says that this 1992 sculpture "was born from of a rice ball shape in a conversation with Madoka at the age of five."

Oushi Zokei-Madoka was a gift to Seattle from the city of Kobe, Japan, to commemorate twenty-five years of the Seattle-Kobe sister city relationship.

SIX ARTWORKS SCHEDULED FOR INSTALLATION

Six commissioned artworks scheduled to be installed as part of Seattle's extensive waterfront renovation project were not yet in place as of the publication of this book. Works by Buster Simpson, Oscar Tuazon, Shaun Peterson, Norie Sato, and Stephen Vitiello are being commissioned under Seattle's 1 Percent for Art Program. Leo Burke's creation will be made possible through the King County and Washington State Percent for Art programs.

Located inland of the water's edge and on the east side of the pedestrian path between S Washington Street and Yesler Way, will be Buster Simpson's *Anthropocene Beach*. The Anthropocene is an unofficial, proposed epoch that begins at the point humans starting having a significant impact on the Earth's geology and ecosystems. Climate change is a good example of such a change. Simpson's design has two elements. The most obvious will be a group of complex cast concrete geometric shapes. These are dolosse, heavy cast concrete elements that are used in great numbers along harbor walls and breakwaters to dissipate the erosive force of waves. Simpson made each somewhat anthropomorphic and shaped so that it can be sat upon. Perhaps viewers will look out on Elliott Bay and contemplate rising waters and erosive forces that will occur in our future.

The second element of *Anthropocene Beach* consists of three, thirty-foot-long walls of cast concrete sandbags. These are also designed to be sat upon, but Simpson warns that viewers should enjoy the experience now, because decades into the future these benches may act as barriers to rising waters created by human-created climate change.

Leo Burke's design for passenger queuing stanchions at the King County Water Taxi Terminal at the foot of Yesler Way was inspired by the fact that the dock for Yesler's Mill stood here, huge amounts of lumber were once shipped from here to San Francisco and other ports, timber pilings were used in the process of filling in tidelands to create today's waterfront, and the waters of Puget Sound relate to so much of the region's life and history. Burke will use four-inch distressed California redwood posts, thereby symbolically bringing wood back to Seattle. The stained designs on each will refer to natural staining from tidal action. Over two hundred posts will be linked by wave patterns of braided blue nylon ropes.

Along the edge of the waterfront for three blocks, from Columbia to Madison Streets, will be two sections of wooden posts and beams that Oscar Tuazon designed to refer to longhouses used by the Coast Salish tribes of the Puget Sound region. Proceeding north, between Madison and Spring Streets, will be a section of posts without beams, as if they are remnants of an ancient longhouse. Tuazon's creation will be the length of one of the largest tribal longhouses that existed in the region, a Native reference imposed along this urban setting. The structures will be supplemented with designs created in collaboration with members of various Coast Salish tribes and landscaping that will further refer to the natural environment in which longhouses existed.

Native artist Shaun Peterson (whose Native name is Qwalsius) is known for his contemporary approaches to traditional art forms of the Coast Salish people, and he will create three unique bronze and red cedar figures that will look out over Puget Sound. Each will be a different height: two will be approximately fifteen feet and a third will be just over fourteen

Salish waterfront figures, Shaun Peterson (Courtesy Shaun Peterson)

feet. Peterson says that although they may be reminiscent of the welcoming figures Native villages often placed on the beach to greet visitors arriving for a ceremony or event, his will represent the human family—not members of any one group or tribe—who stand as symbols of unity and peace. Included on the figures and their concrete bases will be incised

Promenade sculpture, Oscar Tuazon (Courtesy Andrew Ten Brink, James Corner Field Operations)

designs inspired by those used in Coast Salish carving, painting, and weaving.

In early discussions about a Native artwork for the waterfront, planners suggested that a totem pole might be nice. However, despite the fact that totem poles are commonplace in this city named for a Salish chief, the Salish people did not carve such poles. The popular designs seen throughout Seattle are from tribes of the Northwest Pacific Coast, not those of Puget Sound. As his sculptures will stand at the edge of a modern, technological city with many international visitors, Peterson elected to combine contemporary forms with designs of the Indigenous people of Puget Sound.

Norie Sato's artwork will be installed across Alaskan Way and one block inland at Union Street and Western Avenue. She will create a thirty-foot-long by twelve-foot-high curved glass wall that will capture and play with the changing angles of light on the waterfront as the sun sets in the west. Within the layers of glass Sato will place a pigmented layer of film to create iridescent color shifting. What the viewer experiences will change according to the level of brightness and the angle of viewing. On gray days passersby will see images on the surface of the glass rather than colors from within. The curvature of Sato's wall will further enhance the experience as people walk by it. Sato's approach was inspired by her experiences over almost thirty years of admiring the play of reflections off the waters of Elliott Bay as she looked out of her studio at Yesler and Western Avenue.

At the west end of a floating dock to be installed next to Pier 62 will be Stephen Vitiello's

Land Buoy Bells. Vitiello is an electronic musician and media artist who works with sound as an artistic medium. His sculpture will consist of five bells, with diameters ranging from twenty-eight to seventy-two inches, that will be created from repurposed metal tanks. They are to be engineered so that a mechanism will strike each at intermittent times depending on the strength of tidal action below. Vitiello seeks to expand the experience of those who visit the site by adding to the activity on the waterfront sounds that in some cases may be barely perceptible. Silence will often reign and then be interrupted by subtle tones from his bells.

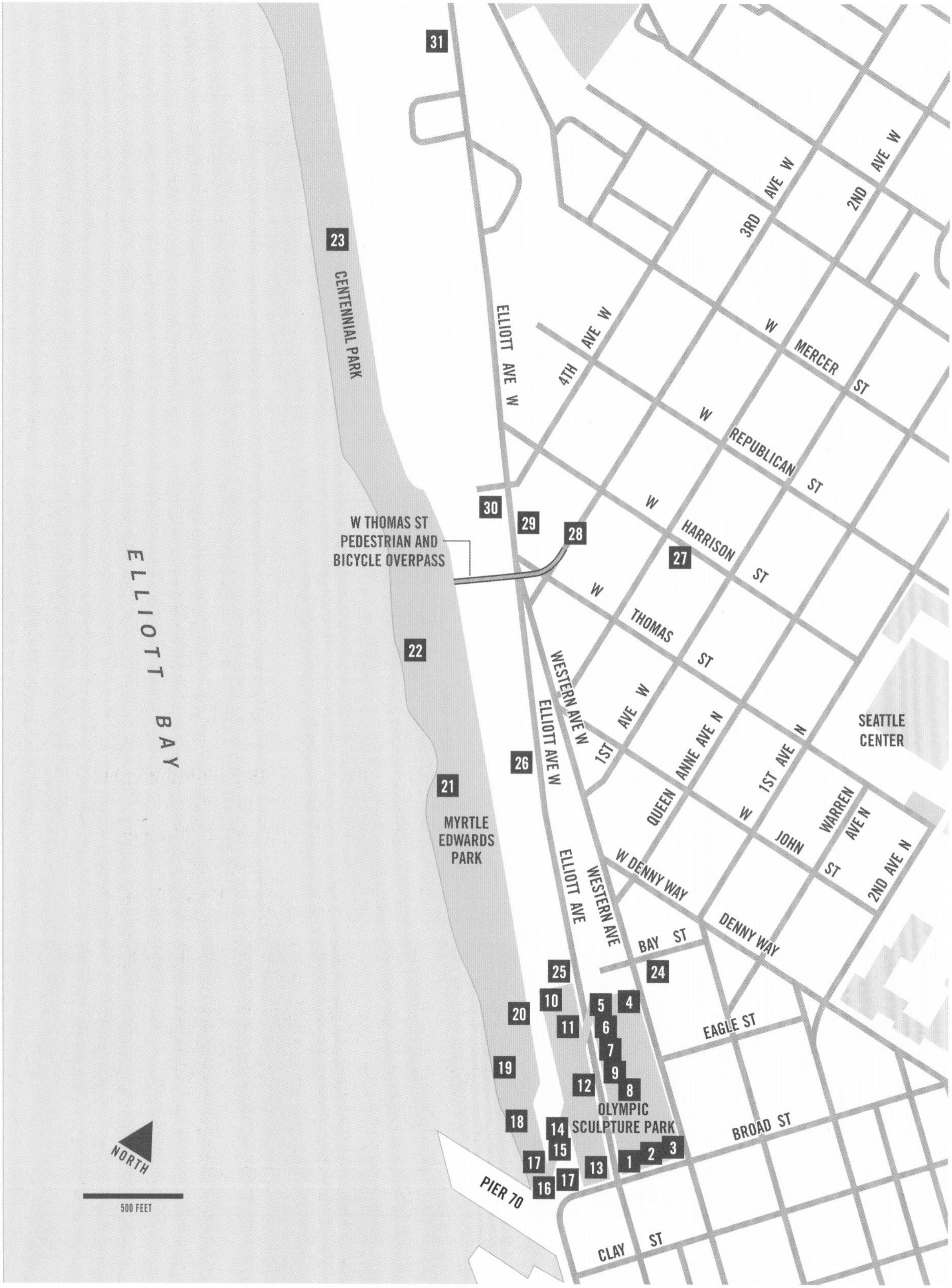

31

23

CENTENNIAL PARK

E L L I O T T   B A Y

30

29

28

27

W THOMAS ST
PEDESTRIAN AND
BICYCLE OVERPASS

22

ELLIOTT AVE W

4TH AVE W

3RD AVE W

2ND AVE W

W MERCER ST

W REPUBLICAN ST

W HARRISON ST

W THOMAS ST

26

21

MYRTLE
EDWARDS
PARK

WESTERN AVE W

ELLIOTT AVE W

1ST AVE W

QUEEN ANNE AVE N

1ST AVE N

SEATTLE
CENTER

WARREN AVE N

2ND AVE N

W JOHN ST

W DENNY WAY

DENNY WAY

ELLIOTT AVE

WESTERN AVE

BAY ST

24

25

10

20

11

5

4

6

7

9

8

EAGLE ST

19

12

OLYMPIC
SCULPTURE PARK

18

14

15

BROAD ST

17

1

2

3

16

17

13

PIER 70

NORTH

500 FEET

CLAY ST

3 OLYMPIC SCULPTURE PARK AND NORTH ENVIRONS

Art is everywhere except it has to pass through a creative mind.

—Louise Nevelson (1899–1988)

THE SEATTLE ART MUSEUM'S OLYMPIC SCULPTURE PARK is a nine-acre site that sits on a former fuel storage and transfer facility. The park extends in a forty-foot grade change from Western Avenue down the hill, across a four-lane roadway and busy railroad tracks, to the last undeveloped section of downtown shoreland. At shore level the property connects to the north with Myrtle Edwards Park and the Port of Seattle's Centennial Park. The Seattle Art Museum (SAM) was able to rally private and local, state, and federal government support to create a sculpture park at the location despite the challenges of extensive environmental cleanup, topography, and separation from the shore.

After seven years of lobbying, planning, and construction, the park opened in January 2007 to much acclaim not only for the art on display but for its architectural design by Weiss/Manfredi and its landscape design by Charles Anderson.

To provide a continuing and scenic connection of all aspects of this park, Weiss/Manfredi created a twenty-two-hundred-foot-long Z-shaped path that begins at the site's southeast corner at PACCAR Pavilion (where SAM presents rotating programs of commissioned artworks), zigs over Elliott Avenue and the railroad tracks, then zags southwest and zigs north to follow the shoreline. That path links Anderson's four landscape zones, each representing a Pacific Northwest ecosystem: the *Valley* is an evergreen forest of trees and plantings found in the moist coastal region; the *Grove* is a forest of quaking aspen selected in part because the sound of their moving leaves will help mask traffic noise; the *Meadow* is a landscape of grasses and wildflowers along both sides of Elliott Avenue; and the *Shore*, which includes native beach grass and pines, is designed not only to promote salmon recovery underwater along the shore but also to provide an accessible beach for human visitors and marine wildlife, including the occasional seal.

Olympic Sculpture Park is part of the Seattle Art Museum, but unlike its brick-and-mortar cousins, this facility has no walls separating it from its surroundings and there is no admission fee. To enable maximum opportunity to commune with nature and enjoy quiet reflection, the park opens thirty minutes before sunrise and closes thirty minutes after sunset. Presiding over the park's highest

point is Alexander Calder's monumental red *Eagle* (3.11). Near the water's edge at the end of Alaskan Way is Louise Bourgeois's unique *Father and Son* (3.16) fountain and Jaume Plensa's sublime *Echo* (3.18). On the grounds in between is a host of sculptures that may inspire or confound. All are worthy of investigation and thought.

3.1 NEUKOM VIVARIUM, 2006

Mark Dion

Mixed media; L 80 ft.
Seattle Art Museum collection
Olympic Sculpture Park

3.1   *Neukom Vivarium,* Mark Dion

3.2 *Split*, Roxy Paine

The Seattle Art Museum describes Mark Dion's *Neukom Vivarium* as "a hybrid work of sculpture, architecture, environmental education, and horticulture that connects art and science." Part of it is an eighty-foot-long greenhouse whose lines echo the angles and shapes of the Olympic Sculpture Park's design. Within the greenhouse is a sixty-foot-long nurse log that provides nutrients to other vegetation as it rots away. The vivarium is all about birth, death, and renewal. "My art," Dion explains, "asks you to think about both nature and sculpture not as objects but as processes." The museum explains that Dion "imagines young visitors coming to see the . . . vivarium, returning while in college, and someday visiting it again with their own children. . . . They would have always entered the same building but never have had the same experience."

Viewers are able to use microscopes and magnifying glasses to more closely investigate the environment of decay and growth in this work. Those tools are provided in a special case designed by Dion that also includes scientific reference books. Tiles along the upper portion of the east wall provide the names of famous naturalists such as John James Audubon, William Beebe, and Rachel Carson. A collection of tiles along retaining walls have scientific illustrations of plants and denizens of the log environment. Those were created by ten artists whose names are listed near the building's north entrance.

Neukom in the sculpture's title refers to Seattle philanthropists Sally and William Neukom, the principal donors who made *Neukom Vivarium* possible.

3.2 SPLIT, 2003

Roxy Paine

Stainless steel; H 50 ft.
Seattle Art Museum collection
Olympic Sculpture Park

With his shiny stainless steel tree in the sculpture park's upper meadow, artist Roxy Paine uses a natural form (complete with broken branches and fungi on the trunk) to comment on the intersection of nature and the industrial world. Paine calls this tree of welded stainless steel pipes a dendroid, and such forms are the culmination of his extensive study of the anatomy of trees and how they grow. In a 2002 interview published by the New York Art Fund, Paine said that this series of works arose from "seeking to explore ideas of permanence and impermanence, death and decay." In the case of *Split*, Paine explains that "it mimics how we increasingly experience nature . . . everything is treated like an element in a machine. I'm interested in the constant desire to control nature, to make it fit into processes, factory processes."

3.3 CURVE XXIV, 1981

Ellsworth Kelly

Steel; H 6 ft. 4 in. × L 19 ft.
Seattle Art Museum collection
Olympic Sculpture Park

During his long career, Ellsworth Kelly achieved fame with his large paintings of precise geometric shapes that often consisted of segments of circles. His subjects arose from observations of shapes and forms around him: the

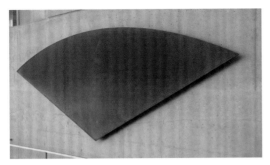

3.3 *Curve XXIV*, Ellsworth Kelly

3.4 *Wake*, Richard Serra

arch of a bridge in Paris, light and shadow on building façades, the rounded edges of a rural hillside, and the outlines of planets in NASA photographs. He was quick to point out that his paintings "don't represent objects . . . they are objects themselves and fragmented perceptions of things." His sculptures, which have been described as monochromatic paintings, take the same approach of reducing images to a bare minimum. *Curve XXIV* is one of a series of sculptures using a fan-shaped portion of a circle that is mounted away from a wall (five inches in this case), to create a shadow extension of the sculpture. It is mounted as if floating in front of a bare concrete wall as Kelly intended it to be when it was commissioned by Seattle collectors Virginia and Bagley Wright for their home.

3.4 WAKE, 2004

Richard Serra

Weathering steel; H 14 ft. 2 in. × W 46 ft. × L 125 ft.
Seattle Art Museum collection
Olympic Sculpture Park

Richard's Serra's three-hundred-ton *Wake* consists of five identical modules of rusted steel forms, each of which is constructed of

massive two-inch-thick curved steel plates bolted together in inverted relation to one another and culminating at each end with a wave form line. Each element is forty-nine feet, six inches long; fourteen feet, two inches high; and six feet wide at its widest point. The individual plates were formed in Germany using massive equipment designed to make ship hulls.

Wake stands in a field of gravel, reminiscent of the Japanese gardens Serra has long admired. In a 1997 interview published by the Dia Center for the Arts in New York, he described the structure of those gardens as "organized with a rigorous mode of placement. . . . The primary characteristic of the garden," he explained, "is that the paths around and through them are curvilinear. The geometry of the site prompts walking in arcs. The articulation of the discrete elements within the field and the sense of the field as a whole emerge only by constant walking and looking."

Curves abound in Serra's *Wake*, which is meant for walking, looking, and engaging in the space. Looking up or along the curves—from the middle of a path or close to a curved steel wall—you may be in awe not only of the massive size but of the relationship between the pieces and their placement in the space. In a

3.5 *Sky Landscape*, Louise Nevelson

Seattle Art Museum publication, Serra explains that "what's important is you moving between them, through them, and around them as they undulate; it's your body moving in relation to their surface that moves."

3.5 SKY LANDSCAPE, 1983

Louise Nevelson

Painted welded aluminum; H 10 ft. × W 6 ft. 2 in. × L 10 ft.
On loan to the Seattle Art Museum
Olympic Sculpture Park

Through almost fifty years of artistic work, Louise Nevelson became famous for her unique assemblages of found elements—at first only wood but later with aluminum and other materials. More often than not, and in the case of *Sky Landscape*, they were painted her favorite color, aristocratic black, which she felt gave a sculpture a feeling of totality and could bring greatness to a work. This sculpture is not limited to its metal shapes. Rather, its shadows are integrated parts of the whole. "Shadow is fleeting," she once remarked. "I give it static life."

3.6   *Perre's Ventaglio III,* Beverly Pepper

Louise Nevelson envisioned her sculptures with an initial mental blueprint, but they were never meticulously planned. They just evolved. In the film *Nevelson in Progress,* an interviewer asked her how she thought of each design. "Darling," she responded, "how do you eat a pear?"

3.6 PERRE'S VENTAGLIO III, 1967

Beverly Pepper

Stainless steel and enamel; H 7 ft. 10 in. × W 8 ft. ×
    L 6 ft. 8 in.
Seattle Art Museum collection
Olympic Sculpture Park

Perre's Ventaglio III is one of three Beverly Pepper sculptures in Seattle's public places and each is from a different period of her long career. Two are in Olympic Sculpture Park, the third is in downtown Seattle (4.6). This sculpture is one of many works Pepper created with highly polished stainless steel frames that have their inner edges covered with blue enamel. Here the forms are fanned out (*ventaglio* is Italian for "fan") and both the voids and the highly polished surfaces incorporate the

surrounding environment into the sculpture, while the painted surfaces seem empty. As a result, *Perre's Ventaglio III* is constantly changing with its surroundings. In Giulio Fratelli's book, *Beverly Pepper,* the artist says that the bright finish "is not simply illusion but the inclusion of the person who is looking at it, so there's a constant exchange going on between the viewer and the work."

3.7 PERSEPHONE UNBOUND, 1999

Beverly Pepper

Cast bronze; H 10 ft. 2 in. × L 2 ft. 7 in.
On loan to the Seattle Art Museum
Olympic Sculpture Park

3.7   *Persephone Unbound,* Beverly Pepper

Beverly Pepper's *Persephone Unbound* rises out of the landscape as a craggy bronze monolith, the central part of which extends up from its rougher lower surfaces. This sculpture is named for the Greek goddess of the underworld who lives upon the earth from spring through harvest and then retreats to the underworld in the fall, much like the receding plants in the fields. Persephone was the daughter of Demeter, goddess of agriculture. According to Greek myth, when Hades, the god of the underworld, abducted Persephone, her mother was so distraught and angry that she refused to let the earth be fruitful until her daughter was returned. But Persephone had eaten pomegranate seeds, the food of the underworld, which made it impossible for her to escape permanently. She was allowed to return only once a year, and her arrival in spring is heralded by the flowering of the earth and the growth of crops. This is the latest of Pepper's works displayed in Seattle's public places (see 3.6 and 4.6)

3.8 TWO PLANE VERTICAL HORIZONTAL VARIATION III, 1973

George Rickey

Stainless steel; H 8 ft. 1 in.
Seattle Art Museum collection
Olympic Sculpture Park

George Rickey's highly polished, precisely balanced stainless steel sculptures may seem passé to many today, but he and Alexander Calder are the two major artists of the last century who brought kinetic sculpture to the forefront of modern art. Rickey used only simple geometric shapes and the form of his sculptures was less important than the balanced, non-mechanized movement of the piece. "I wanted whatever eloquence there was to come out of the performance of the piece," he said, "never out of the shape itself." His sculptures are known for the smooth, natural, and calming tempos created by the wind-generated movement.

In a *New York Times* obituary, art critic Ken Johnson noted that Rickey's work "was often compared with Calder's, but while Calder's abstract mobiles had playful, organic qualities related to Surrealism, Mr. Rickey's geometric forms and machinelike engineering harked back to the early-20th-century Russian movement of Constructivism. . . . It is a curious fact of contemporary art history," Johnson concluded, "that Mr. Rickey left no significant artistic heirs

3.8 *Two Plane Vertical Horizontal Variation III*, George Rickey

3.9 *Mary's Invitation: A Place to Regard Beauty,* Ginny Ruffner

... no sculptor has adopted his innovations with comparably persuasive ambition or elegance." Another George Rickey sculpture can be seen at 1015 Second Avenue (4.9).

3.9 MARY'S INVITATION: A PLACE TO REGARD BEAUTY, 2004

Ginny Ruffner

Coated aluminum; H 4 ft. × L 9 ft.
Seattle Art Museum collection
Olympic Sculpture Park

Ginny Ruffner's curved biomorphic bench on the upper Z path at the sculpture park was commissioned by friends of the late Mary Shirley who, with her husband, Jon, was a driving force behind the creation of the Olympic Sculpture Park. The Shirleys were the park's primary benefactors, which gave them the right to have the park named for them. They chose instead to honor the Olympic Mountains, which can be viewed in all of their splendor from Ruffner's bench, which honors Mary. Ruffner is best known as a prominent glass artist, but she

3.10 *Bunyon's Chess,* Mark di Suvero (Photo by Nathaniel Wilson, courtesy Seattle Art Museum)

works in other mediums and this bench is one of two commissioned sculptures in downtown Seattle (see also 6.2).

3.10 BUNYON'S CHESS, 1965

Mark di Suvero

Stainless steel, wood, and steel chains; H 22 ft.
Seattle Art Museum collection
Olympic Sculpture Park

Bunyon's Chess is an early work by Mark di Suvero, the world-renowned abstract expressionist sculptor. It was the first commission for the then twenty-two-year-old artist, and he created it on site at the Seattle home of art collectors Virginia and Bagley Wright. It is a kinetic work—although movement is often barely perceptible—in which reused wood is held together by cables and chains in a stainless steel frame. Alexander Calder inspired di Suvero to create moving sculptures, and di Suvero has said that having elements

3.11 *Eagle,* Alexander Calder

suspended from the beams of his works and interacting with wind and other forces creates a sense of unity and joy.

3.11 EAGLE, 1971

Alexander Calder

Painted steel; H 38 ft. 9 in. × L 32 ft.
Seattle Art Museum collection
Olympic Sculpture Park

Alexander Calder is perhaps best known for introducing to modern art sculptures of delicately balanced floating shapes that his friend Marcel Duchamp dubbed mobiles. His six-ton *Eagle,* which has become the symbol of SAM's sculpture park, is an abstract stationary form that another friend, Jean Arp, dubbed a stabile. Calder's monumental stabiles, such as *Eagle,* are constructed of bolted steel plates. Although his stabiles do not move, it has been said that they do so impliedly. *Eagle* presides over the city from the highest point of the sculpture park, and from some angles it soars. The museum notes that "*Eagle* displays its curving wings, assertive stance, and pointy beak in a form that is weightless, colorful, and abstract." Viewers are well advised to explore the sculpture from many viewpoints, close up and from afar, and experience its many different shapes and visual impacts.

Eagle was commissioned by Fort Worth National Bank in 1971 and stood in front of its headquarters for many years. When the bank was sold, the sculpture changed ownership and was moved and then ultimately purchased by Seattle art collectors and philanthropists Jon and Mary Shirley, who gave it to the museum in 2000.

3.12 UNTITLED BENCH, 2004/2007

Roy McMakin

Concrete, bronze, and steel with porcelain enamel; H 3 ft.
× W 5 ft × L 5 ft.
Seattle Art Museum collection
Olympic Sculpture Park

This collection of sculptural elements—consisting of a concrete bench, a bronze replica of a plastic garden chair, and an enameled steel replica of a file box—was created in 2004 by Roy McMakin for a project at the University of California, San Francisco. McMakin and Michael Jacobs gave it to SAM in 2006, the

same year that McMakin's *Love & Loss* was installed (3.20). It was placed in its current configuration in 2007.

3.13 STINGER, 1999

Tony Smith

Painted steel; H 6 ft. 6 in. × L 74 ft. 6 in.
Seattle Art Museum collection
Olympic Sculpture Park

Tony Smith's approach to sculpture, creating monumental works with geometric forms such as the tetrahedral and octahedral shapes used to create *Stinger*, was heavily influenced by his career as an architect. The late art critic and museum director Sam Hunter said that "Smith's grasp of formal systems, essentially the interaction of geometric solids, gives his forms an architectural presence quite unlike any other contemporary sculpture. His mathematical configurations and calculations have a way of seeming at once simple and extremely intricate." In this case, Smith has created an open-ended structure (originally titled *Gate*) that seems to be delicately balanced on the point of its diamond edge. Some have said

3.12　Untitled bench, Roy McMakin

3.13　*Stinger,* Tony Smith

3.14 and 3.15   *Wandering Rocks,* Tony Smith; *Seattle Coud Cover,* Teresita Fernández

that those who enter find a more comforting environment than its fortress-like exterior suggests. But whether one views it from within or from outside, it presents a complex collection of angles and shadows that change depending on the time of day or the position taken by the viewer. The Seattle Art Museum reports that Tony Smith named this sculpture for the popular cocktail, "whose sweetness masks its intoxicating effects."

As is true of many of Smith's sculptures, *Stinger* was originally a plywood mock-up. Long after his death, Smith's widow had this and other sculptures fabricated in steel, which was Smith's original desire. She gave *Stinger* to the Seattle Art Museum in 2004. Its original wood mock-up was first installed outside of the Museum of Modern Art in New York in 1968,

the same year Smith's mock-up of *Moses* was placed at the Seattle Center (8.5).

3.14 WANDERING ROCKS, 1974

Tony Smith

Painted steel; various sizes
Seattle Art Museum collection
Olympic Sculpture Park

Tony Smith's *Wandering Rocks* consists of five unique tetrahedral and octahedral shapes that were inspired in part by Japanese gardens. Smith has said that their placement is, to a certain extent, "capricious" (in an earlier wood mock-up he located the largest pieces in one area because that placement imposed the least burden on those who had to move them). However, Smith emphasized that there is always a sense of order, and the arrangement depends on the site. He explained to art critic and museum director Sam Hunter, "You have to take each plane as it comes and find out in what way it will join the other planes. There isn't even a regularity of height. . . . The individual elements are controlled somewhat by a sense of order, for they line up on the same axial grid either parallel or perpendicular to any architectural scheme. They are thus to be viewed both as self-contained objects and in the context of a continuing spatial experience, rather than as a purely arbitrary or haphazard arrangement."

The names and measurements of the pieces that make up *Wandering Rocks* are *Smohawk* (H 3 ft. 7⅜ in. × W 1 ft. 11 in. × L 2 ft. 4 in.), *Shaft* (H 5 ft. 3⅜ in. × W 3 ft. 9½ in. × L 2 ft. 4 in.), *Crocus* (H 3 ft. 7⅜ in. × W 3 ft. 9 in. × L 2 ft. 4 in.), *Slide* (H 5 ft. 4⅜ in. × W 1 ft. 11 in. × L 2 ft. 4 in.), and *Dud* (H 2 ft. 8⅜ in. × W 1 ft. 11 in. × L 6 ft. 11½ in.).

3.15 SEATTLE CLOUD COVER, 2006

Teresita Fernández

Laminated glass with photographic design interlayer;
  H 9 ft. 6 in. × L 200 ft.
Seattle Art Museum collection
Olympic Sculpture Park

Rather than have a mundane barrier on the edge of a pedestrian bridge over railroad tracks, Teresita Fernández combined art and functionality and created *Seattle Cloud Cover,* a band of vibrant color along the east side of the bridge that also extends over pedestrians

and creates a pathway of filtered light along its two-hundred-foot length. The artist provides a filtered view of the city through enhanced photographs taken of clouds and sky above Seattle, but that view is interrupted by lines of small holes through which the real world flickers in and out of view. Fernández wants those experiencing *Seattle Cloud Cover* to feel like they "are moving through a landscape painting or movie rather than within the landscape itself, blurring the lines between your presence as participant and observer."

3.16 FATHER AND SON, 2005

Louise Bourgeois

Water, steel, aluminum, bronze; H 6 ft. 5 in. and H 4 ft. 9 in.
Seattle Art Museum collection
Olympic Sculpture Park

The origin of Louise Bourgeois's *Father and Son* is one of the oddest of any artwork in Seattle. It was commissioned pursuant to a $1 million bequest from the estate of Stu Smailes to the City of Seattle on the condition that it be used for acquiring a sculpture of one or more unclothed, life-size, realistic male figures. The limitation required by the benefactor presented delicate political issues for the city, and the bequest and the task of selecting a piece was transferred to the Seattle Art Museum when it was creating its Olympic Sculpture Park. The museum commissioned French-born American surrealist sculptor Louise Bourgeois to design a fountain. Bourgeois created an artwork that was far removed from anything she had done before or since (she was ninety-three at the time and died five years later).

3.16   *Father and Son*, Louise Bourgeois

In *Father and Son* Bourgeois fashioned two realistic nude figures who reach out to one another, but one or the other is always engulfed in water. The sculpture includes a bronze bell pitched to a perfect F sharp that rings every hour, at which time the exposed figure is engulfed in water and the other is exposed. The two figures remain distant, unable to touch one another. Bourgeois once stated that all of her works arose from a personal or emotional experience, and this creation is not far removed from her life experiences. Her father was cold and domineering over his children and their invalid mother, and his many infidelities included a ten-year affair with his children's governess. This created a lifelong resentment and insecurity in Bourgeois that was at the core of much of her artwork. *New York Times* art critic Holland Carter said that all of her work "shared a set of repeated themes, centered on the human body and its need for nurture and protection in a frightening world."

3.17 EYE BENCHES I, II, III, 1996–97

Louise Bourgeois

Black Zimbabwe granite; various sizes, approx. H 4 ft.
Seattle Art Museum collection
Olympic Sculpture Park

Louise Bourgeois's *Eye Benches I, II, III* are three sets of carved black Zimbabwe granite that sit in the vicinity of her sculpture *Father and Son* and also near Jaume Plensa's *Echo*. They were the artist's gift to the museum in honor of its seventy-fifth anniversary. The museum notes that the enlargement and displacement of the eyes "recall the perspectives of Surrealism, a source for these images. Visitors encounter the disembodied eyes, which seem to follow their every movement, and later discover that the enigmatic sculptural objects provide comfortable outdoor seating."

3.18 ECHO, 2011

Jaume Plensa

Polyester resin and marble dust on steel frame; H 45 ft. 11 in.
Seattle Art Museum collection
Olympic Sculpture Park

The inspiration for Jaume Plensa's grand white head was the Greek myth in which Echo, an excessively talkative mountain nymph, is punished by the goddess Hera. The nymph is condemned to never speak except to repeat the words she has just heard. In a 2011 TED talk, Plensa explained that with his sculpture *Echo* he refers to a problem in today's world: there is much talking, but "with so many messages around . . . we are not any more sure if our words are from ourselves or are just the echo

3.18 *Echo,* Jaume Plensa (Photo by Richard J. Birmingham)

3.19 *Schubert Sonata,* Mark di Suvero (Photo by Richard J. Birmingham)

of something else." He portrayed the nymph with her eyes closed, serene and meditative, to "create a certain quietness, a place where you can listen again to your own words, your own heart." He also wanted to introduce in this sculpture a sense of alien beauty: "Something that arrives from another planet. The idea of beauty without any explanation. Something that would elicit, 'Wow, it's just beautiful' and produce silence in a very noisy time like today."

Echo was created for a park in New York City, a venue Plensa thought was appropriate for a theme about too many words. In Seattle *Echo* stands in a quiet setting looking west at the Olympic Mountains and the peak of Mount Olympus. It is a lovely coincidence for a sculpture that refers to a Greek myth, but its

location implies no message. Plensa emphasizes that she is still intended to inspire us to be introspective and concentrate on our internal voices and feelings. An excellent spot for viewing *Echo* is at the end of Pier 70, which is open to the public and readily accessible from the sidewalk.

Another Plensa sculpture that addresses human communication can be seen in the South Lake Union neighborhood (9.23).

3.19 SCHUBERT SONATA, 1992

Mark di Suvero

Painted and unpainted steel; H 22 ft.
Seattle Art Museum collection
Olympic Sculpture Park

Balanced on a narrow point at the end of a black painted column, a collection of rusted steel ribbons and geometric forms move gently with the wind. This is Mark di Suvero's *Schubert Sonata*, one of a series of works the artist dedicated to classical composers (including his towering red steel *For Handel* at Western Washington University in Bellingham). The ten-foot-diameter top portion has been likened to a floating musical note or score. The design no doubt arose from his practice of creating preliminary designs with rapid brushstrokes of black paint to create the desired, seemingly random, forms. Di Suvero told art critic Barbara Rose that his sculpture is "painting in three dimensions." The artist told author Jan Castro, "I don't like people who interpret my sculptures in an anthropomorphic way—see figures in it. The best part is when people see my work in its own way. [Sculptor] John Chamberlain said to me, 'You do your own calligraphy—steel calligraphy.'"

3.20 LOVE & LOSS, 2006

Roy McMakin

Mixed media; H 40 ft. × W 24 ft.
Seattle Art Museum collection
Olympic Sculpture Park

Love & Loss, by Seattle artist, furniture maker, and architect Roy McMakin, consists of functional benches and tables in the form of letters that help spell out the words of its title. A *v* is

3.20   *Love & Loss,* Roy McMakin

3.21 *Undercurrents,* Laura Haddad and Tom Drugan

formed by the white-painted trunks of a living tree, a bright red neon ampersand rotates between Love and Loss, and the *e* is painted on top of the round table. This is a participatory installation in which love and loss intersect. Rather than merely view it, McMakin wants people to walk through and around its elements. "We live in a world of words and objects," he explains. "How they become special and take on meaning is fascinating to me. My sculptures are functional but they also have content that you discover through participation. You need to put the meaning together by sitting on it, walking through it, and then recomposing what you have seen and experienced in your mind's eye. Only then will the theme—the process of love and loss—be revealed for you to sit here and contemplate."

How that revelation occurs is up to the viewer. One can sit at the round table and concentrate solely on love, or follow the *S* in the pavement and end up on the side of loss. The museum points out that "in the process of sorting out the overall 'image,' the viewer becomes physically absorbed into the work itself."

3.21 UNDERCURRENTS, 2003/2010

Laura Haddad and Tom Drugan (Haddad/Drugan)

Stainless steel and concrete
King County 1 Percent for Art program
King County Combined Sewer Overflow Facility,
  Myrtle Edwards Park

Undercurrents is the public art component of King County's Denny Way/Lake Union Combined Sewer Overflow project, which significantly reduces the amount of untreated storm water that discharges into Lake Union and Elliott Bay. The water flows to its destination through underground pipes and tunnels, hence the name of this multipart installation. Laura Haddad and Tom Drugan endeavor to increase the public's understanding of how the facility relates to their daily lives and the environment.

The focal point of its first phase, completed in 2003, is a concrete plaza that extends to the shore of Elliott Bay. Bisecting the plaza and running over buried outfall pipes is a stainless steel swale containing etched lines that represent swirling currents and eddies of water moving to the bay, along with the script of a poem, titled "Undercurrents," by Laura Haddad. At the western edge of the swale is "h'loo-loo-loo-loo-loo," which is the sound of water in a Native American myth. The artists also placed vertical wave-activated sound pipes among the shoreline rocks below the swale. The gates and fences around the adjacent brick pump house are made of pipe that Haddad and Drugan bent to resemble eddies and shoreline reeds that naturally filter estuaries.

In 2010 a second phase of *Undercurrents* was installed around the mechanical vault at the east end of the artwork. On its south side is a fifty-foot-long wall of etched stainless steel panels aligned with the swale below. The etchings create a pictogram that shows the process of storm water collection, transport, and treatment. It begins with homes where storm water and sewage is collected and then channeled through pipes. Rain caused by a "cloud chamber" is channeled underground by spinning manhole-like parts. The artists note that the smoking pipes, organ pipes, and garden hoses are metaphors for the mechanics of the system.

A collection of coins symbolizes collecting water and also references the many coins that find their way to the county's treatment facilities. Surrounding a pipe organ, which represents the Elliott Bay treatment facility east of the railroad tracks, is a collection of pumps, siphons, and circuitry that help pipe the water across to this site. Etched on the wall's left end are maps of underground pipes on the site and molecules that represent the dechlorination that occurs here. A reed block with five organ pipes represents the vault and vent pipes. The swirling circle and flowing lines at the end refer to the plaza and the water outflow into Elliott Bay.

3.22 ADJACENT, AGAINST, UPON, 1976

Michael Heizer

Granite boulders and concrete; H 9 ft. × W 25 ft. × L 130 ft.
Seattle 1 Percent for Art Program, National Endowment for the Arts, and private funding
Myrtle Edwards Park

Michael Heizer's *Adjacent, Against, Upon* is one of the most unusual artworks in Seattle, and although widely admired now, when it was installed, the piece was considered by many to be an example of modern art gone wild. Created in 1976, it was Heizer's first public art commission and, at the time, the most accessible work by one of the leaders of the Earth Art movement. It is a three-part sculpture with each section consisting of a fifty-eight-ton concrete base and a large granite boulder. *Adjacent* is an irregular pentagon shape that sits next to a pentagon-shaped base. *Against*, a rough trapezoidal form, leans against a trapezoidal base, and the triangular *Upon* rests on top of a triangular base. The boulders (two of which weigh approximately fifty tons, with a third weighing thirty-five tons) were chosen by the artist from quarries near Skykomish, Washington. Heizer explained to author Germano Celant, "The rocks . . . are not touched at all, they were just drilled and broken loose and brought in. . . . They have their own spirit, not mine."

Some have theorized that Heizer's placement of the boulders in relation to the man-made forms has special meaning, perhaps referring to the relationship of man to nature or the separation of our complex industrial society from the natural world. However, Heizer confirmed in a conversation with the author that *Adjacent, Against, Upon* has no meaning or message.

The sculpture is consistent with his comments to Celant that concepts "cloud people's minds more than ever before. . . . Art provides relief from thinking . . . and leaves fixed solutions, never attempting more than itself." It is worth noting that Heizer's placement of elements in an earlier earth sculpture, *Nine Nevada Impressions*, was determined by how matchsticks landed when he dropped them from a height of two feet.

Similarly, in this case Heizer placed the elements simply to give them unique characteristics of their own. In the book *Michael Heizer: Sculpture in Reverse*, Heizer says that to bring a rock "into the context of art . . . you have to articulate it somehow. So if you put it on a base then the base is a pedestal or an armature, the base is only a presentation mode, it

3.22 *Adjacent, Against, Upon,* Michael Heizer

isolates it. Does it kill it? No, I don't think so, in fact it probably enhances it because otherwise it would probably be another rock. . . . You can look at a pile of rock and it looks like a pile of rock. You can take one of those rocks and wash it off . . . and lean it up against the side of your house or just appreciate it like the Japanese do. The thing seems to assume character and you can start to study it and understand it." Heizer's *Black Diorite Negative Wall Sculpture* at the Hyatt Regency Hotel (6.27) is another example of his use of boulders to create sculpture.

> Myrtle Edwards Park ends just after Michael Heizer's sculpture as the trail enters the Port of Seattle's Centennial Park, which adds another forty-one hundred linear feet of the park along the shores of Elliott Bay. The next item of interest as you head north is *Shipmates Light*. Dedicated in 1977, it is a hexagonal concrete cone with inlaid rock on the sides and a large light on top. A bronze memorial plaque by an unknown artist includes a bas relief rendering of a sailing vessel. Principal sponsors were the Maritime Union, the Port of Seattle, and the US Coast Guard.

3.23 TOTEM POLE, 1975

John Hagan, Ed Kasko, and Cliff Thomas

Carved Cedar; H 32 ft.
Port of Seattle collection
Centennial Park

This traditionally carved pole was commissioned by the Port of Seattle and originally stood at Alaska Square Park, a small spot at Pier 48 where the state of Alaska once had a ferry terminal (operations were moved to Bellingham). It was moved to Centennial Park in 2009. The pole was created by three Alaska Natives who carved images related to Alaska and her Native people. A helpful plaque nearby describes the characters depicted. At the top is Eagle, which represents an important Tlingit clan. Below is Brown Bear, who holds a tináa (also known as a "copper"), which is a shield symbolizing wealth and status and in this case refers to Alaska's great size and potential wealth. Next is Killer Whale, who portrays great strength and tenacity. Hawk depicts sharp eyesight and perception of the future. Grizzly Bear is the fifth figure. He is a symbol of bravery, but he holds Mosquito between his paws, warning people that all is not easy and we should be gentle. Last is Strong Boy, who was regarded as stupid and lazy but who exercised and became brave and strong. When his uncle was swallowed by Sea Lion, all of the nephews ran in fear, except for Strong Boy, who tore Sea Lion in half and rescued his uncle.

3.24 HOMAGE TO THE KING OF CATS, 1991

Judith Caldwell

Steel with copper patina
Private commission
3028 Western Avenue

Across from the Olympic Sculpture Park at Western Avenue and Bell Street is a collection

3.25   *Ten Feet into the Future*, David Govedare

of Judith Caldwell's illustrations from Emily Brontë's *Wuthering Heights* rendered in cut steel with a copper patina. The inspiration for these works were drawings by the artist Balthasar Klossowski de Rola, best known as Balthus (1908–2001), for a 1935 publication of the book. Caldwell explains that the drawings "had a wonderful tension, reflecting the struggle between the wild and the tame that is at the heart of the novel." Caldwell's figures are inset in panels along the street level on Western Avenue that screen the parking garage and to the right and left above the entrance.

In several instances parts of the metal illustrations extend out of the frame. In the upper right figure, Heathcliff holds a package out to the character Cathy Linton, who is in the space to the left of the front door. That package is inscribed with the names "Caldwell and Gulassa," the latter for David Gulassa, who fabricated the panels. Cathy reaches up with a package labelled "de Rola," in reference to Balthus. In 1935 Balthus also painted

a self-portrait that he titled *King of Cats*; thus the title of Caldwell's montage, *Homage to the King of Cats*.

3.25 TEN FEET INTO THE FUTURE, 1986

David Govedare

Aluminum; life-size
Private collection
3131 Elliott Avenue Building, on the south end

Ten Feet into the Future shows five joggers in silhouette. A careful look reveals that five different races or ethnic backgrounds are represented. The lead runner is an American Indian, symbolizing that American Indians were here before all other peoples and the artist's view that "in a spiritual sense" the Native American is leading the others—an African American, an Asian, a Hispanic, and a Caucasian—onward into the future.

Ten Feet into the Future was commissioned by the Spokane Chamber of Commerce in 1986 and was placed in front of the Washington State Pavilion at British Columbia's Expo 86. The sculpture is derived from Govedare's much larger work at Spokane's Riverfront Park that extends two city blocks and consists of forty runners. After the conclusion of Expo 86, *Ten Feet into the Future* was purchased by Martin Selig, who owns the adjacent building.

3.26 MOON SONG, 1971

George Tsutakawa

Silicon bronze; H 4 ft. 6 in. × Dia 2 ft. 6 in.
Private commission
101 Elliott Avenue W

Moon Song is the first of three of George Tsutakawa's fountain-sculptures with this spherical design that includes additional forms created by extensions of water off of its curved surfaces. Another stands in the cafeteria of Seattle Central College on Capitol Hill. The third is located at Pennsylvania State University. *Moon Song* was commissioned as a memorial to Bobbi McCallum, an award-winning columnist and reporter for the *Seattle Post-Intelligencer*, which was housed in this building. The name is not derived from its shape. Ms. McCallum's parents asked that it be given that name because "Moon Child" was a pet name they had for their daughter.

3.27 ORTHAGONAL WEAVE, 2017

Austin Smith

Steel and LED lights; max H 8 ft. × L 40 ft.
Private commission
203 W Harrison Street

With *Orthagonal Weave*, sculptor Austin Smith sought to create a sense of movement by adding eight tetrahedron shapes that weave through the building's barren concrete walls next to the sidewalk. Variations of light and shadow are created by the geometric shapes, their attachment slightly away from the wall, and the addition of multicolored lights. The glow of those lights is visible not only from behind but through the three narrow spaces separating the planes of each of these pyramids. It is a site-specific piece, and Smith notes that both the positive and negative spaces of this sculpture are equally important aspects.

3.28 SNOQUAL/MOON THE TRANSFORMER, 2012

Roger Fernandes

Painted cedar, aluminum, and glass; H 10 ft. 8 in.
   × W 4 ft. × L 10 ft. 8 in.
Seattle 1 Percent for Art Program
W Thomas Street Pedestrian Overpass, W Thomas Street and
   Third Avenue W

Roger Fernandes, a Native American storyteller and artist, created this gateway to tell the stories of those who transform their environment. The principal story is from the Snoqualmie Indians, who lived in the Snoqualmie Valley in east King and Snohomish Counties. The structure represents a longhouse. With painted images and incised carving on the two four-by-nine-foot cedar panels, Fernandes refers to stories and symbolism, all in colors that were used by Native people.

The Snoqualmie are known as People of the Moon (Snoqual). Moon, the son of an Earth

3.29 *Triad,* Phillip Levine

design. The bronze wave forms in the sidewalk refer to a basket design that represents salmon swimming in a river.

On the street-side panel Pacific Northwest mountains are rendered as red triangles at the bottom, and the wandering blue path of the Duwamish River, a fruitful resource until white people modified it to its present course, is shown with the black line. This is a reference to the second story of transformation that Fernandes depicts. Unlike the Native peoples who lived harmoniously with the earth, subsequent inhabitants sought to control and "improve" nature. With the circle and cross, Fernandes refers to the fact that Native cultures use the circle "to symbolize the cycle of life and return to completeness," while the intersecting lines of the cross symbolize power.

Fernandes sculpted the image of Snoqual on the connecting lintel out of metal and glass because they are industrial materials that western society deemed more superior than wood and other natural materials.

3.29 TRIAD, 1983

Phillip Levine

Bronze; H 14 ft.
Private commission
Elliott Bay Office Park, 300 Elliott Avenue W

mother and a Star father, is the main character of the creation myth referred to in this sculpture. He was kidnapped and raised by the Dog Salmon people but was able to return to his own people as a young man. After returning, he traveled down the mountains by following rivers to the ocean. Throughout his travels he transformed the world to prepare it for habitation by people. The interior side of the panel closest to the street shows Snoqual making the Salmon people and putting them in the river. In the opposite panel we see him making plants, deer, and mountains. On the back of that panel Fernandes painted a traditional Native basket

With *Triad*, Seattle sculptor Phillip Levine positioned three bronze figures precariously balanced to form an inverse triangle, whose straight lines contract with the curves of the building behind. Levine admires the sculptural ambiguity in *Triad*. Although the figures are sturdy bronze, their position creates an

3.30   *What goes out … always comes back,*
Catherine Mayer

3.31   *11 Straight Lines,* Bernar Venet

impression of lightness. This sculpture was commissioned by Seattle real estate developer Martin Selig, who developed Elliott Bay Office Park.

3.30 WHAT GOES OUT … ALWAYS COMES BACK, 2013

Catherine Mayer

Steel and fiberglass; H 20 ft.
Private commission
333 Elliott Avenue W

The large hand holding a toy paddle with a ball extended up in the air—*What goes out . . . always comes back*—is one of two of Catherine Mayer's whimsical sculptures in Seattle's public places that refer to favorite

things from her childhood. It joined an earlier childhood memory, the seventeen-foot popsicle at Fourth and Blanchard (7.7). This piece is owned by Seattle real estate developer Martin Selig, who developed the adjacent building.

3.31 SELIG SCULPTURE PLAZA

Bernar Venet, Barbara Hepworth, Sorel Etrog, and Gedalia Ben Zvi

Private commission
635/645 Elliott Avenue W

Seattle real estate developer Martin Selig has placed a number of monumental sculptures in the one-acre space between his two buildings at 635 and 645 Elliott Avenue W. Closest to the street is *11 Straight Lines* by French conceptual artist Bernar Venet. The weathered steel

3.31   *Three Obliques (Walk In)*, Barbara Hepworth

forms are one step in the evolution of Venet's use of simple arcs and lines—on the ground, attached to walls, tumbling over one another, or standing vertically—that stand on their own to create art. The position of this nine-ton collection of lines, standing thirty-one feet, ten inches tall, is dictated more by gravity and the nature of the material than by the artist's planning. He intends to affect the viewer with the sculpture's height and mass in this particular setting. He provides neither decoration nor metaphor and suggests nothing.

On the north end of the lawn is *Three Obliques (Walk In)*, a nine-foot, six-inch-tall bronze sculpture by English abstract sculptor Barbara Hepworth. Hepworth's abstract pieces,

like those of her contemporary Henry Moore, have their basis in natural forms, with curved, biomorphic shapes and voids. But in the 1960s she began working with the hard-edged shapes that are displayed in this work. She wanted viewers to walk around this sculpture and observe the interrelated planes and voids and the effect of light and shade on the forms. Hepworth also intended viewers to look into the piece and experience the effect created by its interlocking walls. The holes are an important part of that experience and Hepworth intended them to be used as viewpoints. Doing so is in keeping with her advice that one must view a sculpture by moving around and experiencing it from all angles and in different light conditions. *Three*

3.31 *Fusion,* Gedalia Ben Zvi

3.31   *The Source,* Sorel Etrog

Obliques (Walk In) was conceived in 1969 and cast in 1970. It is one of only two casts. The second is located at Cardiff University in Wales.

At the north edge is *The Source* (W 6 ft. 6 in. × L 13 ft. 10 in.), a cast bronze sculpture created in 1965 by the Romanian-born Canadian artist Sorel Etrog. The theme of Etrog's work is both the human form and the relationship of humankind to the machine and electronics ages. In his preface to *Sorel Etrog: Recent Works*, Canadian philosopher Marshall McLuhan said, "The Etrog world presents the tension between the old organic, visual world and the raw electronic discarnate man" revealing "how the contemporary world undergoes a transformation of the old machine and its consumer products into new vital images of primal art and perception."

On the south end of the lawn is the eighteen-foot-tall bronze sculpture *Fusion*, with which the Czechoslovakian-born Israeli artist Gedalia Ben Zvi expresses some of his thoughts about the behavior of mankind. He had in mind with this work "the unique ability of the human species to melt from individuals into groups and from small families to clans living and working together." That thought is referred to by the group of four people embracing a fifth one and bringing that fifth one into their circle, thus creating what the artist calls the "eternal Fusion." With the indentation in one of the heads, Ben Zvi refers to the power to have an open mind to new ideas and understandings.

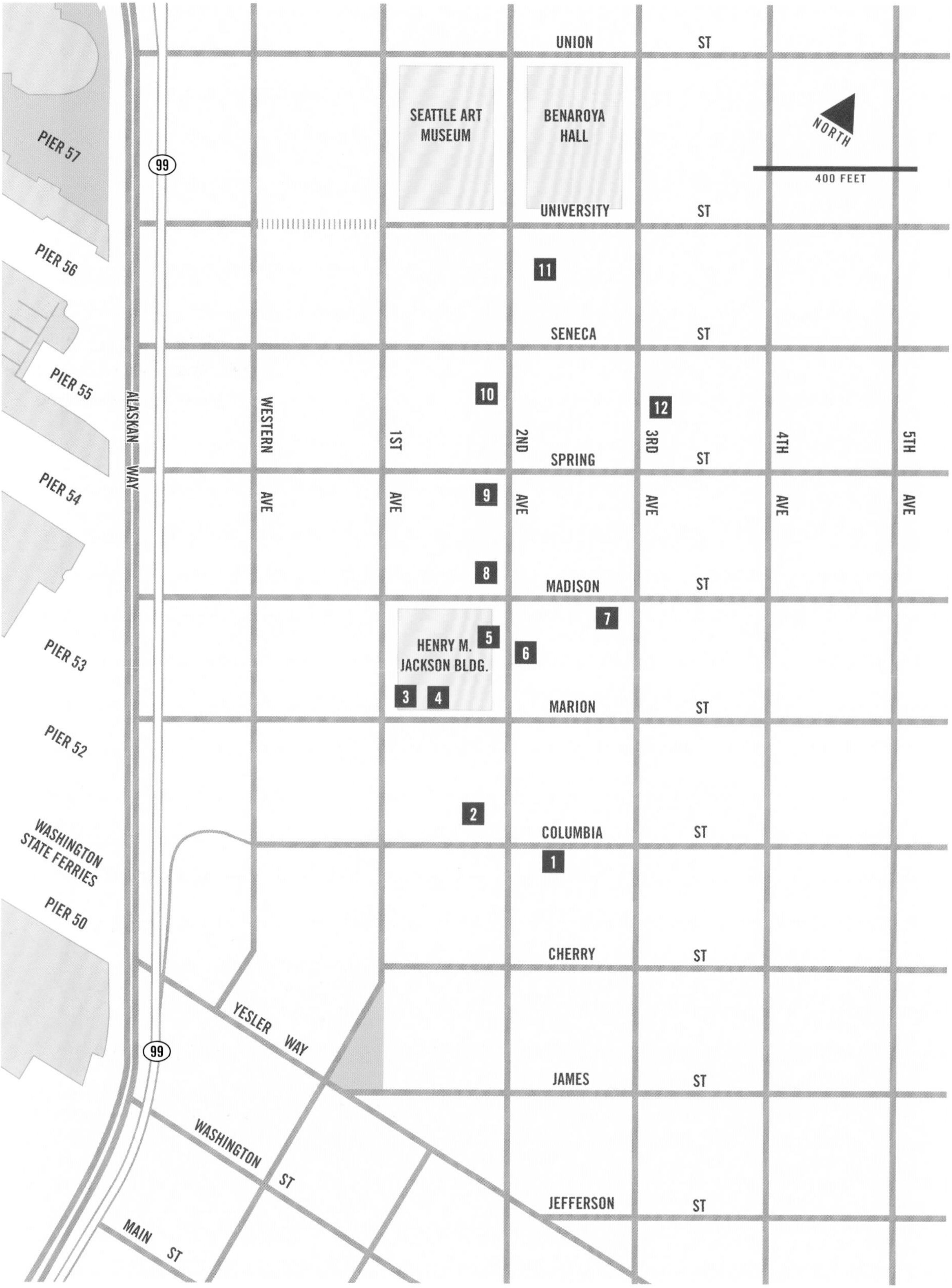

PIER 57

PIER 56

PIER 55

PIER 54

PIER 53

PIER 52

WASHINGTON
STATE FERRIES

PIER 50

99

ALASKAN WAY

99

YESLER WAY

WASHINGTON ST

MAIN ST

WESTERN AVE

1ST AVE

2ND AVE

3RD AVE

4TH AVE

5TH AVE

UNION ST

SEATTLE ART
MUSEUM

BENAROYA
HALL

UNIVERSITY ST

NORTH

400 FEET

11

SENECA ST

10

12

SPRING ST

9

8

MADISON ST

7

HENRY M.
JACKSON BLDG.

5

6

3 **4**

MARION ST

2

COLUMBIA ST

1

CHERRY ST

JAMES ST

JEFFERSON ST

4 WEST OF THIRD AVENUE BETWEEN YESLER AND UNIVERSITY STREETS

Art should be something like a good armchair in which to rest from physical fatigue.

—Henri Matisse (1869–1954)

THE AREA COVERED IN THIS CHAPTER has been an important part of Seattle's downtown business establishment dating back to the late nineteenth century. The city's first privately commissioned artworks were placed here in 1959, and over the years important sculptures by eminent artists have been installed by the US government and by major real estate developers Wright Runstad & Company and Martin Selig, all for public enjoyment.

4.1 RELIEF SCULPTURES, 1924

Morgan Padelford and Mildred Stumer

Cast stone; H 5 ft. 8 in. × L 11 ft.
Commissioned by the Seattle Chamber of Commerce
219 Columbia Street (Second Avenue and Columbia Street)

The entrance of this 1924 Italian Romanesque Renaissance–style building is flanked by two sculptural friezes designed by Morgan Padelford while pursuing his master's degree at the University of Washington. The left-hand panel, designed and executed by Padelford, depicts scenes of Native Northwest residents engaged in various pursuits, including hunting and wood carving. The right-hand group, which is engaged in more modern technological and industrial pursuits, was executed by Olympia-born Mildred Stumer, a young sculptor working in Seattle who followed Padelford's sketches. These sculptures were commissioned by the Seattle Chamber of Commerce, which was the original owner of the building.

4.2 RESTLESS BIRD, 1959

Philip McCracken

Concrete aggregate; H 9 ft. × L 5 ft. 6 in.
Private commission
Norton Building, 801 Second Avenue

When the Norton Building was built in 1959, its architects—Skidmore, Owings, Merrill & Johnson—urged the owner to include artworks in the building's public areas. Acting on that advice, the Northwest Corporation (a Norton Clapp family enterprise) commissioned two artworks. The Norton Building thus became the first private office building in Seattle to have commissioned artworks in its public areas.

The owners were impressed with the young Philip McCracken's contemporary

4.1   *Relief sculpture,* Morgan Padelford

4.3   Untitled sculpture, Harold Balazs

expressions of the Pacific Northwest that were compatible with the elegance of the building's design. *Restless Bird* was the artist's first public commission. This four-ton sculpture, one of McCracken's largest works, is a bird of prey, a recurring subject in many of his creations and creatures that he has studied and admired all of his life. In this case the raptor is poised to strike at an unsuspecting prey.

4.3 UNTITLED SCULPTURE, 1976

Harold Balazs

Welded copper; H 8 ft. × W 2 ft. 6 in. × L 11 ft. 6 in.
Commissioned by the US General Services Administration,
    Art-in-Architecture Program
Jackson Federal Office Building, west side, First Avenue and
    Marion Street

This untitled copper sculpture by Harold Balazs consists of totemic symbols that interlock and grow in all directions, independent of any post or plane. Balazs points out that although we are accustomed to vertical totem poles, totems are symbols that need not be shown only vertically.

"I have always been fascinated with totemic ideas and combinations of disparate figures," he explains. "They show that we are all different, but combined together. . . . This work is a collection of contemporary forms and elements which refer to both that idea and my fascination with combinations of anthropomorphic and mechanical shapes."

4.4 FREEDOM, 1976

Philip McCracken

Cast bronze; H 1 ft. 11½ in.
Commissioned by the US General Services Administration,
    Art-in-Architecture Program
Jackson Federal Office Building, 915 Second Avenue, Marion
    Street side

4.4 *Freedom*, Philip McCracken

4.5 *Landscape of Time*, Isamu Noguchi

Next to the brick stairs, close to the building, and about halfway up the hill, is Philip McCracken's powerful bronze sculpture, *Freedom*, a bird of prey ready to escape from the restrictions of its bronze cage, standing with a look of rage and poised and ready to lunge forward to freedom. In Delores Tarzan Ament's book *600 Moons*, McCracken points out that "although I have done many bird-form sculptures, specific birds seldom appear in my work, and that is true of this piece. It is the birdness as a vehicle for the expression of a vast range of life currents that interests me. Further, this sculpture is not intended to represent a specific religious or political condition, but is meant to be translated into the terms each viewer personally sees as representing his own freedom."

4.5 LANDSCAPE OF TIME, 1975

Isamu Noguchi

Carved granite boulders

Commissioned by the US General Services Administration (Art-in-Architecture Program)

Jackson Federal Office Building, 915 Second Avenue

The design of *Landscape of Time*, by renowned abstract expressionist artist Isamu Noguchi, refers to a Japanese landscape garden and is an example of the breadth of Noguchi's interests in combining art, landscape design, and architecture to create many of his works. The timeworn boulders are meant to inspire thoughtful repose. In fact, these boulders initially stood in the artist's studio garden on the island of Shikoku in Japan. *Landscape of Time* is intended to tie centuries together by combining ancient boulders and modern man-made materials. Noguchi could not place the boulders amidst raked gravel or sand, as he might have in a traditional Japanese garden. The sculpture is surrounded by inlaid bricks and trees.

Noguchi stated that natural stones are "ready-made sculptures for the eyes of connoisseurs." He pointed out that with proper placement anything can become a sculpture. Here, he supplemented the boulders with only a few specially carved grooves. The artist described this sculpture as the ultimate step in his artistic works so far. When he died in 1988 the *New York Times* described Noguchi as "a versatile and prolific sculptor whose earthy stones and meditative gardens bridging East and West have become landmarks of 20th-century art." *Landscape of Time* is the second of two major works in Seattle by Isamu Noguchi. The first is his better-known *Black Sun* in Volunteer Park.

4.6 MOLINE MARKERS: CLAUDIO COLUMN II, DEERE SPLIT COLUMN, TRIANGLE SENTINEL I, LIMA MARKER III, AND MAURO COLUMN II, 1981

Beverly Pepper

Cast iron; H 9 ft. 6 in. to 10 ft. 7 in.
Private collection
Wells Fargo Center, Second Avenue and Madison
    Street plaza

Across the street from Isamu Noguchi's *Landscape of Time* at the Jackson Federal Office Building are sculptures at the other end of the artistic spectrum: Beverly Pepper's five cast iron individually named columns. *Moline Markers* are related to Pepper's four steel columns placed in Todi, Italy, which range from twenty-eight to thirty-six feet in height and weigh five to eight tons. The works here are studio-sized creations the shapes of which may remind some of ancient artifacts, but they were inspired by tools. Pepper chose each shape to serve as a type of sentinel and evoke a sense of ritual ceremony, to serve as what the artist calls "urban altars" through which viewers could pass. In Fratelli Giulio's book, *Beverly Pepper*, the artist says, "The outer reality is the industrial tool, but for the viewer, hopefully their past identity will participate in the present in that they preserve countless archetypical associations." Seattle's *Moline Markers* have been praised as intimate additions to a pedestrian-oriented setting. The decision to place smaller, more intimate works on the building's western steps was made by Wright Runstad & Company, the building's developer.

4.6   *Moline Markers* (detail), Beverly Pepper

Two other Beverly Pepper sculptures, each from a different period of her career, are displayed at the Olympic Sculpture Park (3.6 and 3.7).

4.7 SEATTLE TULIP, 1989

Tom Wesselmann

Painted aluminum; H 18 ft. × L 20 ft.
Private commission
Wells Fargo Center, Third Avenue and Madison Street

This colorful flower is one of the largest sculptures by American pop artist Tom Wesselmann, who established his place in American art history in the 1960s with paintings of flat faceless nudes in billboard colors, some of which incorporated real objects such as clocks or television sets, photomontage effects, and sounds. The

4.7   *Seattle Tulip*, Tom Wesselmann

4.8   *Adam*, Fernando Botero

painted background often included a tulip. In the early 1980s he began turning the subjects of his drawings into sculptures created from cut-out sheets of steel or aluminum. Here his tulip bends and curves as if cut from paper.

Wesselmann had long been working on ideas for a colorful tulip sculpture when Wright Runstad & Company, the building's developer, began searching for an important work to place at this corner. His design for *Seattle Tulip* was readily accepted and this commissioned sculpture—although faded with age—adds needed color to its neighborhood. The three-ton green and red tulip is constructed of three-quarter-inch aluminum sheets.

4.8 ADAM, 1990

Fernando Botero

Cast bronze; H 12 ft. 6 in.
Private collection
1015 Second Avenue

Fernando Botero's *Adam* is an example of the Colombian artist's unmistakable style, in both painting and sculpture, of weighty, inflated human forms, which was influenced by Rubens but goes far beyond the style of that seventeenth-century Flemish artist. The artist has emphasized that he does not portray obesity, rather he depicts volume and sensual form. Botero's works are easily recognizable and as is typical of his works, the surfaces of this corpulent *Adam* are smooth with little emphasis on detail. Botero also created a bronze Eve, and Adam and Eve have been subjects, alone and together, of several of his paintings. *Adam* is owned by real estate developer Martin Selig, and it is the first and only Botero sculpture to be displayed in a Seattle public place.

4.9 L'S ONE UP ONE DOWN EXCENTRIC, 1982

George Rickey

Stainless steel; H 27 ft.; max radius 13 ft. and 14 ft. 7 inches
Private collection
1015 Second Avenue

George Rickey's twenty-seven-foot-tall sculpture *L's One Up One Down Excentric* is a unique commissioned work that the artist created in 1982 for the National Steel Center in downtown Pittsburgh. It stood there for thirty-three years until it was determined that this hard-edged work was incompatible with building renovations. In was then sold at auction to Seattle real estate developer Martin Selig, who owns the adjacent building. Typical of Rickey's sculptures, it is composed of simple straight-edged stainless steel shapes—just two Ls with a blade between them—burnished to catch and reflect sunlight carefully. It is balanced and counterweighted, and seemingly moving as it wishes when inspired by the wind. Rickey told critic John Gruen that he designed his sculptures "to be slow, unhampered, deliberate, but at the same time unpredictable."

At its dedication in 1982, the artist said his intent was to delight and inspire viewers who paused to watch. Rickey told the *Pittsburgh Press* that it is "not intended to be viewed by passing motorists. . . . It is pedestrian-oriented. Time is an element in my art. There is real elapsed time. If you don't spend time looking at it—you may catch it out of the corner of your eye—you haven't seen it."

An earlier George Rickey sculpture can be seen in the Olympic Sculpture Park (3.8).

4.9 *L's One Up One Down Excentric*, George Rickey (Photo by Richard J. Birmingham)

4.10 ETRUSCA, 1989

Manuel Neri

Marble; H 5 ft. 11 in. × W 1 ft. 1 in. × L 1 ft. 9 in.
Private collection
Safeco Center, 1191 Second Avenue

Manuel Neri's *Etrusca*, located at the end of the hallway to the left of the concierge desk, is one of his many sculptures that evoke the Venus de Milo and other classical Greek and Roman forms in an unfinished, abstract fashion. The essential female form is brought forth from the stone, headless and limbless, as are her ancient predecessors, but with a surface intentionally pockmarked as if it is beginning to disintegrate. Many of Neri's sculptures in this genre, whether marble, plaster, or bronze, are accentuated with paint, which the artist has said is in tribute to artists such as Picasso and Willem de

Kooning. In this case, the piece is unadorned marble from Carrara, Italy, the source favored by Michelangelo and where Neri has been a part-time resident.

This sculpture's title is derived from the Etruscan civilization of ancient Italy. *Etrusca* was purchased by building developers Wright Runstad & Company specifically for this lobby. It is Neri's only sculpture in a Seattle public place.

Along the exterior walls of Safeco Center are fifteen bas relief designs of creatures and a Native American woman that were sculpted in 1950 by Seattle artist Everett DuPen. They decorated the entrance archway of the Medical Arts Building at this location for decades. Each is derived from Northwest Coast Indian designs. When Wright Runstad & Company replaced that building in 1991, it not only incorporated the medallions into the new building's façade, it had several more cast to allow the medallions to extend down Seneca Street and along First Avenue.

4.11 NEW ARCHETYPES, 1990

Anne and Patrick Poirier

Stainless steel, granite, concrete; various sizes
Private commission
1201 Third Avenue Tower, Second Avenue side

French artists Anne and Patrick Poirier have gained international fame for their creation of modern renditions of tumbled ancient ruins. In this case, *New Archetypes* is a collection of four Doric columns that have either tumbled

4.10   *Etrusca,* Manuel Neri

down or are on the verge of collapsing. In the fountain behind the columns is a stainless steel arrow, the tip of which is embedded in a boulder. Columns have been the central focus of many Poirier sculptures, and they regard them as "one of the oldest and most universal archetypes in architecture, even of symbolic human thought."

The artists emphasize that even though columns have tumbled to the ground, they "retain the perfection of their forms and their geometry. Archetypes resist all: the wear of Time and the ravages of history." The placement of the columns, they explain, was intended to create "a sort of archaeological landscape of the Present, at once to highlight the variety and simplicity of their form, and to create a sculptural environment . . . to evoke past or future voyages." The Poiriers added the steel arrow that has plummeted from the sky to symbolize the fact that nothing can disturb the order of the columns or alter their perfection.

New Archetypes was commissioned by Wright Runstad & Company, the building's developer. A photo of it appears at the end of the index.

4.12 UNTITLED SCULPTURES, 1972

Jan Zach

Cast aluminum; each H 10 ft. × L 2 ft. 6 in.
Private commission
1122 Third Avenue

The ten-foot-high gray abstract sculptures attached to the building at 1122 Third Avenue are untitled works created in 1972 by Czechoslovakian-born artist Jan Zach. The rough, craggy forms refer to "organic formations of the Pacific Northwest," subjects Zach considered ideal for offsetting the straight lines of the building. These sculptures were commissioned by Pacific Northwest Bell Telephone Company, an AT&T subsidiary that eventually became part of what is now CenturyLink.

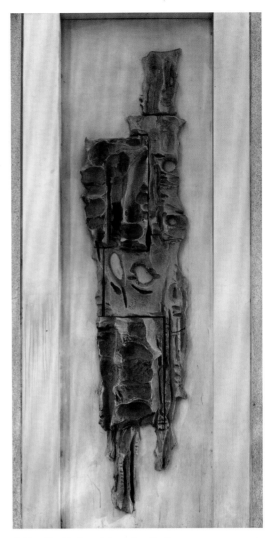

4.12   Untitled sculpture, Jan Zach

NORTH

400 FEET

UNION ST

BENAROYA HALL

UNIVERSITY ST

SENECA ST

SPRING ST

25

24

23

FREEWAY PARK

26

19   18

21   **SEATTLE PUBLIC LIBRARY**

20

22   **WILLIAM K. NAKAMURA COURTHOUSE**

MADISON ST

WESTERN AVE

1ST AVE

2ND AVE

MARION ST

3RD AVE

4TH AVE

5TH AVE

6TH AVE

7TH AVE

COLUMBIA ST

17

16

14   **SEATTLE MUNICIPAL TOWER**

15

CHERRY ST

5   5

13   **SEATTLE CITY HALL BLDG**

12   **SEATTLE JUSTICE CENTER**

11

JAMES ST

YESLER WAY

1   **KING COUNTY COURT HOUSE**

3   **KING COUNTY ADMIN. BLDG**   10

2

9   **KING COUNTY CORRECTIONAL FACILITY**

8

AVE S

1ST

WASHINGTON ST

OCCIDENTAL AVE S

2ND AVE S

3RD AVE S

JEFFERSON ST

CITY HALL PARK

DILLING WAY

4

5

7

TERRACE ST

MAIN ST

YESLER WAY

6

5 EAST OF THIRD AVENUE BETWEEN YESLER AND UNIVERSITY STREETS

As a house is the home of a family, so is the city the home of its inhabitants
and should be furnished with works of art as you would furnish your own home.

—Sir Henry Moore (1898–1986)

WITHIN THE BOUNDARIES OF CHAPTER 5 is the center of municipal and county

government, which has a number of buildings that contain collections of impressive

commissioned artworks. Also included is Seattle's first modern skyscraper with its iconic

Henry Moore sculpture and the main branch of the Seattle Public Library, in front of which

is the first of more than seventy fountains placed around the world by Seattle sculptor

George Tsutakawa.

5.1 KING COUNTY COURTHOUSE WORKS

Max P. Nielsen, Douglas Cooper, Linda Beaumont, Grégoire Picher, and Patricia Clark

516 Third Avenue

At the Third Avenue entrance to the King County Courthouse is a bas relief bronze plaque that depicts Seattle pioneer Henry Yesler, who died in 1892 at his home, which stood on this site. Yesler served as Seattle mayor from 1874 to 1875 and again from 1885 to 1886 (terms were short back then). He also served as Seattle's first auditor in 1853. Yesler is best known for his business endeavors, having created Seattle's first steam-powered sawmill in 1852 (on the Seattle waterfront at the foot of what is now known as Yesler Way), its first water system in 1854, and later a mill on Union Bay in what is now Laurelhurst. Created in 1916, this plaque was Max P. Nielsen's last sculpture. He died the next year.

The courthouse's Third Avenue lobby has a collection of educational and inspirational artworks created in 2005 by Douglas Cooper and Linda Beaumont that are part of the county's 1 Percent for Art collection. The artists helped turn a bland venue into something grand, reminiscent of federal Works Progress Administration–commissioned works in government buildings from the 1930s. Entry requires passing through security, but the security staff is friendly and accommodating. A pamphlet about the artworks featured should

5.1   *Truth Crushed to the Earth Will Rise Again,* Linda Beaumont

5.1   *From These Hills, from These Waters* (detail), Douglas Cooper

be available from the information desk inside the entrance.

Along both sides of the halls leading to the elevator lobby and on the lobby walls is Douglas Cooper's *From These Hills, from These Waters,* a collection of murals drawn in charcoal and graphite that provide imaginary scenes from the past in Seattle and King County. These are not illustrations. Rather they are panoramic scenes with exaggerated perspectives that combine past, current, and imagined subjects, many of whom are historical icons and well-known figures and celebrities. The people were drawn by Grégoire Picher, and Patricia Clark

assisted Cooper on creating the geographic and architectural features.

Included are detailed scenes of Lake Union, Lake Washington, and Elliott Bay and some figures stretch over from adjacent panels. Subjects include the streamlined ferry *Kalakala* and a gigantic Tom Hanks reaching for a telephone being handed to him by the young actor who played his son in the movie *Sleepless in Seattle.* In the left foreground of one panel is Hiram Chittenden, the driving force behind the construction of the government locks, who reaches to place a boat in the ship canal. In a later portion we see Chittenden again, placing the boat from the first mural at the entrance to *his* locks. In another corridor mural is Seattle native Jimi Hendrix, Ray Charles (who played his first gig when he lived in Seattle from 1948 to 1950), and Kurt Cobain.

Historical figures and themes abound in these murals. Principal topics include how people live on and near our local waters, the 1909 Alaska-Yukon-Pacific Exposition (Seattle's first world's fair), mining and logging at Tiger Mountain, the Aurora and Fremont Bridges and Fremont, Safeco Field and scenes of Seattle, the Snoqualmie Valley and Falls, ice climbing in the Cascades, natural resources and the generation of wealth in the region,

the strive for fair distribution of wealth (with Dr. Martin Luther King Jr. in the foreground), ancient and modern use of natural resources, early Seattle, and Seattle's regrade projects.

On the floor of the courthouse's Third Avenue lobby is *Truth Crushed to the Earth Will Rise Again*, Linda Beaumont's tribute to Dr. Martin Luther King Jr., for whom the county is named. Created in 2005, the main focus is a sixteen-foot circle of yellow sienna marble in the lobby's center that has etched into it a photograph of Dr. King giving his "I Have a Dream" speech. In the foreground are some of the 250,000 people who were present on that day. The photo was taken by Flip Schulke, who traveled with King through many of the most important events of civil rights history in the 1960s. The enlarged image is imprecise and fades from focus, which Beaumont likens to "a worn image on an old coin [which] holds the essence of that time." She describes the etched image of the event as "a soft focus lens into our collective memories."

On either side of that circle are eight-foot-diameter circles of water-jet cut marble in a radiating design of triangles that is reminiscent of a sunflower. In the center of each is an eighteen-inch circle of cast and mirror-backed glass. The surrounding black terrazzo contains chips of white marble and iridescent Venetian glass, and the white elements contain flecks of mother of pearl and amber-colored mirrored glass.

The artist's final tribute to Dr. King is the etched glass portrait in the corridor leading to the Third Avenue exit. The civil rights leader looks toward that exit and etched into the bronze frame is Mahatma Gandhi's advice: "Be the change you want to see in the world."

5.1   *Henry Yesler,* Max P. Nielsen

5.2   *Untitled mural panel*, Harold Balazs

Beaumont placed the photo here with the hope that those leaving the building might be inspired by the ideals of King and Gandhi.

P. 14

5.2 UNTITLED MURAL PANELS, 1979

Harold Balazs

Vitreous enamel on steel; 2 panels H 12 ft. × W 8 ft., one
    panel H 8 ft. × W 8 ft.
King County 1 Percent for Art Program
King County Administration Building, 500 Fourth Avenue

The three enamel panels at the Fourth Avenue entrance to the King County Administration Building were commissioned for placement in a vertical row on a high bare concrete space at the Kingdome, Seattle's first multiuse stadium. When Harold Balazs saw the colorless concrete area where his work would be placed, he said to himself, "My God. What a nice place for a bouquet of flowers . . . a little gentleness to

these gray surroundings." What he created is a three-part mural of colorful flowers. Before the Kingdome's demolition in 2000, King County removed the panels and installed them separately on the Fourth Avenue side of the administration building, where they can shine in the daylight and add color to drab surroundings.

One mural has been referred to as "Rhododendrons," but Balazs did not name the panels. He does not believe that his art needs to have a message or a name. It is sufficient simply to "take one corner of the world and make it more beautiful than another."

5.3 KING COUNTY ADMINISTRATION BUILDING INTERIOR WORKS

Robert Sperry and Alden Mason

King County Administration Building, 500 Fourth Avenue

Inside the Fourth Avenue lobby of the King County Administration Building are major works by two prominent Pacific Northwest artists of the mid- to late twentieth century. To the right inside is *Untitled #625*, a 1985 ceramic tile mural by Robert Sperry. The thirty-foot-long piece is a monumental example of the artist's innovative skill in ceramic art. A combination of sculpture and painting, it is composed of 176 black panels painted with a thick white slip (semifluid clay) and then fired. The result is a collection of geometric shapes and abstract images, accentuated by a crackled white surface, which gives an appearance of floating over black voids. *New York Times* critic Ruth J. Katz said of Sperry's technique: "The cracked and crater-like surface of this black-and-white volcanic landscape evokes images of relentless geological activity. The blistered

5.3   *Lunar Promenade,* Alden Mason

5.3   *Untitled #625,* Robert Sperry

and mottled crust periodically dissolves into tranquil plains."

This mural was commissioned by the King County Arts Commission as part of an annual Honors Award Program that saluted outstanding local artists. Sperry spent two years designing and constructing this, his largest mural. Two other works in this medium can be seen in the lobby of the Sheraton Hotel (6.3) and his large ceramic tower stands near the University of Washington's UW Tower building in the University District.

At the end of the lobby is *Lunar Promenade* created by Alden Mason in 1989. This seventeen-foot, six-inch-long painting presents a rare opportunity in Seattle's public places to see the energetic and vibrant spur-of-the-moment images created by one of the Pacific Northwest's most renowned and prolific artists. This large acrylic work is a collection of strange, whimsical images of humans, birds, and animals that illustrate both his lifelong love of nature as well as his desire to create subjects that he described as "more vulgar and wild" than pretty. The paint for his works at this point in his career was applied thickly and then mixed around to create seemingly uncontrolled and random lines, figures, and fields of colors. To many, such figures bring to mind painter Arshile Gorky. But as Seattle art critic Regina

Hackett opined, "if you took the figures out, you'd still have a beautiful painting."

What are the subjects? They were created quickly and, in many instances, long after his paintings were created Mason couldn't confirm the identity of some. But they show his love of nature and colors and the influence of his travels to tropical climes. "I have seen the exotic birds, animals, and humankind of Africa, New Guinea, Australia, South America, and, of course, in our own backyard," he wrote in his proposal for this painting. "I hope to convey a sense of the surreal interaction of each, the 'Bird of the Spirit' that exists in all nature."

Those attending performances at McCaw Hall can see on the walls of the Prelude restaurant Alden Mason's *Seattle City Light Promenade*, which consists of four large paintings from the same period.

5.4 BREWING STORM, PACIFIC COAST TRAIL; STAND OF FIRS, CUMBERLAND; LONGACRES, KENT, 2007

Glenn Rudolph

Etched granite
King County 1 Percent for Art Program
Chinook Building, 401 Fifth Avenue

To the unobservant, the shiny surface of the black granite wall on the Jefferson Street side of the Chinook Building may appear to be dirty and streaked. Closer examination reveals a reproduction of two photographs etched into the surface and augmented with white pigment. Up the hill is *Stand of Firs, Cumberland*, a photo of a stand of firs in a clear-cut on the foothills above Black Diamond, east of Cumberland, Washington, that is illuminated by the sun breaking out on an overcast day. *Brewing Storm, Pacific Coast Trail* is the more visible vertical photograph at the lower corner. It shows an electrical storm forming on the crest of the Cascade Mountains at Stampede Pass (the original photograph is inside the building at the end of the right-hand hallway off the lobby). Extending along the edge of the building's south side is a subtle photo titled *Longacres, Kent*. Its subject is the infield of the Longacres horseracing track, taken long after it was demolished, with a Hawthorne tree standing in the center.

5.4 *Brewing Storm, Pacific Coast Trail*, Glenn Rudolph

5.5   *Rotations*, Anna Valentina Murch

5.5   *Confluences*, Anna Valentina Murch

5.5 CONFLUENCES, 2007; ROTATIONS, 2009

Anna Valentina Murch

Painted steel; patinaed steel with LED lights
King County 1 Percent for Art Program
Chinook Building lobby, 401 Fifth Avenue

The eighty-four-foot, three-inch-long collection of white painted steel forms suspended from the ceiling of the Chinook Building lobby make up *Confluences*, which artist Anna Valentina Murch described as swirling eddies of shadows and light that reflect the complexity of social services housed in this building. The dynamic relationship between the communities served are represented by the series of centers that ripple out, coexisting with all the other centers. "One form interlocks another," she said, "changing as you pass through it, collectively activating the space." Murch gave each of the curved forms a parallel piece that is slightly smaller, and the pairs of shapes are set at different angles to each other depending on the radius of the curve on the plane view and radius of the curve of the sections. The sculpture also extends beyond the shapes with the

5.7   *Tumbling Figure: Five Stages*, Michael Spafford

use of strategically placed lighting and perforated surfaces that create moiré patterns.

On the lobby's north wall is *Rotations*, a nearly twelve-foot-long companion piece that is a collection of circles and swirling lines cut into patinaed steel and accentuated by LED lighting.

5.6 SONGBIRD, 2009

John Henry

Painted steel; H 85 ft.
Private commission
Fifth and Yesler Building

The eighty-five-foot powder blue sculpture adjacent to the Yesler Way overpass was commissioned by building developer Martin Selig for this site. Tennessee sculptor John Henry visited the location on numerous occasions before designing the piece. He sought to create a sculpture that would command the site while complementing the building's design and not overpowering its surroundings. *Songbird* is composed of two large panels and two long bars that thrust skyward, with a titled panel and two shorter bars seemingly delicately balanced at precarious angles.

5.7 TUMBLING FIGURE: FIVE STAGES, 1979

Michael Spafford

Painted aluminum; H 70 ft. × L 10 ft.
King County 1 Percent for Art Program
Parking garage at 415 Sixth Avenue (west side)

Michael Spafford's *Tumbling Figure: Five Stages* was commissioned in 1979 and installed on a high bare concrete elevator shaft at the

5.8   *Torus Torum*, Benson Shaw

Kingdome, Seattle's first multiuse stadium, where all could see the falling figure at five stages of its plunge. The design—an interpretation of Icarus falling from the sky—is an example of the artist's use of Greco-Roman mythology as a visual framework for thought and feeling. Spafford explains that he uses myths to express dualism, metamorphosis, the confrontation of opposites, the struggle for achievement, and the ultimate failure of a heroic effort. This energetic mural consists of seventeen black-painted aluminum sections attached flush against the walls. Before the Kingdome was demolished in 2000, the piece was removed and in 2005 was installed in this new and better home.

5.8 TORUS TORUM, 1984

Benson Shaw

Cast concrete panels; each section H 8 ft. 11 in. × L 17 ft. 8 in.
*King County 1 Percent for Art Program and the National
  Endowment for the Arts*
King County Correctional Facility, 500 Fifth Avenue, south
  entry plaza

Benson Shaw's *Torus Torum* is a relief sculpture placed within two bays of the south entry plaza of the King County Correctional Facility. One bay contains a symmetrical collection of smooth curves and circles. The other bay displays a disassembled version of the former. Shaw gave his creation what he describes as "a snooty Latin title." *Torus*, he explains, is Latin for a "doughnut shape." *Torum* is his made-up word referring to the "torn-up version" of the torus. The end result is a massive work that softens the plaza's harsh concrete angles.

Each sculpture consists of eight cast concrete panels (each appearing to consist of four panels) created using a method invented by the artist. The material used is glass-fiber-reinforced concrete, referred to in the construction industry as GFRC. The panels were made by spraying a slurry of sand, cement, and chopped glass fibers onto the sculpture mold. After several sprayings, a sufficient thickness accumulates and a steel frame is permanently attached to the back of the still-wet material. Shaw lightly textured the surface of *Torus Torum* by sandblasting.

5.9   *Jail House Garden*, Martha Schwartz

5.9 JAIL HOUSE GARDEN, 1987

Martha Schwartz

Ceramic tile

*King County 1 Percent for Art Program and the National
    Endowment for the Arts*

King County Correctional Facility, 500 Fifth Avenue, north
    entry plaza

The colorful plaza on the correctional facility's north side is a surreal version of a formal European garden. Instead of the topiary shrubs of such gardens, Martha Schwartz used geometric shapes made of a rich dark-green tile. The same tile is used for the "shrubbery" border surrounding live plantings near Fifth Avenue. Inlaid throughout this imaginary garden are colorful ceramic pathways in yellow, mauve, blue, and shades of green. The building's walls are tiled in similar colors, and one path seems to lead through a huge arched hedge. The artist explains that, like any other garden design, her *Jail House Garden* was designed with the goal that it "entertain, amuse, and yet impart a sense of mystery." Over the years Schwartz's ceramics have retained their lush colors and continue to present visitors with some respite from the unpleasantness within the facility.

5.10 SAND WORM, 1986

George Tsutakawa

Stainless steel; H 3 ft. 6 in. × W 7 ft. × L 8 ft. 5 in.
King County 1 Percent for Art Program
King County Administration Building, 500 Fourth Avenue,
    Fifth Avenue entrance

5.10   *Sand Worm*, George Tsutakawa

This undulating stainless steel sculpture by Seattle artist George Tsutakawa is different from his other public artworks, most of which are fountains, but in only rare instances are they stainless steel. This piece was originally created as a children's play sculpture and placed in Luther Burbank Park on Mercer Island. It was very popular with children, but unfortunately, stainless steel's ability to retain solar heat made its surfaces too hot. Liability concerns resulted in its transfer to this location. *Sand Worm* was made possible by the grant of a King County Arts Commission Honors Award.

5.11 POINTS OF VIEW, 2002

Pam Beyette, Michael Davis, Norie Sato, and Richard Turner.

Granite and bronze; H 28 ft.
Seattle 1 Percent for Art Program
Seattle Municipal Court building lobby, 600 Fifth Avenue

Visitors entering the Municipal Court building face a conical granite form that rises from a raw gray base, evolves into rough-hewn concentric rings, and culminates with a polished tapered tip. A sense of tension is created as the stone spire almost connects with the point of a more refined, smooth, inverted bronze cone suspended from the ceiling. Fragmented arcs engraved in the granite tile floor emanate from the sculpture's base. The artist team responsible for the work designed it to "suggest the ongoing dialogue, between compassion and justice, natural law and the rule of man, the ideal of the judicial system, and the difficulty creating true balance within society." The floor marks (part of which are now often under a floor mat) were added to "symbolize the rippling effect of the individual's action on society." Note that the form of *Points of View* is referred to in the building's front door handles.

5.12 CODES & PROTOCOLS, 2002

Pam Beyette, Michael Davis, Norie Sato, and Richard Turner

Bronze, limestone, cast glass, plaster, and stainless steel
Seattle 1 Percent for Art Program
Seattle Justice Center lobby, 610 Fifth Avenue

Codes & Protocols is collection of bronze and stone elements in the Police Department lobby that refer to the department's complex role of protecting and serving the public. The artists chose these materials to convey a sense of permanence, weight, and stability and to refer to the familiar and reliable service that citizens expect from their police. On a pedestal against the right wall inside the entrance is a cast bronze police hat and antique keys. The bronze

5.12 *Codes & Protocols* (detail), Pam Beyette, Michael Davis, Norie Sato, and Richard Turner

5.13 SEATTLE CITY HALL INTERIOR WORKS

Eric Robertson, Lois Graham, Beliz Brother, James Carpenter, Nobuho Nagasawa

600 Fifth Avenue

panel behind is a basket weave design inspired by police belts and holsters. The same pattern is used on the building's front door handles.

Also on the south wall are lines of bronze medallions (created by R. W. "Bill" Bane) showing officers at work in such areas as the Communications Center and the Canine, Harbor, Motorcycle, Bicycle, and Mounted Patrol units.

The wall to the left of the entrance includes the same basket weave panel and has a bronze sculpture of a split open rock containing a cast glass rendition of a Seattle police officer's badge. Words and numbers surrounding the badge are codes that police use in their interdepartmental communications. For instance, 244 OCEAN stands for "noise, oral warning given" and 450 ADAM stands for "DWI, physical arrest."

To the left of the reception desk is a memorial wall with plaques showing the names of Seattle police officers who died in the line of duty, beginning with David Sires in 1881. Sires was shot by a man he was attempting to arrest for disorderly conduct.

Seattle City Hall has a broad array of artworks. Some are permanent, others are displayed temporarily, including many from the city's extensive Portable Works Collection, which is funded by the city's 1 Percent for Art Program. There are seven works in the building's lobby and on the second level, accessible via the lobby staircase. Six works were commissioned in 2003 for the new building. The sixth, Lois Graham's *Sargasso Stir*, was originally placed in the Seattle Opera House (which was replaced by McCaw Hall) and moved here when City Hall was completed.

At the northeast corner of the Fifth Avenue lobby is *Evolving Wing and the Gravity of Presence*, by Vancouver, British Columbia, artist Eric Robertson. His references to Native culture in this seventy-two-foot-long piece are obvious, but the sculpture is a more complicated collection of contemporary and traditional symbols that Robertson describes as "a visual journey about honor, connection, contradiction, and continuum." The canoes refer to the 1989 Paddle to Seattle, a journey of traditionally carved canoes in which members from numerous tribes around the region paddled to Seattle to ensure a Native presence in the state's centennial celebration. It became an annual event that grew to include Indigenous people from Canada, Mexico, Greenland, Japan, and Russia.

5.13 *Blue Glass Passage*, James Carpenter

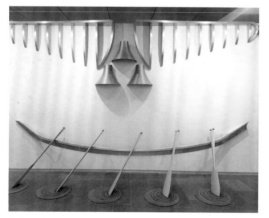

5.13 *Evolving Wing and the Gravity of Presence* (detail), Eric Robertson

5.13 *return*, Beliz Brother

The Paddle to Seattle is represented by the aluminum edges (gunnels) of four large canoes powered by yellow cedar paddles, the blades of which rest in ripples of carved stone. At each end of the long, curved wall, eleven-foot-high cedar paddles rise vertically, a gesture that pays tribute to the Duwamish and Suquamish people. Above the canoe on the left is a series of wooden ribs that bring to mind the ribs of wooden boats. They evolve into aluminum ribs in the shape of airplane wings, referencing the aerospace industry that has been present in Seattle since the Boeing Company was founded in 1916. They also represent the wing flaps of two space shuttles, *Columbia* and *Discovery*, which are also the names of early sailing vessels that plied North Pacific coast waters. In the center are three spun copper cones in the shape of traditional Native woven cedar bark hats. They also resemble a space shuttle's three main thrusters.

Located on the wall behind the Eric Robertson sculpture is *Sargasso Stir*, a 1985 work by the late abstract expressionist Lois Graham. This massive oil painting on linen (19 ft. 6 in.) is typical of Graham's style, with its brilliant green colors accented with bright contrasting slashes of reds and oranges, all applied thickly with a palette knife or brush and supplemented with thick strokes of paint and scratches to create texture. In her last public statement about her art, for a 2007 exhibit at Seattle's Foster/White Gallery, she said, "I like to play with paint. I love to push it around to see what happens. To me, oil paint seems like a living organism: infinite modulations and transformations are possible. I try to evoke directly intense feelings, states of mind, which can't be easily put into words."

The six sepia-toned bands that make up the curved wall on the south side of the lobby is *return*, one of two city-themed works created by Beliz Brother for City Hall. *return* consists of seventy-four photographic images sandwiched between two layers of tempered glass. Brother collected the images from local archival collections, and she notes that each "reveals a fragment of the city's built and natural environment. The images together form a very

personal view of a walk through the city now, thirty years ago, fifty or more years ago."

Up the stairs on the second level is *continuum*, Beliz Brother's eight-by-ten-foot collage of photographic images that portray cultural and historical aspects of the city over time. Close inspection reveals that its pattern of blue and black tones on a white field is a collection of more than five thousand small photos of Seattleites throughout the city's history. The artist created this mural to express "the continuum of Seattle's cultural history."

New York artist James Carpenter has achieved acclaim for his use of glass as art in architecture. In the case of *Blue Glass Passage*, he created a sixty-foot-long walkway above the lobby that is made of blue laminated-glass panels. They are suspended by steel cables and supported by a steel beam. Clear glass on each side allows pedestrians to look out on grand views to the west. Carpenter refers to the sleek span as a "bar of captured light, floating through the lobby." He explains, "The artwork reinforces the placement of City Hall high on the hill and the views it provides of Puget Sound and the Olympic Mountains beyond. The . . . floor of the bridge . . . conceptually make[s] the connection as a transposed slice of water."

Hanging above a stairway at the northwest corner of the lobby level is *Water Weaving Light Cycle*, created by Nobuho Nagasawa in 2005. It is an undulating collection of optical fiber woven by traditional kimono weavers in Japan that has been supplemented with audio components and stainless steel cable. In the daytime this forty-six-foot-long form appears to be merely woven white fabric. At night, the sculpture simulates flowing water with blue light and the sounds of waves and the environment recorded in Seattle's

Golden Gardens and Lincoln and Carkeek Parks. The pulsating hues of blue light that cascade up and down the tapestry and the recorded sounds are linked and synchronized with the ebb and flow of waves and activity changes according to weather conditions through a link to a National Oceanic and Atmospheric Administration website. Nagasawa describes *Water Weaving Light Cycle as* "living architecture in action" and says that it "emulates cascading water and the rhythms of waves breaking on the shores of nearby Puget Sound."

Beliz Brother's third commission for City Hall is *illumine*, which hangs inside a rectangular glass cube on the northwest corner of City Hall at Fourth Avenue and Cherry Street. Within that structure are two-foot-diameter dichroic glass disks that hang from eleven steel cables. *Illumine* means "to give light or to illuminate," and Brother intended to have the rotating and twisting disks "create an artwork that brings the city and its people, through reflection, into the City Hall building, at the same time creating a transparent abstraction of color and light."

5.14 SEATTLE MUNICIPAL TOWER INTERIOR WORKS

Anna Skibska, Everett DuPen, Elias Schultz, and Harold Balazs

700 Fifth Avenue

Hanging from the ceiling in front of the upper wall inside the Fifth Avenue entrance of the Seattle Municipal Tower is *Gravity Law*, a three-part sculpture created by Anna Skibska. What may appear to be lines of twisted metal wire are examples of Skibska's innovative ethereal works of glass webbing and space. They were created using a glass technique called flameworking (or lampworking) in which glass rods are heated with a torch and then stretched into thin lines. Skibska has referred to her sculptures as geometric spiders' webs in which she simultaneously wraps

5.14   *Carved panels,* Everett DuPen

space, embraces time, and traps light. In this case the glass ranges in color from clear to very light brown or amber. Each element is accentuated with overhead lighting, and the highlights on each form change with variations in outside lighting. Imperceptible air currents make Skibska's delicate yet durable forms slightly sway.

Gravity Law was created in 2004 for the Rainier Beach branch of the Seattle Public Library, but in 2017 the shapes of the elements were changed and the work was installed at its present location.

Down the entry stairs are Everett DuPen's carved walnut panels, which were commissioned screens for the 1962 City Hall lobby (demolished in 2001). The theme of DuPen's work is nature's fertility, represented by Pacific Northwest plant life. The designs include undulating seaweed and unfolding buds on growing land plants. Bronze framing originally encompassed each of the three-inch-thick carvings. Now the ten elements are displayed together without frames and the seven-by-ten-foot collection floats off a long wall, providing more of a visual impact than did the original configuration. DuPen carved these screens with the help of his friend Elias Schultz.

Inside and to the left of the glass doors are three decorative abstract bronze screens created in 1962 by Harold Balazs. They were commissioned by the Seattle Civic Arts Committee for the Seattle Opera House, which was built for the Seattle World's Fair in 1962. That building was demolished and replaced by McCaw Hall. Each of the screens are eight feet by eight feet and the surfaces of their interwoven strips of bronze alternate

between smooth and those supplemented with bronze welding patterns.

This lower floor of the Seattle Municipal Tower and the floor above are worthy of investigation as the city has various permanent and portable artworks on display.

5.15 UNTITLED, 1990

Parks Anderson

Steel and stainless steel; H 44 ft.
Private commission
Seattle Municipal Tower, Fifth Avenue and Cherry Street,
     entrance to southwest corner plaza

This sculpture, Parks Anderson's largest, stands one floor above Fifth Avenue and straddles the top of the stairway to the southwest corner plaza. Its two steel legs, one of which is in the shape of a tuning fork, form an equilateral triangle with the top landing. At its apex are three stainless steel forms that swing randomly as the winds blow through the plaza. Anderson notes that the three forms are just off balance enough to turn slightly and create a balletic rocking and then return to their original point by force of gravity. This sculpture was commissioned by the building's developer, Sarkowsky Investment Corporation.

5.16 GATE AND SILVER LADY, 2014

Peter Millett

Galvanized steel, weathered steel; Gate: H 6 ft. 5 in. × W 1 ft.
     9 in. × L 4 ft. ; Silver Lady: H 6 ft. 11 in. × W 2 ft. × L 2 ft.
City of Seattle collection
Seattle Municipal Tower, Fifth Avenue and Columbia Street,
     entrance to northwest corner plaza

5.16   *Gate*, Peter Millett

5.16   *Silver Lady*, Peter Millett

Two sculptures by Seattle artist Peter Millett stand hidden away in a small plaza at the Seattle Municipal Tower. Both are examples of what Millett describes as his exploration of "a geometric language of shape and space." *Gate* is a multifaceted sculpture of weathered steel that consists of three primary forms that transition from a hexagon on one end to an equilateral triangle on the other through an alternating series of triangles and trapezoids. It presents the viewer with twenty-one planes, and studying it from different angles reveals its complexity, with forms that seem to alter with changes in light and shadow. Millett once remarked that a curator called his work "deconstructed architecture." "I'm not sure what that means," he says, "but I like the sounds of it."

Silver Lady is another collection of multifaceted forms, in this case five galvanized steel elements stacked in a narrow, nearly seven-foot-tall torqued column. Viewers are presented with six planes in each of its sections, standing atop a base of twelve planes. This too is a complex structure, the shape of which seems to change depending on the varying degrees of light and shadows present and the angle from which one observes it.

5.17 THE CENTER HOLDS, 2017

Julie Speidel

Bronze; H 14 ft. × W 9 ft. × L 10 ft. 2 in.
Private commission
F5 Tower, 801 Fifth Avenue

5.17 *The Center Holds,* Julie Speidel

When Julie Speidel created *The Center Holds,* she was thinking about the changes and related turmoil created by the rapid development of downtown Seattle and the fact that the F5 Tower is constructed around two historical buildings, the Rainier Club and First United Methodist Church, the latter of which had been threatened with demolition. The Seattle native (her father was Bill Speidel, author, historic preservationist, and founder of Seattle's Underground Tour) thought about the William Butler Yeats poem, "The Second Coming." It is a pessimistic work by that Irish poet, written after World War I and at the beginning of the fight for Irish independence, which includes the line "Things fall apart; the centre cannot hold." In this case the center did hold, and Speidel's sculpture stands on the hill amid modern buildings filled with the latest technologies and architectural treasures that have been saved for future generations.

The Center Holds was commissioned by Daniels Real Estate, the building's developers, who wanted rounded forms to offset the building's rectangular edges. Speidel created a sculpture with three elements that curve around and fold into and around one another. Overall, she sought to create something that was provocative and strong when viewed from all angles, including from within the building's glass enclosed lobby.

5.18 THREE-PIECE SCULPTURE: VERTEBRAE, 1968

Henry Moore

Bronze; H 9 ft. × W 10 ft. 7 in. × L 24 ft.
Seattle Art Museum collection
Safeco Plaza, 1001 Fourth Avenue

When Seattle-First National Bank began plans in the mid-1960s to build the city's first modern skyscraper at 1001 Fourth Avenue, it also began collecting art to grace its future headquarters. A budget of $300,000 was set aside for art in the building's public places. Nothing like it had been done before in Seattle. The resulting collection of works by locally, nationally, and internationally known artists took its place with the finest corporate collections in America. Twenty years later financial catastrophe required that Seafirst sell its headquarters building. Fortunately, some of original artworks have remained.

What was selected for the bank's Fourth Avenue plaza was *Three-Piece Sculpture: Vertebrae,* a new sculpture by Henry Moore, the dean of twentieth-century British sculptors.

5.18　*Three-Piece Sculpture: Vertebrae*, Henry Moore

Two other sculptures were considered for the plaza: Barnett Newman's *Broken Obelisk*, now at the University of Washington, and Michael Heizer's *Adjacent, Against, Upon*, now at Myrtle Edwards Park (3.22). Bank officials, architects, and art collectors who were selecting the public artwork for the new building chose Moore's curvilinear sculpture to offset the stark lines of the building.

This horizontal sculpture is reminiscent of the many reclining female figures for which Moore was perhaps best known. Moore did not believe sculptural subjects had to be limited to animate objects, and he applied the stretched and hollowed approach that he had taken with human forms in the previous decade to other natural forms such as shells and bones. In the book *Henry Moore Sculpture*, Moore had this to say about *Vertebrae*: "Each of the forms, although different, has the same basic shape.

Just as in a backbone which may be made up of twenty segments where each one is roughly like the others but not exactly the same. . . . This is why I call these sculptures *Vertebrae*."

Seattle's *Vertebrae* is one of four such sculptures; one remains on the late artist's estate in England, another sits outside the Israeli National Museum in Jerusalem, and a third resides at the Hirshhorn Museum and Sculpture Garden in Washington, DC. Each is unique in that the three sections are positioned differently. Moore did not believe that a single arrangement was required. In fact, Donald Winkelman, the building's principal architect, reported that slight warping of the sculpture necessitated a placement that was different from Moore's plan. Moore asked Winkelman to suggest the placement, which Moore approved before installation was complete.

The history of Seattle's *Vertebrae* provides a good example of how a modern artwork initially unloved by many ("It's just bones!!") became a city icon worth fighting to preserve. In 1986 it was sold to a Japanese collector, but the public outcry over the secret sale and planned removal of this important artwork resulted in its repurchase and eventual donation to the Seattle Art Museum.

5.19 SAFECO PLAZA INTERIOR WORKS

James W. Washington Jr. and George Tsutakawa

Safeco Plaza, 1001 Fourth Avenue

The four carved black granite benches in the exterior courtyard off of the northwest side of this building's Fourth Avenue lobby are fine examples of the unique sculptural style of Seattle artist James W. Washington Jr. Created between 1968 and 1969, he sought to express in each his thoughts about the creation of life and the interrelationship between all creatures. The theme, which he calls the "kinship of all life," has been emphasized in many of his works since 1968 (see 6.3). Washington's subjects include a crocodile, chicks emerging from eggs, a human head, a rabbit, a lamb, young birds of prey, seahorses, and a coelacanth (a rare prehistoric fish once thought extinct). These simply carved figures show the influence on Washington of ancient carvings that he first saw during a tour of Mexico in the early 1950s. Only the essential form is carved. Detail is left to the viewer's imagination.

Between Washington's benches are two sculptures by George Tsutakawa. They were created in 1968 as fountains and originally

5.20   *Fountain of Wisdom*, George Tsutakawa
(Photo by Richard J. Birmingham)

placed on the building's south side. High winds prohibited their use as fountains, and when they were moved to this location, they were placed as sculptures.

5.20 FOUNTAIN OF WISDOM, 1960

George Tsutakawa

Silicon bronze; H 9 ft. × W 5 ft. 6 in.
Seattle Public Library collection
Seattle Public Library, 1000 Fourth Avenue

Fountain of Wisdom is George Tsutakawa's first fountain-sculpture and marks the beginning of a successful career as an internationally known creator of such works. This creation displays the central idea in the design of all Tsutakawa fountains: that water should be integrated into the sculpture, not just sprayed at it or from it. "Water is part of the sculpture—that's one of my strong beliefs," Tsutakawa explained. "The old European, so-called Roman, fountains used cast bronze figures . . . women, horses, fish, with water either squirting onto them or pouring out of an urn or squirting out of a mouth. The water and sculpture are unrelated. I started to think of water as another element of the work . . . . It had to function as part of the total design. One way to do that was to have the water forced out to become part of the design. By doing that, the water can dominate and command the total space around the sculpture . . . not to mention the color, sound, and deflection of the water, which are all tremendously exciting things. Water is the most exciting element we have."

In the case of this fountain, Tsutakawa explained that the gushing water "represents knowledge, the material source. . . . The library is the source of that knowledge. The total representation is of the universe. The top curved dish represents heaven; the round form beneath it represents earth. Beneath it all is the five-fingered basin representing man. Knowledge is flowing down to him . . . . He's trying to catch knowledge to obtain wisdom, but no matter how much knowledge he catches, so much is lost." However, that which is lost will be recirculated, as the water in this fountain recirculates.

Fountain of Wisdom was commissioned for the Fifth Avenue entrance to the library's second building on this site, which was built in 1960. It was moved to this new location when the current library building was built in 2004.

5.21 SEATTLE PUBLIC CENTRAL LIBRARY INTERIOR WORKS

Ann Hamilton, Mandy Greer, James FitzGerald and Margaret Tomkins, Everett DuPen, Tony Oursler, George Legrady, Lynne Yamamoto, and Frank Okada

1000 Fourth Avenue

Some consider Seattle's Central Library, designed by architect Rem Koolhaas and completed in 2004, to be both a building and a sculpture. It was selected as *Time* magazine's 2004 Building of the Year and hailed by New York Times architecture critic Herbert Muschamp as the "most exciting new building it has been my honor to review in more than 30 years of writing about architecture." A number of artworks were commissioned for its interior spaces through Seattle's 1 Percent for Art Program.

Inside of the library's entrance and to the right is *LEW Wood Floor*, Ann Hamilton's unique flooring, which is her tribute to the production and reading of hard copy books. She reports that her intent was to mark the technological transition from books to digital technologies "by imbedding in the membrane of the library's surface work that in texture and form remembers and evokes a tactile experience of book production and reading." Within the sections of its seventy-two hundred square feet are first lines from books within the library, all set backward as they would have been set in a typesetter's block. The artist explains that "the experience of reading backwards also demonstrates the experience of learning to read as a process wherein abstract symbols become, in time, transparent and meaningful words and sentences." The books that make up the dominant textual sources—fiction and nonfiction,

5.21   *Making Visible the Invisible,* George Legrady

5.21   *Braincast,* Tony Oursler

5.21   *Babe,* Mandy Greer

5.21   *LEW Wood Floor* (detail), Ann Hamilton

poetry and musical lyrics—fall under the library category of "Literacy/ESL (English as a Second Language)/World languages" or LEW, hence the name of the artwork, *LEW Wood Floor.* The languages included in the design—English, French, German, Italian, Russian, Spanish, Arabic, Chinese, Japanese, Korean, and Vietnamese—are the most frequently used in the LEW collection.

In the children's center, inside the Fourth Avenue entrance and to the left, are three wall-mounted sculptures of fabric, steel, and papier mâché that were created by the innovative fabric and multidisciplinary artist Mandy Greer. Each was inspired by a folktale found in the library's collection. Mounted on a concrete column is a bust of Paul Bunyan's blue ox, *Babe,* faced with blue felted wool and adorned with glass and plastic beads, buttons, and sequins. The tips of *Babe's* horns culminate with blue pom-poms and his harness is faced with blue plaid. Greer has *Babe* looking down inquisitively. He represents discovery through investigation of one's surroundings.

The red *Phoenix Fairy,* perched on a red branch above the librarian's information desk, is covered with individually crafted red fabric feathers and layers of translucent red fabric, sequins, and glitter. Its tail end is ablaze with red peacock-like feathers accented with yellow and turquoise. The phoenix is the mythical bird that is continually reborn from the ashes of its predecessor. Greer notes that this sculpture represents "the continual rebirth of knowledge."

Greer's *Magical Grove* is a green felt-covered tree with sparkling bright pink flowers growing out of a concrete column. Greer chose this theme, which was inspired by a Persian folktale, to symbolize how the "seed" of an idea can expand into something vibrant.

Through the doors to the right of *Magical Grove* is a twenty-seven-foot-long sculptural screen created by James FitzGerald and Margaret Tomkins in 1960 for the earlier library building. It is an array of 125 panels created from sand-cast bronze, etched brass, and fused layers of colored glass with a frame of polished brass. The work presents a multitude

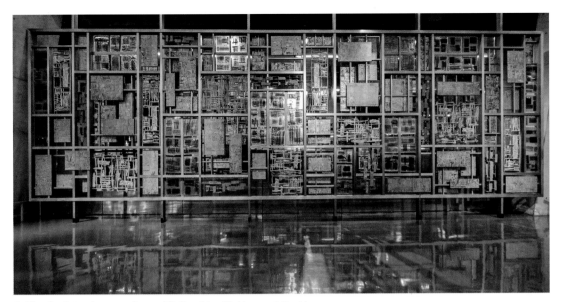

5.21 Sculptural screen, James FitzGerald, with Margaret Tomkins

of shapes and visual effects and colors, further accentuated in this contemporary placement by the installation of mirrors behind it. This work holds a special place in FitzGerald's career. It was his first major public commission since 1938, when he designed the tunnel reliefs for the original Mercer Island floating bridge tunnel, and it was the cause of a fire that destroyed his studio and many of his artworks and those of his wife, Margaret Tomkins. This screen is actually FitzGerald's second because much of the original was destroyed in that fire.

On the wall to the right of the screen is a bronze plaque honoring George Rochester (1888–1929), a prominent lawyer and judge who was an influential member of the Seattle Library Board from 1900 to 1912. The plaque was created by Everett DuPen in 1966.

Along the glowing escalator walls between levels 3 and 5 is *Braincast*, a three-part video sculpture created in 2004 by Tony Oursler, a New York–based multimedia artist known for his innovative video artworks. A ripped-open portion of the wall reveals oval white forms mounted amid studs, pipes, and wiring that project video images of faces and facial features onto three-dimensional forms and semitransparent Plexiglass. The mystical aura created by these disembodied images is increased with the addition of softly spoken recitations of poetry. With *Braincast*, Oursler sought to "inspire contemplation upon the transmission of information, while reflecting upon the tradition of the public library and its expanding role as the transmitter of myriad information in spoken, printed, recorded, and digital form."

Another innovative artwork that refers to the library's place in the increasingly technical world is *Making Visible the Invisible*, an electronic installation by George Legrady. Located near the top of the escalator on level 5, on the glass wall above the librarian's reference desk, are six large liquid crystal display screens that visualize statistical analyses of what resources

5.21 *Shiva II*, Frank Okada

patrons are checking out of the library. Legrady does so by providing four visualizations. *Vital Statistics*, shows the number of books, DVDs, CDs, videos, and other sources that have been checked out within the past hour and the past day. The passage of time is reflected by changes in background colors on the screen. *Floating Titles* displays the titles of books and other materials checked out in the past hour. In *Dot Matrix Rain*, checked-out resources are divided into the Dewey Decimal system classification numbers (000 to 999) and pop up on the screen at their numerical classification. Titles of books excluded from that system, such as fiction, fall from the top and fade at the bottom of the screen. The *Keyword Map Attack* screen displays keywords for items that have been checked out. It is color coded and spatially plotted according to the Dewey Decimal system order and usage. Legrady's creation starts working an hour after

5.22 *Tregaseal*, Julie Speidel

the library opens, at which time it has enough statistical information to display.

On the south side of level 10, mounted high up on a black wall at the top of the escalator, is Lynne Yamamoto's *Memory*, a row of card catalog cabinets of the style used in libraries before computerized cataloging. This white fiberglass rendition of antique elements is appropriately located near where the library stores its collection of early Seattle history resources.

On the west side of that wall is *Shiva II*, a large oil painting on canvas by Frank Okada, a prominent Pacific Northwest abstract expressionist. Okada gave this 1972 painting in honor of his brother John Okada (1923–71) who wrote the 1957 novel *No-No Boy*.

5.22 TREGASEAL, 1998

Julie Speidel

Welded bronze; H 4 ft. × W 4 ft. × L 24 ft.
US General Services Administration commission
William Kenzo Nakamura US Courthouse, 1010 Fifth Avenue

Tregaseal was commissioned to honor the memory of Morell Edward Sharp (1920–80) who was a highly regarded state and federal court judge in Washington State for many years. Judge Sharp was not only an important jurist but also a beloved and active member of his community who worked for many causes. Sculptor Julie Speidel thought of the many components of his life when she designed this four-part sculpture made up of ten unique elements. The lines between each element flow into the adjacent piece, creating an image of floating shapes that seem poised to either settle into one another or float apart. Shapes and spaces are further delineated and emphasized

by changing levels of shade and natural light. Speidel made the four elements asymmetrical to ensure "that they aren't too grounded in their environment."

The inspiration for this and many other Speidel sculptures has been ancient forms she has seen in Europe and Asia, especially those in the British Isles, where she lived for many years. The name *Tregaseal* comes from a restored prehistoric circle of granite stones near Cornwall, England. Although those stones did not specifically influence the design of this sculpture, Speidel did have in mind the fact that ancient people found sites that spoke to them and marked their importance and sacred nature by placing stones there.

5.23 NARAMORE FOUNTAIN, 1966

George Tsutakawa

Welded silicon bronze; H 15 ft.
Gift to the city
Sixth Avenue and Seneca Street

In 1966 Floyd Naramore, a prominent Seattle architect and founder of what is now the NBBJ architectural firm, commissioned George Tsutakawa to create this fountain (the artist's twentieth) for presentation to the city. Tsutakawa created it with two purposes in mind: to please its viewers and to make water an integral part of its form. Tsutakawa's primary innovation here is the forcing of water onto and against curved bronze shapes, thereby creating flared sheets of water that extend the bronze forms. "As a design without water, it's a more conventional work," he explains, "but the water forced up against the sides and over the leaves is unique. Not many fountains have that."

5.23 *Naramore Fountain,* George Tsutakawa

Naramore Fountain is also unusual for the manner in which it is displayed. Rather than placing it at eye level, Tsutakawa and Perry Johanson, the Seattle architect (another cofounder of NBBJ) who designed the setting, placed it on a concave rock aggregate platform above eye level. Rocks quarried from the Cascades were added to the platform to give the effect of a flowing mountain stream.

5.24 WIND ON WATER, 1971

Norman Warsinske

Steel with gold leaf; H 5 ft. × L 10 ft.
Unico Properties collection
IBM Building lobby, 1200 Fifth Avenue

The only artwork in the IBM Building's white marble lobby is Norman Warsinske's *Wind on Water.* Standing above the elevator bay, his sculpture portrays the motion created by wind upon the sea, a force that, Warsinske noted, "creates a feeling of joy for those who observe it." That theme was translated into this simple, yet elegant, sculpture. It is the largest of the works in Warsinske's "Wind Series," the subject of two exhibitions of his sculptures.

The simplicity of the lobby design is consistent with the clear vertical lines of this building, which was designed by architect Minoru Yamasaki (1912–86), a Seattle native and Garfield High School graduate. Yamasaki also designed the Pacific Science Center and the nearby pedestal-based Rainier Tower. His most famous work was the World Trade Center in New York City, which was completed in 1973. That ill-fated landmark had vertical lines extending up the sides of both buildings, elements reminiscent of Yamasaki's Seattle designs.

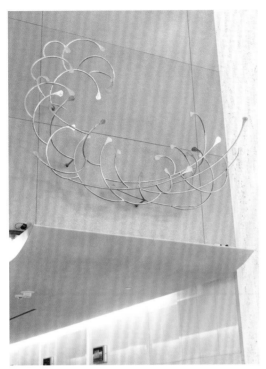

5.24 *Wind on Water,* Norman Warsinske

5.25 IBM FOUNTAIN, 1964

James FitzGerald

Cast bronze; H 6 ft. 10 in. × L 18 ft. 6 in.
Unico Properties collection
IBM Building, 1200 Fifth Avenue, lower plaza, corner of Fifth
    Avenue and University Street

The fountain-sculpture that James FitzGerald created for IBM's new Seattle building in 1964 is constructed of welded sections of craggy cast bronze shapes that are similar to those of his fountain at Cornish Playhouse at Seattle Center (8.26). In both cases water appears to have eroded away the cast bronze forms. Here, however, water leakage issues made it impractical to continue operating it as a fountain and FitzGerald's creation is now a sculpture surrounded by plants.

5.25 *IBM Fountain,* James FitzGerald

5.26   Freeway Park waterfalls, Lawrence Halprin & Associates

5.26 FREEWAY PARK WATERFALLS, 1976

Lawrence Halprin & Associates

Concrete

Freeway Park, Sixth to Eighth Avenues, between University
    and Seneca Streets

When Interstate 5 was cut through Seattle in the 1960s, the environmental planning we know today was not a predominant influence. Thus, suggestions that the freeway be covered over to create usable space were quickly dismissed. However, by the end of that decade Seattle voters passed one of the city's Forward Thrust bond issues that included plans for a small park at the edge of the freeway between Seneca and University Streets. That idea grew to encompass a much grander 5.4-acre park, the nation's first to be built over a freeway. It was designed by the San Francisco landscape architecture firm of Lawrence Halprin & Associates.

The park consists of a series of plazas that are enclosed by board-formed concrete walls and planting containers, the horizontal and vertical lines of which remind some of Mayan ruins. The central portion is devoted to three waterfalls that recirculate a combined total of twenty-seven thousand gallons a minute.

They are titled *Central Plaza Canyon*, *East Plaza Water Display*, and *Central Plaza Cascade*. These roaring waterfalls effectively drowned out the sounds of the freeway below. In a 1977 interview with *Newsweek* magazine, Halprin commented that the rushing waterfalls "affect us in the same way as does a wild animal in the zoo, pacing back and forth in his cage, beautiful and quietly desperate, controlled, but with implications of wild danger."

Lawrence Halprin & Associates was also the principal landscape designer of the Seattle World's Fair and designed the *Joseph Drumheller Fountain* at the University of Washington.

The principal architect on this project was Angela Danadjieva, a Bulgarian-born and now California-based landscape architect who achieved considerable recognition for her work on this and similar projects. She also designed the extension to the Washington State Convention and Trade Center and the earlier half-acre addition to the park across the freeway and above the city parking garage. Funds for the first addition were given to the city by the PACCAR Foundation in memory of Paul Pigott, former chief officer of PACCAR Corporation. A later addition was constructed with federal funds authorized in 1984 by the Federal-Aid Highway Act.

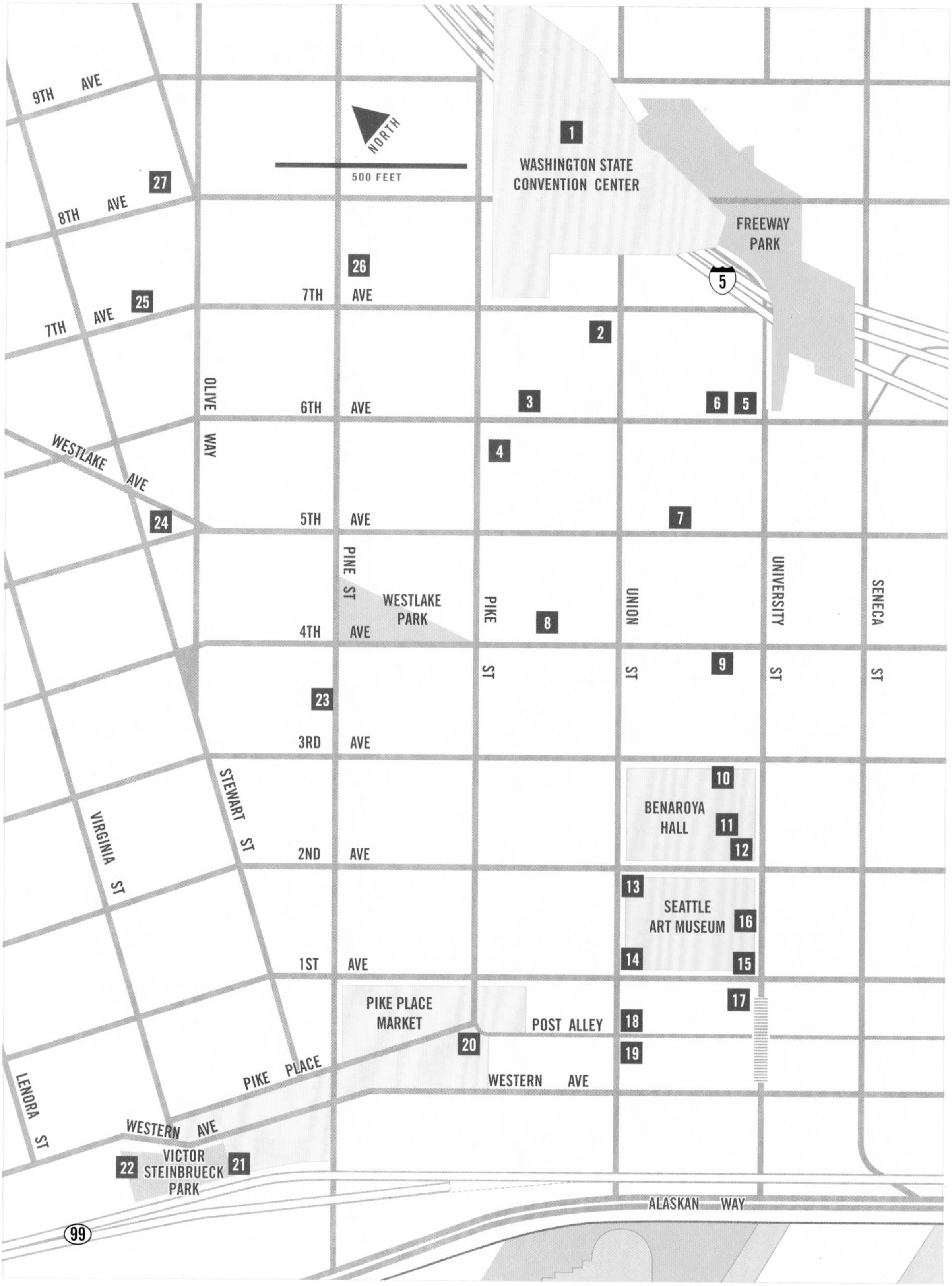

NORTH

500 FEET

9TH AVE

8TH AVE

[27]

7TH AVE

[25]

WESTLAKE AVE

[24]

OLIVE WAY

[26] **7TH AVE**

[1] **WASHINGTON STATE CONVENTION CENTER**

FREEWAY PARK

[5]

[2]

6TH AVE

[3]

[6] [5]

[4]

5TH AVE

[7]

PINE ST

WESTLAKE PARK

PIKE ST

UNION ST

UNIVERSITY ST

SENECA ST

4TH AVE

[8]

[9]

[23]

3RD AVE

STEWART ST

VIRGINIA ST

2ND AVE

[10]

BENAROYA HALL

[11]

[12]

[13]

SEATTLE ART MUSEUM

[16]

[14]

[15]

1ST AVE

[17]

PIKE PLACE MARKET

POST ALLEY

[18]

[20]

[19]

PIKE PLACE

WESTERN AVE

LENORA ST

WESTERN AVE

[22] **VICTOR STEINBRUECK PARK** [21]

ALASKAN WAY

(99)

6 UNIVERSITY STREET TO STEWART STREET

Painting is the only bridge linking the painter's mind with that of the viewer.

—Eugene Delacroix (1798–1863)

THIS CHAPTER STARTS WITH THREE VENUES—the Washington State Convention and Trade Center, the Sheraton Hotel, and US Bank Centre—each of which has a readily accessible, museum quality collection of works by Pacific Northwest artists. These venues are close to one another and worthy of a combined tour. Readily accessible commissioned artworks can also be found in a number of other buildings, including Benaroya Hall, the Seattle Art Museum, and Pike Place Market.

6.1 WASHINGTON STATE CONVENTION CENTER WORKS

Seventh Avenue and Pike Street

Several commissioned artworks were included in the Washington State Convention Center when it was completed in 1988. Later expansions of the center provided a vast amount of wall space for displaying art, and the facility now has an impressive collection of art by a wide range of artists working in many mediums. The increased availability of space with the center's expansion was an artistic aha moment according to Phyllis Lamphere, who headed up initial efforts to amass the collection. She explains that representatives from all of the arts commissions, private collections, museums, and arts patrons were called together and asked, "Can you help us build a collection for these walls?" The center accumulated a collection (some of it on loan) that includes many of the best known Pacific Northwest artists who established critically acclaimed careers in the twentieth century.

Those who wish to explore the facility will find works by a wide range of artists, including Eustace Ziegler, Hilda Morris, Margaret Tomkins, Kenneth Callahan, Guy Anderson, Alden Mason, Richard Gilkey, Paul Horiuchi, Neil Meitzler, Glen Alps, James Lee Hanson, Michael Spafford, Doris Chase, Francis Celentano, Paul and Dante Marioni, Patti Warashina, Robert Sperry, Jacob Lawrence, Dale Chihuly, Nancy Mee, and Alfredo Arreguin. Signage is well placed to identify them, and the only restriction on viewing is that some may be in areas that are temporarily unavailable due to convention activities. The collection also includes a number of glass

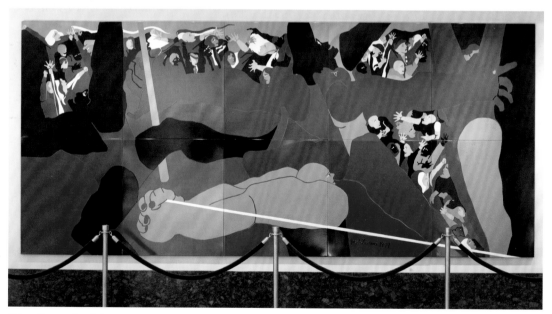

6.1   *Games,* Jacob Lawrence

6.1   *Lebeg*, Ann Gardner

6.1   *Seattle George Monument*, Buster Simpson

pieces from local studios and others associated with the Pilchuck Glass School.

Two large sculptures welcome visitors at the center's entrance at the corner of Seventh and Pike. Hanging from the ceiling eighty-five feet above the lobby floor is Ann Gardner's *Lebeg*, a sixty-five-foot-tall mobile of nine elliptical forms covered in half-inch colored glass tiles with foil backs that shimmer in the light. The sculpture's name is Hungarian for "slight movement in the air," and the forms are very slowly moved by a small motor. The terrazzo floor below is Gardner's design. *Lebeg* was created in 2001 and funded by the Washington State Art in Public Places Program.

Near the elevators is *Myth of the Sea*, a large bronze sculpture created in 1970 by the late Hilda Morris and loaned by the Tacoma Art Museum. Morris was an abstract expressionist who was hailed as the leading Oregon sculptor of her time. Her craggy forms with voids and spires were described by a *Portland Oregonian* art reviewer as "more found than created, as though some particularly wise and lucky archeologist or geologist had rescued it, undamaged and spirit intact, from the past."

At the top of the escalators at level 3 is Jacob Lawrence's monumental *Games*, an eighteen-foot-long vitreous enamel on steel mural created in 1979 for the Kingdome. The boldly

6.1   *Skagit Valley Triptych* (part), Richard Gilkey

colored work (the artist's first in this medium) abounds with athletic activities and physical competition, with massive athletes in the foreground and an excited crowd in the background. No specific sport is represented in this mural. Rather, Lawrence vividly portrays the excitement and action of sports in general with his carefully placed interlocking shapes and spaces.

At level 4 is Richard Gilkey's sixty-foot-long *Skagit Valley Triptych* a 1974 work that provides three separate views of his beloved Skagit Valley north of Seattle. All are united by composition and theme and painted in his distinctive style of thick, subtle colors applied with palette knives rather than brushes.

An original commissioned sculpture at the center is Buster Simpson's *Seattle George Monument,* located outside of level 4 at the edge of Freeway Park. His twenty-eight-foot-high creation consists of a steel mesh cube topped with twenty-four aluminum profiles of Chief Seattle's head. The monument includes a supporting cone and tripod, in reference to Washington's career as a surveyor, and the sculpture is placed on a grid aligned to the Willamette Meridian, the main survey line of

Washington and Oregon. Simpson has said that the cone and tripod also refer to the shape of an inverted Native American lodge. The wind vane that turns around the Seattle profile is cut in the shape of a profile of George Washington's head. Simpson envisioned Seattle's profile disappearing under a blanket of ivy that would grow up over the years and be trimmed by the turning wind vane into the shape of Washington's profile. After over a quarter of a century, the ivy has not grown up, but the profiles remain intriguing.

Between the Convention Center and Simpson's sculpture is a large basalt assemblage created by landscape architect Angela Danadjieva (see 5.26). Reminiscent of a classical Chinese landscape painting, Danadjieva's creation is part of the James R. and Mary Lou Ellis Plaza, which is dedicated to the enduring work of the Seattle attorney Jim Ellis and his wife. Ellis was a leader in the campaigns that created both Freeway Park and the convention center as well as the clean-up of a polluted Lake Washington in the 1950s, and the creation of the Mountain to Sound Greenway along Interstate 90 corridor in the 1980s.

6.2 THE URBAN GARDEN, 2011

Ginny Ruffner

Painted steel and aluminum; H 27 ft.
Private commission
Seventh Avenue and Union Street

The Sheraton Hotel has often been criticized for an exterior that is inhospitable to pedestrians. In 2011 the hotel embarked on a program to improve its perimeter and a major step toward that goal was the installation of Ginny Ruffner's kinetic sculpture, *The Urban Garden*. Ruffner created a colorful collection of flowers—a purple tulip, a rotating yellow daisy, bluebells that open and close—that grow out of a nine-foot-high clay-colored pot, with a tipping red watering can that pours water onto a green leaf. The computer-controlled workings are visible through a window in the flowerpot. Ruffner is primarily known as a glass artist and is her largest and her first moving sculpture, *The Urban Garden*. She explains that moving objects are more intriguing, and she wanted a piece that could be easily accessed visually from many points of view. Ruffner notes that this sculpture reflects her feeling that Seattle is a beautiful, growing, flourishing place.

6.2   *The Urban Garden,* Ginny Ruffner

6.3 THE SHERATON HOTEL COLLECTION

Sheraton Hotel, Sixth Avenue, between Union and Pike Streets

When the Sheraton Hotel opened its doors in 1982, it presented Seattle citizens and visitors with the most elaborate collection of art in any hotel in the region. Its collection has grown since then, and it remains available for public view. Throughout the hotel's lobby level are original works on paper or canvas by major names in twentieth-century Pacific Northwest art history including Mark Tobey, Kenneth Callahan, Richard Gilkey, Margaret Tomkins, Guy Anderson, William Cumming, Leo Kenney, Carl Morris, Walter Isaacs, Ambrose Patterson, William Ivey, Paul Horiuchi, Morris Graves, Louis Bunce, Jacob Lawrence, and Peter Millett.

Inside the Sixth Avenue entrance, at the Pike Street (north) end of the Sheraton's lobby level, and to the left is the Fountain Wine Bar & Lounge. That name refers to George

Tsutakawa's silicon bronze *Northwest Fountain* (1981) installed within. At its entrance is Tsutakawa's sumi ink painting of Mount Rainier (1980). Along a wall to the right of the entrance is *The Four Philosophical Elements*, a four-part series of assemblages created by Dennis Evans in 2013. A sign on the wall describes the rich symbolism Evans incorporated into each piece.

In a glass case at the end of the Fountain Wine Bar & Lounge is Nancy Mee's *Transition of Venus*. The fifteen-foot-long glass and copper sculpture, created in 1982, is a fine example of the artist's use of vertical columns of thick glass shards fused together and often twisting and contorting. Mee explains that the continuing theme in her sculptures at that time is the transition between beauty and deformity, and the columns refer to deformed backbones often caused by scoliosis, a spinal abnormality that develops in younger women. This theme is derived from images Mee often saw as a college student when she worked as a photocopier at the University of Washington Medical School library.

Behind the reception desk is Alden Mason's twenty-four-foot-long painting *Big Chief Seattle*. Painted in 1982, it is one of the largest examples of his unique style of covering the canvas with richly colored acrylic paint squiggles.

Inside the lobby's Sixth Avenue entrance to the right is *Obelisk with Phoenix and Esoteric Symbols*, a sculpture created by James Washington Jr. in 1982. This red granite monolith has a collection of the esoteric symbols for which Washington was known. Creatures on its top include a reclining rabbit and a hatching bird. Designs on its front, back, and sides include a phoenix, symbolizing destruction and recreation or reincarnation; a loaf and a fish, symbolizing Christ feeding the multitudes; two arrows pointing in opposite directions that represent the circle of life; and geometric shapes and numbers that refer to Washington's personal philosophy.

On the south side of the lobby is a twenty-seven-piece collection of glass created between 1980 and 1982 at the world-famous Pilchuck

6.3   *Obelisk with Phoenix and Esoteric Symbols*, James Washington Jr.

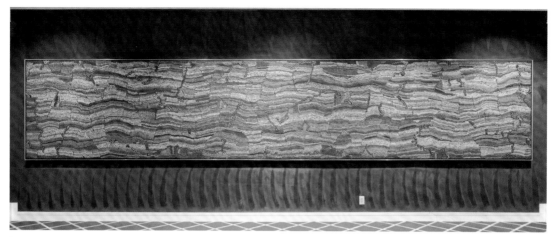

6.3 *Big Chief Seattle,* Alden Mason

6.3 *Veil of the Siren, Disguise of the Mime (Genesis),* Mary Ann Peters

Glass School, located north of Seattle in Stanwood. Also on view in a large case is *Flower Form #2,* a collection of blown white glass forms by Dale Chihuly, one of the deans of studio glass art and a cofounder of the Pilchuck Glass School. Paintings and reproductions of paintings by Dale Chihuly can be seen on the lobby level and throughout the rest of the hotel.

Also in the south lobby, towards the hotel's Union Street Tower, are two sixty-four-square-inch untitled murals created by Robert Sperry in 1982. They are splendid examples of the artist's distinctive treatment of ceramic tiles with a thick layer of slip (semifluid clay) to create a crackle glaze. The resulting effect is reminiscent of the surface of a dry lakebed. These two

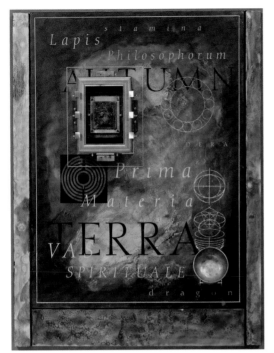

6.3   *The Four Philosophical Elements, Autumn and Winter* (top); *Spring and Summer* (bottom) Dennis Evans
(Courtesy Dennis Evans)

6.3 Untitled mural, Robert Sperry

murals are composed of separate panels, as is also true of Sperry's massive mural created for the King County Administration Building in 1985 (5.3).

On the conference and banquet room level above the lobby on the Sixth Avenue side is *Veil of the Siren, Disguise of the Mime (Genesis)*, by Mary Ann Peters. At the top of the escalator on the third floor is *Projections 7 (Tides)* by Jeffrey Bishop. It is typical of Bishop's work at the time with its brightly colored floating geometric shapes that project into a deep, dark background. Both of these paintings were completed in 1982.

Another major work, along the Sixth Avenue side, is William Hoppe's 1980 painting *Latitude Zero*, an eighteen-foot diptych that is a grid design of subdued colors.

6.4   *Artifact Series #14, Offering,* William Morris

6.4 PILCHUCK COLLECTION OF GLASS

US Bank Centre, 1420 Fifth Avenue

A very fine collection of art glass can be seen on the first three floors of the US Bank Centre across Sixth Avenue from the Sheraton Hotel. In 1989 the building's developers commissioned recognized artists affiliated with the renowned Pilchuck Glass School in Stanwood, Washington, to create glass art for their building. The collection is made up of almost forty works by artists from throughout the United States and Europe. Most of the works are located in separate display cases around the second floor, and information about each is displayed in the case or nearby.

While for the most part the artworks display the natural beauty of glass, William Morris's *Artifact Series #14, Offering,* the ten-foot-long installation located just beyond the top of the first to second floor escalator, is an early example of his ability to push the medium past traditional boundaries. Morris presents what appears to be an ancient site with prehistoric remnants partially framed by parts of a huge ribcage—as if the viewer has stumbled across an archeological dig containing human skeletal remains and artifacts, prehistoric evidence of an event, perhaps a ritual, the reason for which can never be known.

On the opposite side of the second floor is an immense, twelve-foot-long, seventeen-foot-high case containing Dale Chihuly's *Puget Sound Persian Installation,* a collection of his now-famous crumpled, thin glass disks of

6.4   *Vertical Interior Fold*, Lino Tagliapietra

6.4   *Urn*, Thomas Farbanish

6.4   *Whopper*, Dante Marioni

6.4   *Magic Woman*, Dan Dailey

saturated rich colors with spiraling concentric lines.

The escalator from second to third floor is flanked on each side by *The Duel*, a mixed-media installation by Norie Sato. When operating correctly, the ghostly twelve-foot-high columns of etched glass, neon, and plastic laminate are lit from below by television images.

Hanging over the Fifth and Sixth Avenue entrance rotunda are two large commissioned mixed-media sculptures created in 1989. At the east (Sixth Avenue) entrance is *Sun Ring*, an eighteen-foot-diameter creation by Paula Rees. The theme of her design is Helios, the god of the Sun, taking the sun across the sky. On the west side, is Graham Graham's twenty-foot-tall, fourteen-foot-diameter *Celestial Vessel*, which refers to constellations traveling across the night sky.

6.5 NEWARI I AND NEWARI II, 1982

Lee Kelly

Stainless steel; each H 7 ft. 9 in. × L 5 ft.
Private collection
One Union Square, 600 University Street, elevator lobbies

The two stainless steel sculptures in the One Union Square elevator lobbies are named in honor of the Indigenous people of the Kathmandu Valley and its surrounding areas in Nepal who are called the Newar and who speak a language known as Nepal Bhasa and Newari. At one time, Lee Kelly visited that region regularly to hike, mountain climb, and create small polished bronze sculptures cast by Newari artisans. These are Kelly's first stainless steel sculptures in Seattle's public places and each has accentuated sanded textured surfaces with

white neon backlighting. They were commissioned by the building's developer, Unico properties. Kelly's other works in Seattle (on Capitol Hill and at the University of Washington) are outdoors and made of rusted weathering steel.

6.6 SALMON DANCE, 1996

Ron Petty

Bronze; approx. H 9 ft.
Private collection
One Union Square, 600 University Street, Sixth Avenue lobby

Ron Petty's *Salmon Dance* is a series of four classical columns on top of which are three bronze salmon swirling through currents, perhaps spawning upriver. Each group is "dancing" together in unique poses. They were commissioned by the building's developer, Unico Properties. Petty has created a number of sculptures featuring creatures of our local seas, the best known of which is the *Seattle Fishermen's Memorial* at Fishermen's Terminal.

6.7 SEATTLE'S MEMORIAL BRONZE PLAQUES AND MEDALLIONS

The central downtown Seattle area is home to a collection of bronze plaques and medallions, most of which were placed in memory of twentieth-century business leaders, and they are worthy of a brief tour. Start at the Skinner Building, the 1926 Renaissance revival gem at 1326 Fifth Avenue. Inside its lobby is a bronze bas relief profile of its namesake, David E. Skinner (1867–1933), known as "D.E." It was created in 1926 by New York sculptor Leo Lentelli and placed there by Skinner's friends

6.5   *Newari sculpture*, Lee Kelly

6.6 *Salmon Dance*, Ron Petty

Skinner & Eddy, Skinner's holdings included the Port Blakely Mill and Skinner & Eddy Shipbuilding on Harbor Island, which was an important shipbuilding firm throughout World War I. The company's later interests included the Alaska Steamship Company.

On the north wall outside of the Skinner Building's entrance is a bronze bas relief bust of *David E. ("Ned") Skinner II* (1920–88), created in 1990 by Everett DuPen. Ned Skinner was the grandson of D.E. and made what became the Skinner Corporation into a major Pacific Northwest commercial and real estate enterprise. He and his wife, Kayla, were prominent Seattle promoters and philanthropists. Skinner was an original investor in the Space Needle, a major supporter of the 1962 Seattle World's Fair, and one of the investors who acquired what became known as the Seattle Seahawks football team.

From the Skinner Building entrance, take the stairs at the Fifth Avenue Theater's entrance down to the Rainier Concourse, the tunnel that extends from Rainier Tower to the Two Union Square office building. The concourse walls are adorned with a collection of photographs from early Seattle. At the western end is one of the terra-cotta American Indian heads that graced the upper façade of the White-Henry-Stuart Building that was demolished to make way for the Rainier Tower. This particular head is not complete. The tunnel's low ceiling required removal of its lowest section. A complete head, and information about such architectural embellishments, can be found at 6.9.

Bronze plaques in the concourse salute businessmen who, through their involvement with the Metropolitan Building Corporation, had a major impact on the development of the

in the Metropolitan Building Corporation, of which he was a director. The company was created to develop the Metropolitan Tract, the original site of the University of Washington that consisted of the ten-acre rectangular section of land bordered by Seneca Street, Third Avenue, Union Street, and Sixth Avenue, which is still owned by the university. As a partner in

6.7   *Albert Sperry Kerry,* Alonzo Victor Lewis

6.7   *D.E. ("Ned") Skinner II,* Everett DuPen

Metropolitan Tract. From 1908 to 1915 the company constructed the Stuart Building, the Cobb Building, the Stimson Building, the Seattle Ice Arena, and the Metropolitan Theatre. In 1962 the Metropolitan Tract was expanded to include the garage for what is now the Fairmont Olympic Hotel. Seattle sculptor Max P. Nielsen created the bronze relief medallion (circa 1916) of Chester F. White, a lumberman and original investor in the company. Nearby is a bronze profile of David E. Skinner created in 1926 by the Austrian sculptor Hugo Taglang. Compare Taglang's refined, classical approach (some may see a resemblance to a formal profile of England's King George VI) to that of the rougher surface of Leo Lentelli's rendition of Skinner referred to above.

Also included are bas reliefs (the sculptors of which are not identified) of John Francis

Douglas, the founder of the Metropolitan Building Co., which leased the university's Metropolitan Tract properties from 1908 to 1954, and lumber and real estate magnates C. D. Stimson and C. W. Stimson (C. D.'s nephew). These medallions once stood on now-demolished buildings in the area. The most recent medallion shows Roger Stevens in profile. Stevens was the founder of what became Unico Properties, created in 1953 to manage and develop the property.

Nearby at the west side of the Fairmont Olympic Hotel's entry driveway off of University Street is a plaque honoring Albert Sperry Kerry (1866–1939), one of Seattle's leading businessmen, whose properties included what is now Kerry Park on Queen Anne Hill (donated to the city by Kerry and his wife, Katherine, in 1927). The plaque was placed in this location because

Kerry, as president of the Community Hotel Corporation, was instrumental in the financing and construction of the Olympic Hotel, which was completed in 1924. A successful lumberman, Kerry's holdings included extensive timberlands and mill operations in Washington and Oregon. Local sculptor Alonzo Victor Lewis was commissioned to create the plaque shortly after Kerry's death.

The oddest story behind any plaque in Seattle is the tribute to Hannah Newman at the corner of Sixth Avenue and Union Street on the Washington Athletic Club building. The subject is shown in profile above the inscription: "Mrs. Hannah Newman, with courage and faith in the development of our city owned this ground from pioneer days until the erection of this building – 1930." This plaque was commissioned by Hannah's husband, John "Packer Jack" Newman (1863–1931), a Klondike gold rush packer and muleskinner. During his time in Alaska, Newman fell in love with Mollie Walsh, a charming young woman who ran a grub tent in White Pass during the Klondike gold rush. She was known as the "Angel of White Pass" for her efforts providing hot meals to tired and hungry prospectors. She ended up marrying another man and moved to Seattle. In 1902 her husband murdered her.

In 1930, a year before his death, the sixty-seven-year-old Newman commissioned James Wehn to create a bust of Mollie, which still stands in Mollie Walsh Park in Skagway, Alaska. Hannah was reportedly miffed at the attention paid by her husband to his first love. This inspired him to have Wehn create the Hannah Newman plaque. One hopes that peace prevailed in the Newman household.

6.7   *D.E. Skinner,* Hugo Taglang

Three other downtown plaques honoring Seattle businessmen can be found outside of the retail core. One, by James Wehn, is in the lobby of the Seattle Tower at 1218 Third Avenue, and it pays tribute to brothers *David Bruce Morgan* (1869–1943) and *Tasso Mayne Morgan* (1862–1918). The Morgans founded the Northern Life Insurance Company in Seattle in 1905. D. B. Morgan was in charge of the successful company when this twenty-seven-story art deco tower was completed in 1929. As noted on the plaque, it was placed there in 1931 by friends of the two men. It is presumed that Wehn finished it that year or in 1930.

In the lobby of the Hoge Building, at 705 Second Avenue, is a bronze bas relief profile of *James Hoge* (1871–1929). His business interests included part ownership of the *Seattle Post-Intelligencer* newspaper and the founding of the Union Savings and Trust Bank, which eventually merged with other banks to become the First Seattle Dexter Horton National Bank, of which he was chairman when he died in 1929. The bank eventually

6.8   *Stained glass window*, Anton Rez

changed its name to Seattle-First National Bank, which was a prominent bank in this country until financial reverses led to its acquisition by Bank of America in 1982. The date on the lobby plaque is 1926, three years before Hoge's death. There are no records identifying the sculptor, whose initials "JWP" appear over Hoge's right shoulder. It may have been Chicago sculptor John Wallace Purcell. A list of artworks in Seattle public places created in 1956 by the Argus Publishing Co. says the artist was Jessie Phillips; however, records show that she was a young painter and illustrator of medical records, not a sculptor. John Wallace

Purcell was an active sculptor at the time who worked in bronze. He was an instructor at the Art Institute of Chicago from 1925 to 1944 and exhibited his sculptures throughout that period. James Hoge's grandson believes it is likely that his grandfather would have selected an artist from "back East."

6.8 STAINED GLASS WINDOW, CA. 1920S

Anton Rez

Stained glass; approx. H 15 ft. 6 in. × L 8 ft. 6 in.
Private collection
1414 Fourth Avenue

On the Fourth Avenue side of the Motif Hotel building, on the east side of the lobby near the doors onto the alley, is an often-overlooked stained glass window created in the late 1920s by Anton Rez (1896–1963). The detailed work depicts people laboring in major areas of regional commerce. This window was originally installed in the Joshua Green Building on Fourth Avenue. It was moved to its current location when People's National Bank, created by shipping and banking magnate Joshua Green (1869–1975), relocated its headquarters into its new building in 1972. Rez was Joshua Green's son-in-law, and he used the pool table at what is now the Stimson-Green mansion to lay out the stained glass design.

6.9 AMERICAN INDIAN HEAD, CA. 1909

Victor Schneider

Terra-cotta; H 8 ft. 9 in. × L 3 ft. 5 in.
1309 Fourth Avenue

6.9   American Indian head, Victor Schneider

This large terra-cotta American Indian head was one of many that decorated the White-Henry-Stuart Building, which was across Fourth Avenue between University and Union Streets. Before the building's demolition in 1976, a number of heads were removed and purchased to enable future viewers to see how Seattle's grand old buildings were decorated. Similar heads can still be seen intact on the upper portions of the Cobb Building, at the corner of Fourth Avenue and University Street just south of this location. These heads, and many other terra-cotta adornments on Seattle buildings of the period, were executed by Victor Schneider, a Seattle artisan whose expertise was creating the terra-cotta architectural decoration that was so popular in the early 1900s. Each head weighs about eight hundred pounds and consists of eighteen parts.

A slightly different design from the same building stands inside the Pike Street side of the Washington State Convention Center (see 6.1).

6.10 BENAROYA HALL

Dale Chihuly and Anna Valentina Murch

Third Avenue between University and Union Streets

The chandeliers at each end of the Benaroya Hall lobby are Dale Chihuly's *Crystal Cascade*, two maelstroms of swirling clear patterned glass (with some flecks of gold leaf) that are vibrantly illuminated by lighting. Chihuly's works were a gift for the new symphony hall from Seattle philanthropists Jack and Rebecca Benaroya.

In the five twenty-by-twenty-five-foot niches in the upper walls of the arcade is *Sky Tones*, by Anna Valentina Murch, a piece best seen at night. The artist used colored lighting that modulates and dissolves to create the illusion of seeing sky through a building. The curved corners of each niche help dramatize the effect by adding the illusion of more depth and space. Murch had the lights programmed to respond to the comings and goings of the Benaroya audience. In the evening, the glow of her creation provides a visual experience for those inside and outside of the hall. *Sky Tones* was funded by Seattle's 1 Percent for Art program.

6.11 METRO STATION ARTWORKS, 1990

Bill Bell, Robert Teeple, and Vicki Scuri, with station architect Mark Spitzer

Mixed media
Metro Transit commission
University Street Station, Second Avenue and
   University Street

Mezzanine-level artworks in the University Street Station are the most high-tech creations of the 1990 Metro tunnel project. Boston artist Bill Bell installed twenty-four 16-by-32.5-inch computer-operated bars of lights that flash on and off and groupings of lightbulbs that flash sequentially across the wall to create unexpected patterns of movement, such as a running animal. Bell embedded the bars into the marble tile wall in what he described as "a random vertical pattern resembling falling red raindrops." Seattle artist Robert Teeple installed *Electric Lascaux*, a series of twenty-eight electronic displays in eight electronically operated light boxes that have light-emitting diodes flashing schematics and diagrams of twentieth-century technology as well as words and human faces.

The walls on the mezzanine level are graced with black-and-white granite designs by Seattle artist Vicki Scuri. She also created computer-etched designs on stainless steel door panels, which she likens to Braille or circuit board patterns. The reverse of those designs is etched on nearby black granite panels on benches.

The University Street Station also includes The Beltline, Vicki Scuri's elaborate graphic design of black, red, and speckled white-and-brown granite that covers parts of the walls and creates trace-like patterns on the floor. The designs change at doorways and where benches and information panels are located and continue up the escalators. Scuri describes her work as "a kit, with different modules placed in different manners . . . made up of asymmetrical designs for symmetrical spaces, that wrap around the station like an elastic band, or beltline."

6.10   *Sky Tones*, Anna Valentina Murch

6.10   *Crystal Cascade* (north), Dale Chihuly

Those attending an event at Benaroya Hall can pause at the main stairway and admire Robert Rauschenberg's monumental *Echo*, a twelve-by-forty-five-foot silkscreen transfer on polylaminate created in 1998 for the hall. Rauschenberg's artistic premise—that the commonplace has aesthetic potential—is evident in *Echo*, and he incorporated in it a collection of disparate photographic images of common subjects. Some are symbolic, others are not, and some arose from his involvement in photography, set and costume design, musical composition, and choreography—he worked for many years with Merce Cunningham as well as with Paul Taylor and Trisha Brown. In the 1960s Rauschenberg collaborated on several occasions with the composer John Cage. Thus, we see a photo of a John Cage manuscript, with text by Gertrude Stein (from the artist's private collection), and a Tibetan musical score. Also included are images of windswept palm trees, from his home in Florida, and trees in a swamp. He has said that those palms refer to the stormy scenes of a Wagner opera, while the calm swamp refers to pastoral pieces. Silkscreened photos of trumpets and violins can also be seen. A few other subjects include a bicycle, Gothic cathedrals, machinery, and a New York homeless woman pushing a grocery cart.

Echo was a commissioned gift for the new symphony hall from Virginia and Bagley Wright, prominent Seattle art collectors and philanthropists.

6.12 GARDEN OF REMEMBRANCE, 1998

Robert Murase

Granite, concrete, and landscaping
Gift to the City
Benaroya Hall, Second Avenue and University Street

When Benaroya Hall was being designed, there were no plans to create anything on the L-shaped half-acre section of property at the southwest corner of the block. Seattle philanthropist Priscilla "Patsy" Bullitt Collins donated the funds to create a war memorial on the site. She wrote that her interest in doing so was not to make a political statement or to create a memorial to war, rather, "it is a reminder of war's costs and terrible pain." Collins's fiancé died in World War II. The end result is a place of reflection that honors Washington State residents who died in American wars from World War II on. The garden includes smooth granite walls and benches with rough-hewn granite elements and boulders, together with waterfalls, channels, and pools, all graced with deciduous trees and plantings. The engraved names of the thousands who died are oriented so that they are bathed in the glow of the western sun.

Engravings on granite walls include quotations of great thinkers, portions of soldiers' letters home, and a passage from Laurence Binyon's poem "For the Fallen." Engraved on the long wall in the north section is part of Archibald MacLeish's poem "The Young Dead Soldiers Do Not Speak."

Whether our lives and our deaths were for peace and a new hope, or for nothing, we cannot say . . . We leave you our deaths. Give

6.12   *Garden of Remembrance*, Robert Murase

them their meaning. We were young. We have died. Remember us.

Garden of Remembrance was designed by the late Robert Murase, one of the region's most highly regarded landscape designers. Murase was influenced by the stone sculptures of Isamu Noguchi, but at the root of Murase's designs are his Japanese ancestry and his sensitive use of stone and water to create elements present in Japanese gardens—meditative simplicity and the illusion of nature. Seattle architect John Nesholm described Murase, who hand selected each stone at the quarry and placed it on this site, as "a poet of stone and water."

6.13 PULSE 15, 2011

Charles Loomis

Stainless steel and glass; H 8 ft. × W 8 ft. × L 12 ft.
Private commission
Russell Investments Center lobby, 1301 Second Avenue

Pulse 15 is the vibrant collection of curved glass-covered rectangles that floats above the Russell Investments Center lobby. Each element consists of twenty-six pieces of kiln-formed glass attached to metal trusses and each is attached independently to create a whole in which no part touches the other. External lighting adds to the sculpture's presence. With

6.13 *Pulse 15,* Charles Loomis

this design, artist Charles Loomis refers to the vibrancy of Seattle's business community and the fact that Russell Investments is located in the heart of Seattle.

6.14 MIRROR, 2013

Doug Aitken

LED tiles and photographic imagery
Seattle Art Museum collection
Seattle Art Museum, corner of First Avenue and Union Street

Doug Aitken's *Mirror* on the northwest corner of the museum's exterior wall is an ever-changing collection of photographic images that turns the building into what Aitken describes as a living museum. The principal feature is a huge screen that wraps around the corner at First Avenue and Union Street and shows photographic imagery compiled by the artist from hundreds of hours of footage he took throughout the city and the state. The images and what is done with them are created by a computer system that responds to changes to, and the levels of intensity of, many things happening at the time, such as weather and atmospheric conditions, pedestrian and vehicle traffic, and lighting conditions. The combinations of imagery are all unique and are not repeated. Much of *Mirror*'s twelve-story height includes vertical bands of LED strips of vibrant lighting that move up and down the side of the museum. Best seen at night, Aitken describes his creation as liquid architecture.

Aitkin created the work to "move on its own and constantly create its own sequences,

6.14   *Mirror*, Doug Aitken (Photo by Benjamin Benschneider, courtesy Seattle Art Museum)

patterns and composition. Like a minimalist musical composition. . . . However," he said, "the work must generate its own tempos and patterns feeding off the landscape, movement, temperature, light or darkness, wind or many other live organic things around it. Like choreography with no music, the images are left to define the composition and patterns live, today, tomorrow, and into the future."

Mirror was a commissioned gift of Bagley Wright who, in partnership with his wife, Virginia, was one of the region's most supportive patrons of the arts. Virginia Wright reported that when Aitken presented his concept to the museum, "Bagley immediately thought it was a great idea that would transform the building. I think he was right."

6.15 *Hammering Man*, Jonathan Borofsky

6.15 HAMMERING MAN, 1992

Jonathan Borofsky

Painted steel and aluminum; H 48 ft.
City of Seattle Collection
Seattle Art Museum, corner of First Avenue and
University Street

Standing at the corner of First Avenue and University Street is *Hammering Man*, a forty-eight-foot-high black silhouette created by American artist Jonathan Borofsky. Borofsky's working man holds a hammer in his hand, and his mechanized aluminum arm moves methodically up and down four times a minute. Borofsky has explained that "the boring, monotonous repetition of the moving arm implies the fate of the mechanistic world," while the man "symbolizes the underpaid worker in this new, computerized revolution. The migrant worker who picks the food we eat, the construction worker who builds our buildings, the maid who cleans offices every evening, the shoemaker—they all use their hands like an artist."

A three-horsepower electric motor runs the arm from 7:00 a.m. to 10:00 p.m. daily, and it rests each evening and into the early hours of the morning—and on Labor Day. "At its heart, society reveres the worker," Borofsky explains, "*Hammering Man* is the worker in all of us. . . . Let this sculpture be a symbol for all the people of Seattle working with others on the planet to create a happier and more enlightened humanity."

Seattle's *Hammering Man* is part of Borofsky's goal of having this sculpture placed all over the world, hammering simultaneously

to pay tribute to workers and to connect people throughout the world. A larger version hammers in Frankfurt, Germany (Seattle's is the second largest on the planet). Others of varying sizes have been erected in Japan, Switzerland, New York, Los Angeles, Minneapolis, and Washington, DC. Borofsky does not believe it is important to have an artist's name on a work. However, in keeping with his longtime preoccupation with numbers, each *Hammering Man* has a unique number painted on its base. Seattle's number is 3277164.

Funding for *Hammering Man* was provided by Seattle 1 Percent for Art funds, the Virginia Wright Fund, the Museum Development Authority, and private donations. It was commissioned as part of "In Public: Seattle 1991," a project to celebrate Seattle's public art program.

6.16 CHINESE TOMB GUARDIANS, FIFTEENTH TO EIGHTEENTH CENTURIES

Chinese artisans

Carved marble
Seattle Art Museum collection
Seattle Art Museum, corner of First Avenue and
University Street

On a grand stairway inside the Seattle Art Museum, accessible through the doors at the corner of First Avenue and University Street and viewable through the windows of the Seattle Art Museum up the hill along University Street, are six impressive carved marble figures. They once stood along avenues called the Spirit Path, which led to important

6.17 *Moment,* Buster Simpson

Chinese tombs. Along those avenues were statues of real and mythological creatures, as well as warriors and government officials, which guided the soul of the deceased and those paying homage to him or her along the path to the monument. More statues stood at the entrance and within the tombs to serve the deceased and ensure that what comforts existed in life could be enjoyed after death. The pair of camels and the pair of rams reportedly led to the tomb of Prince Zhu Gaosui, near Beijing. The prince, who died in 1436, was the third son of the Yongle emperor, whose reign during the Ming dynasty lasted from 1404 to 1424. The human figures are a civil officer and a military officer and were created in the late seventeenth or eighteenth century, during the Qing dynasty. As was the custom, they stood on one side of the avenue and faced identical sculptures on the other side.

These and four other funerary sculptures were brought to Seattle in 1933 by Dr. Richard Fuller, who, with his mother, Mrs. Eugene Fuller, founded the Seattle Art Museum. Pairs of tiger and lion sculptures are displayed in the museum's Volunteer Park facility. All of the sculptures were purchased from Gump's in San Francisco and stood for decades in front of the Volunteer Park museum. They were removed in 1987 for restorative work after years of deteriorating in the elements. The six downtown figures were placed in their new home in 1990. Because of their size, they were installed on the grand stairway before the building's final walls were in place. They were then encased in wooden boxes, and the building was constructed around them.

6.17 MOMENT, 2000

Buster Simpson

Stainless steel; H 16 ft. × Dia 2 ft. 10 in to 6 ft. 6 in.
Harbor Steps, north side, below First Avenue and
   University Street

Buster Simpson's *Moment* consists of two separate stainless steel coils that twist upward inside two cones composed of thin vertical stainless steel strips. A sense of movement is created as the viewer progresses around the piece, the result of a moiré pattern created by superimposing the similar unaligned sheets of metal strips. A beacon of light from beneath adds drama to the piece at night.

6.18 FOUR SEASONS HOTEL

99 Union Street

Standing at the far western end of Union Street, overlooking Elliott Bay is Gerard Tsutakawa's eleven-and-a-half-foot-high welded bronze *Thunderbolt*, which was created in 2008. The owners of this Four Seasons Hotel wanted Tsutakawa to create a work for this particular spot. He chose the upward thrusting form as a strong silhouette against the sky and further enhanced the shape by giving it a golden patina.

An impressive collection of works by Pacific Northwest artists are on display within the hotel, beginning with the lobby. Kenneth Callahan's *Wind Song* is an energetic collection of broad sumi-inspired brushstrokes in blue, brown, and reddish tones amid spontaneous calligraphic swirls and strokes of black.

6.18   *Wind Song,* Kenneth Callahan

6.18   *Brown Bingo,* Alden Mason

Brown Bingo, by Alden Mason, is an example of his widely acclaimed Burpee Garden series in which he used diluted oil paint to create exuberant pools of transparent colors. Paul Horiuchi's *Massive Silence* is a six-paneled screen with his signature collage medium that includes torn pieces of mulberry and rice paper. *Night*, an oil painting by Gaylen Hanson, shows the dark sky and landscape of Hanson's beloved Palouse region in southeastern Washington illuminated by a full moon. And *Evening Light*, a still life by Morris Graves, is a lithography, photolithography, and silkscreen reproduction that looks like his original 1992 work. Also on display is a large untitled oil painting created by Portland-based Carl Morris, a dean of Pacific Northwest abstract expressionism.

Around the corner to the left inside the entrance is a group of black-and-white photos of major Pacific Northwest artists of the same period represented in the hotel collection. These were taken by Mary Randlett, an artistic photographer who captured on film all of the major names in Pacific Northwest art. Some of those represented in the collection can be seen in Randlett's photos. If you number each row one to five from left to right, Alden Mason is fifth in the top row. In the middle row, Johsel Namkung is second, Morris Graves and Mark Tobey are fourth, and Kenneth Callahan is fifth. Carl Morris and his wife, sculptor Hilda Morris, are the subjects of the bottom row, number two.

At the top of the nearby stairs are two complementary black-and-white works. On the right is *Sumi Painting*, painted in 1959 by Mark Tobey, the patriarch of the Northwest School of art, the influences of which include Asian philosophy and religion. Next to it is *Tinkum Road*, a black-and-white photograph taken in 1986 by

6.18   *Thunderbolt*, Gerard Tsutakawa

Johsel Namkung. It is reminiscent of a classical Chinese landscape painting. Namkung was a friend of many of the Northwest School artists, including Mark Tobey, with whom he practiced sumi painting. His photographic art was hailed for its creative execution and often painterly qualities.

6.19 SEATTLE GARDEN, 1988

Ann Sperry

Painted galvanized steel; H 4 ft. 6 in. × L 334 ft.
Seattle 1 Percent for Art Program
Seattle City Light Union Street Substation,
Post Alley and Union Street

Just below the Four Seasons Hotel and readily visible from the stairs leading down from the end of Union Street is New York sculptor Ann Sperry's *Seattle Garden*, a collection of painted steel flowers on top of the wall around an electrical substation. One of Seattle City Light's

goals was to keep transients out of its substation, and Sperry created what she describes as "an impenetrable botanical fence." Her sheet steel plants consist of welded triangular sections topped with round flowers of various sizes. This fantasy garden is painted silver, and portions of some of the flowers are painted with splotches of subdued hues.

6.20 PIKE PLACE MARKET

85 Pike Street

Five artworks at the Pike Place Market are featured here, and the most famous is Georgia Gerber's *Rachel the Pig* (*Market Foundation Piggy Bank*), a life-size, 550-pound bronze pig that was chosen through a competition to commission a piggy bank for contributions to the Market Foundation, which supports human service agencies in the market. The model for Gerber's sculpture was a friendly old sow

6.19   *Seattle Garden* (detail), Ann Sperry

6.20   *Rachel the Pig (Market Foundation Piggy Bank)*, Georgia Gerber

who lived near Gerber's home on Whidbey Island. Gerber explains that she always strives to engage the viewer's imagination and likes to have her sculpture invite an interaction with its audience. The success of this piece is evident from the fact that Rachel has become the symbol for the market and one of the most photographed, and sat upon, sculptures in the city. Her form was used to make a large number of fiberglass replicas that were painted by artists and sold at a Pigs on Parade auction to benefit the market. Many of them are still displayed throughout the city.

A second bronze pig sculpture by Georgia Gerber, created in 2011, is the 700-pound *Billie*, a friendly looking pig who sits upright with splayed front legs at the southern end of the market's new second level pavilion, just south of Steinbrueck Park.

A lesser known but important artwork at the market is Aki Sogabe's five-part, thirty-six-foot-long mural *Song of the Earth*, which is located on the rafters above the market's Pike Street entrance. It highlights the fact that before World War II and the internment of West Coast Japanese Americans, the majority of farmers who sold produce at the Pike Place Market were of Japanese descent, and they had a significant impact on the development of the market. Their internment and the resulting loss of their property ended an era that was impossible to revive. The first panel, *Song of the Earth,* shows workers clearing and preparing the ground. In the second panel, *Song of the Farmers,* farmers work the land. In *Song of Joy* we see Japanese Americans selling produce at the market. *Song of Sorrow* is a wartime scene of empty fields with Mount Rainier in the background. The last panel, *Song of Memory,* shows a line of Japanese, one of whom is a saluting American soldier.

Aki Sogabe is a local artist who is a master of *kiri-e,* the Japanese art of paper cutting. Her original paper works were enlarged and transferred to the three-by-five-foot steel panels in enamel porcelain. *Song of the Earth* was commissioned by the Japanese American Citizens League, among others, and was dedicated

in 1999 on February 19, which is the Day of Remembrance for Japanese Americans. February 19, 1942, was the date of Executive Order 9066, requiring the internment of US residents of Japanese ancestry (see 1.10).

Just inside the market entrance at 1433 First Avenue, south of the main entrance, is Richard Beyer's seven-foot-tall *Sasquatch* sculpture. He carved this mythological creature of Pacific Northwest forests in the 1970s, and it is the earliest of his many works in Seattle's public places. Early in his career Beyer sold smaller versions of his Sasquatch carving from a stall at the Pike Place Market.

Hanging from the atrium ceiling above Beyer's *Sasquatch* is Pat Wickline's twenty-

6.20   *Seattle Squid,* Pat Wickline

seven-foot-long *Seattle Squid*. Wickline has long been fascinated with squid, in particular the largest varieties, such as the giant squid, which can grow well over fifty feet long. It is the largest invertebrate on earth and has the largest eyes in the animal kingdom. This sculpture, created in 2001 of hammered copper, shows the squid as it would look swimming through the ocean depths, with eight arms and two longer arms with tentacles on the ends for grabbing prey.

The most unusual light fixtures in the city can be found on the stairs west of the Pike Street entrance (behind and to the right of *Rachel the Pig*) that lead down to Western Avenue. They are seven stainless steel sculptures of individuals holding onto lights. This collection, created in 2011 by Dan Webb, is called *Short Cut 7*, and the artist placed them in unlikely positions—walking up walls, upside down on an overhang, standing at an open door inset into the concrete wall—to be discovered by pedestrians on the ordinary, plain stairwells.

Three artworks can be seen down on the Western Avenue side of the market. The most prominent is *Western Tapestry*, John Fleming's 250-foot-long mural of 1,670 colorful aluminum strips that extends along the east side of the avenue. Its four-inch-wide aluminum strips of varying lengths hang in twenty sections along the eastern side of the avenue. Blue, red, and green lights glow behind them. Fleming worked with approximately two hundred people from the community who painted their own unique designs on the strips, and then he arranged them into this vibrant tapestry extending along what was once a barren stretch of concrete.

At the downhill end of *Western Tapestry*, at the base of the staircase, is *A Point*, an often

6.20   *A Point*, Michael Oren

unnoticed carved stone sculpture created in 1992 by Michael Oren (1948–98). This four-foot-high sculpture includes swirling waters and a city on a hill. The mountain form at the top is a precisely carved triangle on the reverse side. This piece reportedly honors Indigenous people of the area and may refer to the sacred nature of the spot where it is located. Oren was part of a residential artists' community that lived and worked from studios formerly located at the market. His friends installed *A Point* in his honor after the artist died in a motorcycle accident.

Across the avenue (at 1901 Western Avenue) is an entrance to the new west wing of Pike Place Market. Inside on the right-hand wall and up the stairs to the right is a set of colorful mosaic tile murals by Vashon Island artist Clare Dohna. At the entry level she salutes the bounty of the sea with a multitude of fish. Up the stairs and to the left off of the first landing is a mural of lovely birds, flowers, and insects.

6.20   *Western Tapestry*, John Fleming

6.20   *Song of the Earth (Song of the Farmers)*, Aki Sogabe

6.20   Tile murals, Clare Dohna

On the upper landing are nine framed murals of fruits and vegetables, with a few insects here and there.

6.21 TOTEM POLES, 1984

James Bender, Victor Steinbrueck, and Marvin Oliver

Carved cedar; each H 50 ft.
City of Seattle collection
Steinbrueck Park, north end of Pike Place Market

The totem poles in Steinbrueck Park show two approaches to totem pole design: the northern one is a traditional Northwest Coast Haida design, while the southern pole is smooth and topped with two eight-foot-high figures of a male and female farmer. The traditional pole was created by James Bender after a concept developed by Marvin Oliver. Bender and Seattle architect Victor Steinbrueck designed the adjacent pole. Bender carved both poles from trees that Marvin Oliver had selected and prepared for carving.

The traditional pole does not depict a legend, although its figures can be interpreted to stand for qualities of strength and abundance and other attributes of the city and the market. From the top, the figures are Raven holding a Salish woman's spinning whorl, Human holding a potlatch copper of prosperity, Little Human (a messenger), Killer Whale with a human face in its blowhole, Little Raven, and Bear holding Hawk.

The nontraditional southern pole was inspired by an Alaskan pole near Ketchikan that depicts Abraham Lincoln standing at the top of an otherwise unadorned pole; the Alaska Natives honored Lincoln by placing him at the

6.21   Totem pole, James Bender and Marvin Oliver

6.21   Totem pole, James Bender

top. In this case, the men and women who sell at the market are honored. The man and woman on the Seattle pole each wear "Honored Farmer-1984" badges that are similar to those the Friends of the Market presented to old-time farmers in 1981.

Victor Steinbrueck designed this park with Seattle landscape architect Richard Haag and included these poles as an integral part of the park's design to frame the scenes of Puget Sound and the distant Olympic mountains and the frequent colorful sunsets beyond. Steinbrueck described them as "a tribute to the cultural contributions and the heritage of our Native Americans." He also designed the green wrought-iron fence behind the totem poles that incorporates abstract floral designs. After Victor Steinbrueck's death in 1985, the park was named for him, a fitting tribute to the man who led the fight to save the market from destruction and replacement by developers.

6.22 TREE OF LIFE, 2012

Clark Wiegman

Patinated stainless steel; H 12 ft. 5 in. × L 6 ft. 5 in.
Gift to the City
Steinbrueck Park, north end of Pike Place Market

Clark Wiegman's *Tree of Life* was created to honor the many homeless individuals who die in Seattle each year. It is the central part of the Homeless Remembrance Project which was made possible through the efforts of Women in Black and WHEEL (Women's Housing and Equality Enhancement League). Tree of Life is in the shape of leaves, but many see the shape of a heart. Wiegman says that the sculptural form came to him more or less unconsciously during meetings with those involved with the project, and he didn't intentionally refer to a heart. What is clear is the cut-out shapes of maple leaves that refer to the second part of the project. Those cut-out spaces symbolize the hundreds of bronze leaf shapes that have been placed throughout the city, each one of which is a memorial to a Seattle homeless person who died while living on the street. The leaf placed closest to this sculpture is at Second Avenue and Bell Street. *Tree of Life* is stainless steel with a patina to make it look like bronze. It stands in the center of a base of tempered glass.

6.22   *Tree of Life,* Clark Wiegman

6.23 WESTLAKE METRO STATION ARTWORKS, 1990

Heather Ramsay, Bill Whipple, Roger Shimomura, Fay Jones, Gene Gentry McMahon, Jack Mackie, and Vicki Scuri

Mixed media
Metro Transit commission
Westlake Station, Pine Street at Westlake Mall

At street level near the Westlake transit tunnel are two sculptural street clocks. Installed when the Metro transit tunnel was constructed in 1990, Heather Ramsay's fourteen-foot-high *Pendulum Clock,* of steel with a copper finish,

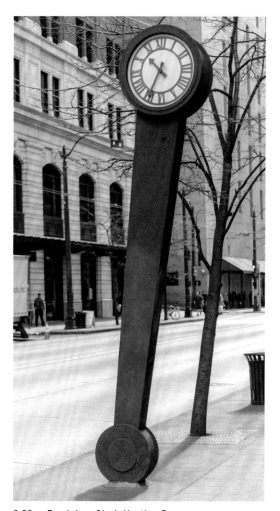

6.23   *Pendulum Clock,* Heather Ramsay

stands at Third Avenue and University Street. It seems delicately balanced on a rounded base and leans at an angle inspired by how the passage of time made the Leaning Tower of Pisa lean. Running up each side are little brass mice that Ramsay included to "evoke a nursery rhyme and the relative distance each of us has traveled in time since childhood." Bill Whipple's seventeen-foot-high *Question Mark Clock,* installed in 1988 at Fifth Avenue and

6.23   Untitled mural, Roger Shimomura

Pine Street, has its face framed by the top portion of a seven-foot-high stainless steel question mark that stands on a granite base.

Inside the tunnel station are three vivacious ten-by-thirty-five-foot murals of vitreous enamel tiles created by Roger Shimomura in 1990. A vibrant combination of images from traditional Japanese woodblock prints and twentieth-century American life, the tiles include iconic examples of comic book and pop art, as well as his three children. Shimomura is best known for his complex and often humorous works that refer to the cultural clashes related to the assimilation of Japanese Americans into American society and his belief that this country is more of a "tossed salad" than a melting pot of cultures. The artist points out that this earlier work is an introduction to "more crystalized" bi-cultural themes of later years that emphasize the value of Japanese Americans retaining links to their heritage and culture.

In an effort to bring sunshine underground, Fay Jones used bright yellow and blue as the principal colors in her mural that depicts a scene of oversized people dancing in front of the waterfront. She explains that her work is a "humorous and theatrical interpretation of Seattle as a waterfront city." Retail sales is the theme of Gene Gentry McMahon's mural and she refers to the bombardment of images one gets from passing retail displays.

A 32-by-116-foot section of the south station wall is covered with overhanging vines, leaves, and flowers created in terra-cotta tiles designed by Seattle artist Jack Mackie. Mackie also created the designs that were sandblasted into granite benches on the station platform level. Each bench appears to have been draped with patterned cloth.

Vicki Scuri's repeated series of twenty low-relief patterns composed of approximately twenty-five thousand cream-colored, one-square-foot tiles covers the station's platform-level walls in geometric designs that wrap around corners like fabric. Forty different tile designs that include shirt designs, portions of

Japanese dress patterns and kimonos, zippers, and stitching are arranged in six-foot-square grids to create the twenty larger patterns. Viewed from different angles, the light upon the impressed forms changes the appearance of the creation. In addition, some tiles are blank and others are cropped, adding to Scuri's desired effect of a "patterned garment" for the station.

Across the tracks and east of the John Harte McGraw statue, next to the covered Seattle streetcar stop is *Sequence/Consequence*, Seattle's only subterranean artwork. From a distance it appears to be only a round disk embedded in the concrete, but just beneath its etched glass hatch cover is a neon double helix form than spirals into the ground. The artists included mirrors in the design to help create a seemingly endless field of light. *Sequence/Consequence* was created in 2009 by the artistic trio of John Sutton, Ben Beres, and Zac Culler, who work under the name SuttonBeresCuller. It was commissioned through Seattle's 1 Percent for Art Program.

6.24 JOHN HARTE MCGRAW, 1912

Richard Brooks

Cast bronze; sculpture H 6 ft. × L 4 ft. × W 4 ft.
City of Seattle collection
McGraw Square, Fifth Avenue and Stewart Street

John Harte McGraw (1850–1910) was a prominent figure in early Seattle history. A lawyer, businessman, and law enforcement officer, he was also the state's second governor

(1893–1897). McGraw served as president of the First National Bank of Seattle and was president of the Seattle Chamber of Commerce. He was an avid and effective supporter of plans to build the Lake Washington Ship Canal. As King County sheriff, he protected life and property during the Seattle fire in 1889 and was a major figure in keeping the peace during anti-Chinese disturbances in the mid-1880s, which culminated in violent but thwarted attempts by angry citizens to drive the Chinese out of town. In his book *Seattle, Past to Present*, Roger Sale writes that "during the worst of the February [1886] troubles, Sheriff John McGraw was consistently sensible, cool, and strong."

After McGraw's death, citizens raised funds to commission prominent New York sculptor Richard Brooks to create this statue. It shows the governor with his overcoat draped over one arm and his right hand pressed down on a sheaf of documents on a small pedestal. It was cast in Paris and dedicated on July 22, 1913. Brooks also sculpted the William H. Seward statue in Volunteer Park.

6.25 1700 SEVENTH AVENUE BUILDING LOBBY

Deborah Butterfield, Deloss Webber, Joseph McDonnell, and Ann Gardner

Private collection

When Clise Properties built the 1700 Seventh Avenue Building, it graced the lobby with five significant artworks. In the center of the space is Deborah Butterfield's *Green River,* a majestic horse, sculpted in 2000 from discarded worn, rusted, and twisted metal. Seven feet high and ten feet long, it is typical of Butterfield's horse

6.24 *John Harte McGraw*, Richard Brooks

portraiture. She is known for her ability to capture the essence of each animal and imbue her subject with a unique energetic presence. Her horses are never running. Butterfield, an avid horse rider, does not believe that a sculptor can convincingly capture the power and grace of a running horse.

Adjacent to Butterfield's horse is Deloss Webber's *Events and Incidents, Sphere #3, #5, #6*—three solid wood spheres of different sizes, each inlaid with bamboo strips. They are part of a series created in 2014 after Webber had gone through a divorce and lost a daughter. Webber says that although small, they "represent a sense of weight and resolution . . . each could be a burden or an obstacle to surmount. . . . What doesn't crush you," he says, "may give you a higher elevation from which to view your world."

On the south wall of the building's lobby is Joseph McDonnell's painted aluminum sculpture, *Homage to Matisse*, created in 2000. When McDonnell visited a Henri Matisse retrospective in New York he was "blown away" by the French master's vibrant collages of paper cutouts. He visited the exhibit three times, and afterward he started making his own collages, cutting shapes out of thin aluminum and painting them to enhance each element. McDonnell describes them as "three-dimensional paintings floating on a wall like leaves before the wind." They are mounted on a bronze panel, which adds depth to the floating assemblages.

On the north lobby wall is McDonnell's *Shad Run II*, created in 2004. The origins of this collection of swirling, glistening stainless steel shapes are his memories of spawning American shad swimming up the Hudson

6.25   *Shad Run II,* Joseph McDonnell

River. The swirled surface texturing adds to the feeling of movement.

In the elevator lobbies are Ann Gardner's *Yin and Yang,* four-foot-high panels of iridescent glass tiles created in 2001 specifically for these spaces. *Yang* is gold and silver with joined convex panels bending in at the center. *Yin* consists of concave panels of bronze and bluish tones with the center bending outward. Gardner explains that the contrasting shapes "speak to the concept of how seemingly contrary ideas are opposite yet related to one another."

6.25   *Homage to Matisse,* Joseph McDonnell

6.25   *Green River*, Deborah Butterfield, with *Events and Incidents, Sphere #3, #5, #6* (detail). (Photo by Richard J. Birmingham)

6.26 THE SCULPTOR, 2014

Tom Otterness

Stainless steel on limestone; H 1 ft. 7 in. × L 3 ft. 8 in.
Private collection
Grand Hyatt Hotel, 721 Pine Street

The Sculptor is the main character in a 2014 exhibition of more than twenty of Tom Otterness's sculptures that related to the ancient story of Pygmalion, a sculptor who becomes enchanted with his carving of a beautiful woman. His prayers to the god Aphrodite for a bride are answered when his lovely sculpture comes to life. The roles are reversed in the Otterness exhibit and the sculptor is a woman, carved in his typical cartoonish style, standing on a limestone block and holding a mallet in one hand and a pencil in the other. She will finally succeed in creating the perfect man,

6.26　*The Sculptor,* Tom Otterness

natural boulders that stand on their own to assume whatever character and inspire whatever response the viewer creates (see 3.22). He made his first negative wall sculpture in 1968 in order to "create an absence and then refill the same void." *Black Diorite Negative Wall Sculpture* was brought to Seattle from New York by the Gagosian Gallery for its exhibit at the 2017 Seattle Art Fair. Prominent real estate developer and art collector Richard Hedreen was immediately taken with it and purchased it for his new hotel building. Because of its massive size, Heizer's sculpture was installed early in the lobby construction process.

Hedreen's other major purchase for the hotel is *Bring Me the Sunset in a Cup,*

after several failed attempts, and bring him to life with a kiss. *The Sculptor* was purchased by Richard Hedreen, who developed the hotel property.

6.27　HYATT REGENCY ARTWORKS

Michael Heizer and Cecily Brown

Private collection
Hyatt Regency Hotel, 808 Howell Street

Inset into the wall of the Hyatt Regency Hotel lobby is Michael Heizer's *Black Diorite Negative Wall Sculpture,* an unadorned, 5.7-ton black diorite granite boulder set into a thirty-one-inch-deep rectangular box of rusted steel. Heizer did nothing to the boulder's natural pockmarked and craggy surface. This is consistent with his long history of creating sculpture with huge

6.27　*Black Diorite Negative Wall Sculpture,* Michael Heizer (Photo by Fredrik Nilsen, courtesy Gagosian Gallery)

6.27 *Bring Me the Sunset in a Cup,* Cecily Brown (Courtesy Paula Cooper Gallery)

a thirty-three-foot-long, ten-foot-high oil on linen triptych by London-born and New York–based artist Cecily Brown. Her vigorous and bold brushstrokes create vast fields of abstraction interspersed with hints of the human form. The abstract aspects of her painting style have been described as suggestive of Willem de Kooning and Oskar Kokoschka. Brown has said that she wants her paintings to grab attention and be impossible to merely walk past. Completed in 2018, this is one of her largest paintings and, thanks to the hotel's large lobby windows, it attracts the attention of many.

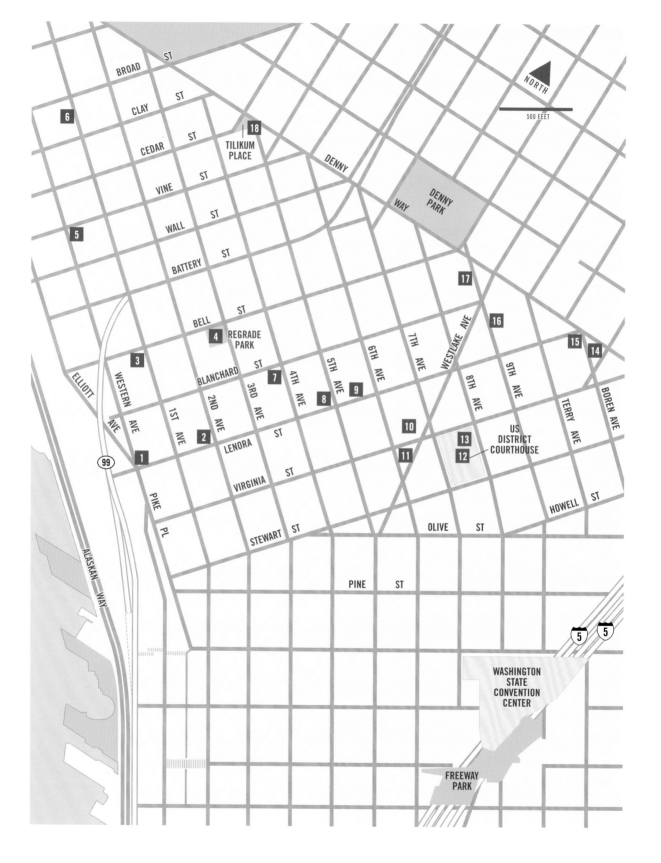

7 BELLTOWN AND THE DENNY TRIANGLE

Architecture, sculpture, painting, music, and poetry may truly be called the efflorescence of civilized life.

—Herbert Spencer (1820–1903)

BELLTOWN AND THE DENNY TRIANGLE ARE LOCATED on flat terrain that was once Denny Hill, an obstacle that the city decided was a hindrance to downtown development. So, that obstacle was removed, in stages, between 1897 and 1930. For decades afterward it was a relatively quiet area on the edge of downtown, with small buildings and warehouses and a lot of parking lots. In recent decades it has undergone extensive development and along with the construction of many new buildings has come the addition of many new artworks in the neighborhoods' public places.

7.1　*Angie's Umbrella*, Jim Pridgeon and Benson Shaw

7.1 ANGIE'S UMBRELLA, 2003

Jim Pridgeon and Benson Shaw

Stainless steel and aluminum; H 30 ft. 8 in.
Gift to the city and city grant
Western Avenue and Lenora Street

When the Belltown neighborhood wanted a sculpture for the small traffic triangle just north of Pike Place Market, artist Jim Pridgeon proposed a wind-powered, rotating, inside-out umbrella. Once the proposal was accepted, he teamed up with fellow Seattle artist Benson Shaw, who designed how it would work. The nineteen-foot-long umbrella, with its red-coated perforated aluminum "fabric," is delicately balanced and rotates on the tip of its handle. The piece reminds many of experiences with umbrellas when the wind whips up from Elliott Bay through the canyons of downtown Seattle skyscrapers. This sculpture is named in honor of Angie Pridgeon, the artist's mother. *Angie's Umbrella* was made possible by the Denny Hill Association, which is part of the Belltown Community Council, and a matching grant from the Seattle Department of Neighborhoods.

7.2 BRICK MURALS, 1986

Mara Smith

Carved brick
Private commission
Second Avenue and Lenora Street

7.2   Brick murals (detail), Mara Smith

The large brick building at the northwest corner of Second Avenue and Lenora Street has few windows because it houses communications equipment for CenturyLink. Rather than leave the walls blank at street level, CenturyLink's predecessor, Pacific Northwest Bell, commissioned sculptor Mara Smith to create historical and scenic murals of carved brick. Her six scenes wrap around the building corner from Lenora to First Avenue. Starting at the Lenora Street end, Smith has depicted Alexander Graham Bell's invention of the telephone, the growing Seattle waterfront, William Boeing and aviation in Seattle, historic Pioneer Square, bustling Pike Place Market, and the Hiram Chittenden Locks. Each scene was carved before the brick was fired.

7.3 LOW TIDE, 2012

Laura Brodax

Ceramic tile mural; L 20 ft. 6 in.
Private commission
2233 First Avenue, at Bell Street, northeast corner on hill

Laura Brodax's *Low Tide* is an illustration of reflections off the shallow waters and beach at low tide, with a rocky beach in the foreground. The scene was first photographed and then it was screen printed onto one-foot-square porcelain tiles with hand applied colors.

7.4 GYRO JACK, 1979

Lloyd Hamrol

Concrete; H 9 ft.
Seattle 1 Percent for Art Program and private sources
Regrade Park, Third Avenue and Bell Street

California artist Lloyd Hamrol created *Gyro Jack*, a nine-foot-tall participatory sculpture, to encourage play, relaxation, and contemplation. The sculpture consists of four tilted arcs of graduated sizes, ranging from eight to sixteen feet in diameter, and a narrowing path spirals up the sides. At the top of this eighty-four-ton sculpture is an indentation designed for relaxed viewing of the surroundings. Unfortunately, as the neighborhood changed over the years, the park was deemed unsuitable for families with children and was changed to its current function as an off-leash dog park.

At its dedication in 1979, Hamrol pointed out that his work is more than a concrete construction. "It moves if you let it. It invites you to explore. It represents a past which is part of the important changes leading to the present." The last comment refers to Hamrol's intention that *Gyro Jack* reflect the history of the Denny Regrade, which is what remains of Denny Hill after it was regraded in the early part of the twentieth century.

Also on the park's north side is *The Dogs*, a group of carved sandstone dogs created by Richard Beyer in 1978. Each crouches and awaits the reappearance of a little rat that hides underneath the bottom step.

7.5 BECKONING CISTERN, 2002

Buster Simpson

Aluminum and concrete; H 10 ft. × Dia 6 ft.
Seattle 1 Percent for Art Program
81 Vine Street

Buster Simpson has created a number of innovative sculptures designed to redirect water from building roofs. With *Beckoning Cistern*, he has fabricated a bright blue corrugated aluminum cistern and capped it with five curved "fingers," the gesture of which Simpson likens to the beckoning hand of God in Michelangelo's *Creation of Adam* in the Sistine Chapel. The index finger receives water from the building's downspout. When the tank overflows, water drains from the thumb of the hand into the planter below, and then down the hill through a series of troughs.

Extending down the brick walls of the 81 Vine Street building are Simpson's "vertical planters," unique corrugated aluminum structures connected to the building's downspouts. These are other elements of Simpson's environmental art and they act as bio-filtration systems that filter water draining off the roof before it makes its way into the city's storm sewers.

The water from Simpson's creations makes its way underground to the western portion of the block, just beyond the curved concrete mosaic sign that says *Cistern Steps*, where it remerges and travels along concrete troughs to a granite basin at the corner of Vine Street and Elliott Avenue, next to the Belltown P-Patch. Simpson's *Beckoning Cistern*, and the *Cistern*

7.4   *Gyro Jack*, Lloyd Hamrol

7.7 *Popsicle,* Catherine Mayer

Steps, are components of the Growing Vine Street revitalization effort, in which property owners, neighborhood groups, and various city departments worked together in an effort to make Vine a green street. The elements combine to emphasize water conservation and natural cleansing of storm water through planted drainage systems.

7.6 WATER TABLE/WATER GLASS, 2001

Buster Simpson

Stainless steel, glass, granite, water, and horsetail; table H 3
  ft. L/W 4 ft.; glass H 8 ft. × Dia 4 ft.
Private commission
2801 First Avenue

Buster Simpson's *Water Table/Water Glass* takes a unique and creative approach to diverting water from a building roof. On the south side of the building plaza, water from the roof of the adjacent building runs through a large stainless steel downspout and empties into an eight-foot-high green tilted water glass to create a unique fountain. Water pours out of the water glass into a trough that extends into the landscaped interior court. The sculpture's circular base is planted with horsetail (also known as scouring rush), a metaphor for natural cleansing because it was used by Native Americans to scour pots.

In the north half of the plaza, the downspout extends into the ground and remerges as a leg of Simpson's stainless steel and black granite *Water Table,* which has its name etched and drilled onto its surface. When it's dry, the table is just a table. When it rains, water shoots out of the holes that spell *water,* and then falls into a drain that connects to *Water Glass.* Simpson's design called for a more developed shallow wetland landscape that would be nurtured by the two water features. However, he explains that "the stewardship of the residents" was necessary to implement that aspect, and it was not to be.

7.7 POPSICLE, 2011

Catherine Mayer

Steel and colored epoxy resin; H 17 ft.
Private commission
Fourth Avenue and Blanchard Street, northwest corner

The red popsicle at the corner of Fourth Avenue and Blanchard Street is the creation of Seattle artist Catherine Mayer. She selected the subject not only to refer to memories from her childhood in New Orleans but also to memories of viewers who have enjoyed double popsicles on wooden sticks—whether alone or split to share with a friend. The subject matter, its bright color, and its precariously balanced placement are all part of Mayer's desire to inspire positive, perhaps surprised, reactions from passersby. Another of her childhood memories can be seen at 3.30. *Popsicle* is owned by Seattle real estate developer Martin Selig, who developed the adjacent building.

7.8 THOLIAN WEB, 2013

Ned Kahn

Stainless steel; approx. H 32 ft. × L 80 ft.
Private commission
2105 Fifth Avenue

On a calm day the exterior cladding above the Martin Apartments retail level looks like a decorative architectural element, but on a windy day, the wind is visible as thousands of small stainless steel tiles ripple across the surface of the building's façade. This subtle, complicated work is an example of artist Ned Kahn's interest in capturing the mysteriousness of the world around us and allowing viewers to observe and interact with natural processes. "I am intrigued with the way patterns can emerge when things flow," he says. "These patterns are not static objects, they are patterns of behavior—recurring themes in nature." In order to achieve the desired effect, each tile in Tholian Web is finely perforated and hangs loosely on the supporting frame.

Tholian Web was commissioned by Vulcan Real Estate, the Paul Allen real estate company that developed the property. Kahn knew that

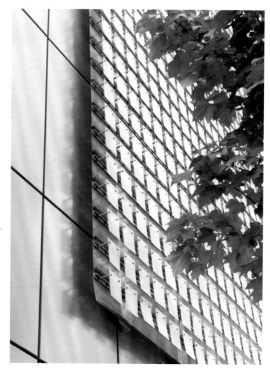

7.8   *Tholian Web* (detail), Ned Kahn

Paul Allen is an avid fan of *Star Trek* and named this sculpture after an award-winning *Star Trek* episode in which the starship *Enterprise* must escape from a destructive web of energy created by threatening Tholians.

7.9 OLD TIME JAZZ SCENE, 2013

Bart Turner

Forged and galvanized steel; H 8 ft. × L 13 ft.
Private commission
Alley off Lenora Street behind Via6 Apartments,
    2121 Sixth Avenue

Just inside the alley off of Lenora Street behind the Via6 Apartments is a steel cut-out mural showing a jazz nightclub scene from the 1940s or '50s—an odd location perhaps,

7.9   *Old Time Jazz Scene,* Bart Turner

but an outstanding cover for a building vent. Some may think the singer is Billie Holliday, complete with the typical flower adorning her hair, but Seattle artist Bart Turner reports that no one in particular is depicted. He says the design is the result of studying a wide collection of vintage photographs, which inspired a composition that he "reduced down to the essentials to make the sculpture have contrast like a photograph." The figures are shaped and cut from galvanized steel and placed in the frame as if the viewer is looking into the club through a window, with a cropped view of the end of the trombone and the top of the bass. Turner added more depth by rubbing in black paint and then burnishing the metal. *Old Time Jazz Scene* was commissioned by Via6 Apartments and is appropriately located near Jazz Alley, Seattle's longtime jazz venue at 2033 Sixth Avenue.

The violet-colored steel saxophone, with notes bursting forth from its bell, at the southwest corner of Sixth Avenue and Lenora Street was created by Seattle designer and artist Mike Phifer. It is in front of Jazz Alley, the popular jazz venue that commissioned the work.

7.10 PETROS, 2015

Julie Speidel

Stainless steel
Private commission
2030 Sixth Avenue and 2021 Seventh Avenue

With *Petros,* the collection of three sets of stainless steel sculptures on the Sixth and Seventh Avenue sides of Amazon's Doppler Building plaza, Julie Speidel is paying homage to the

7.10 *Petros* (west and east sides), Julie Speidel

glacial erratic left behind by the Vashon Glacier (18,050–13,050 BCE) the last glacier that helped form the geography of the Salish Sea region. Erratics are rocks that differ from the local geology, having been brought from afar through glacial action. Placed among hard-edged architecture, Speidel describes them as "fundamental visual connections between the continuum of time and the accomplishments of human endeavor."

The principal elements of *Petros* stand on stilts on the Seventh Avenue side and are twenty-five feet tall. Speidel gave them such height to allow viewers to interact with them from underneath and to refer to the Cascade Mountains to the east as viewers on the Sixth Avenue side see them peeking above the staircase. Similarly, Speidel invites viewers to walk around the other elements and experience their burnished, multifaceted forms from different angles.

Petros was commissioned by Amazon for its new building. Its name is the Greek word for

boulder or rock and the original Greek version of the name Peter.

7.11 CLOUD HAIKU, 2011

Squeak Meisel

Painted bronze
Seattle 1 Percent for Art Program
Pedestrian triangle at Westlake and Seventh Avenue
  and Virginia Street

The eight white painted life-size bronze pillows that make up Squeak Meisel's *cloud haiku* were inspired by both Japanese garden design and cloud watching. Seven of the pillows have been placed in plantings while one stands alone on the sidewalk. Meisel describes his sculpture as an urban Zen garden and he hopes that its unexpected combination of imagery and materials will inspire a sense of wonderment in pedestrians and people driving by. "Look here, look from across the street," he advises. "Allow yourself to observe the pillows to align

7.11 *cloud haiku*, Squeak Meisel

7.12 *Pillar Arc*, Ming Fay

and unfold like a secret dance with cars, plants, objects, and pedestrians."

7.12 PILLAR ARC, 2004

Ming Fay

Cast aluminum; H 27 ft. 6 in.
US General Services Administration, Art-in-Architecture
  Program commission
US Courthouse, 700 Stewart Street

Pillar Arc, the gray abstract monolith in the US Courthouse plaza, raises many questions about its subject matter and the artist's intent. Its creator, Shanghai-born and New York City–based

sculptor Ming Fay, is known for converting single small items from nature into monumental references to their natural and cultural environment. In this case, he was inspired by a single scale of a cedar tree cone. *Pillar Arc* is the abstract shape of that scale balanced on its pointed end, and it stands as a monument to one of the Pacific Northwest's great cedar trees, rising out of a depression surrounded by deciduous trees. Ming has said that with "the exaggeration of size, scale, and its juxtaposition, I hope to emphasize the inherent beauty, nuance, and poetry of the form."

Ming Fay chose a form related to cedar because of that tree's important cultural and historical significance in this region. For centuries it was an essential material to the Native American sustenance and culture, providing pliable bark for weaving and durable wood for structures, canoes, implements, and important artwork; it was also a major timber source for non-Natives and a major export.

7.13 US COURTHOUSE INTERIOR WORKS

Michael Fajans, Ed Carpenter, Richard Gilkey, and Sung-ho Choi

US General Services Administration, Art-in-Architecture Program commission; private donation
700 Stewart Street

When the new US Courthouse was completed in 2004, 1 percent of its $170 million construction budget was used to fund artwork commissioned under the US General Services Administration, Art-in-Architecture Program. The commissioned art includes *Pillar Arc* (7.12) and several interior works, which were all created in 2004. To see them requires passing through a security check inside the entrance, but fear not, it is a simple process and the security guards welcome visitors who want to look at artworks. However, you can't take photographs.

After passing through security, visitors can explore *Three Sets of Twelve,* Michael Fajans's grand three-story mural that pays tribute to the American jury system. The first of his three paintings is on the lobby level, and the other two are on the second and third floors. Each painting is on cherrywood veneer and is eighty feet long and nine feet high. The subjects are the finely rendered realistic depictions

for which Fajans was known, all meticulously painted with airbrushed acrylic. *Three Sets of Twelve* shows the transformation of people as they leave their daily occupations upon entering the courthouse and assuming their roles as jurors.

On the lobby level are twelve Seattle residents from diverse backgrounds, each seated at his or her place of work. Painted twice life-size, their names and occupations are Leon, microbiologist; Cathy, stenographer; Reid, potter; Kay, architect; Joe, camera repairman; Roberta, cellist; Daniel, computer operator; Walter, shoemaker; Mattie, bus driver; Chris, heavy-equipment operator; Thu-Van, garment worker; and Phil, window

7.13   *Leaf,* Ed Carpenter (Photo by Carol M. Highsmith)

7.13   *Three Sets of Twelve* (lobby level), Michael Fajans (Photo by Carol M. Highsmith)

washer. Each portrait includes items that their subjects use in their daily work.

On the second level Fajans painted eleven unique versions of the jury box chair used in the courtroom: a tiny chair, an upside-down chair, a chair out of focus, the left half of a chair, the right half of a chair, a chair comprised of a set of bricks, the space left by a chair removed, a huge chair, a transparent chair, a photo-negative chair, and the shadow of a chair. One other image is the computer operator's wheelchair. Note that for his second-floor creation, Fajans made the background unique by placing the cherry panels so that their grains alternate in a checkerboard pattern.

On the third level, the people are life-size, painted in black and white, and seated as a jury of twelve looking out with an objective gaze as light shines upon them and shadows cast behind them. They are a unified group prepared to consider the evidence presented to them. Fajans explains that the vertical grain in the wood panels on the first floor suggests non-intersection, while the horizontal grain at this third level suggests interconnection.

It may not be apparent that the ascending steel frame and cables with strips of dichroic glass inside courthouse's east atrium refer to anything in particular. This is Ed Carpenter's *Leaf*, and the principal shape in the center is that of a fifty-four-foot-high leaf, with strands radiating out on both sides to the office levels above. Its origin was the artist's walk through the forest as he thought about shapes that would fit into this tall, thin atrium. He encountered alder leaves on the ground and began thinking about the alder's special restorative role in the forest. Alders are the first to grow after a forest fire, a clear-cut, or a landslide, and they add nitrogen to the soil and help prevent erosion. Carpenter says that the network of cables refers to the way the parts of the court system are connected and the sculpture is in part a metaphor for the restorative role and "humanistic aspects" of the judicial system.

Also in the atrium is large acrylic on canvas painting by Northwest artist Richard Gilkey, a master of painting scenes of the Skagit Valley north of Seattle. This is an ethereal, abstract composition that Gilkey painted later in his life.

Inset in a wood-paneled wall inside the workstation across from the clerk's office, is *Quiltroad*, a long, rectangular painting that appears to be a quilt of forty-two different patterns. Korean-born, New York City–based artist Sung-ho Choi created this mural with traditional textile patterns from different countries and cultures and combined those samples into a woven checkerboard pattern to create what the artist describes as "a colorful and harmonious quilt" that embodies his vision for a more peaceful world.

7.14 SERVANT CHRIST, 1986

Jimilu Mason

Bronze; H 3 ft. 10 in. × L 2 ft. 4 in.
Private collection
Recovery Café, 2022 Boren Avenue (at Fairview)

At the southern tip of the Recovery Café building is a contemporary image of Jesus, kneeling and barefoot, wearing a sweatshirt and jeans. Before him is a bowl of water and he looks up, offering to wash the feet of passersby. Water flows up into Jesus's left hand and down into the bowl. Recovery Café is a support center whose members are struggling with addiction and mental illness. The plaque in front of the statue notes that it "represents the humility, loving kindness and service which is at the heart of Recovery Café."

This bronze sculpture is a replica of the one in front of Christ House in Washington, DC. It

7.15   *Merce*, Steve Jensen

was a gift from an anonymous donor who had seen it in the US capital and commissioned this duplicate in 2010. It is the only public sculpture in Seattle by Jimilu Mason, whose work is widely represented throughout the DC area, as well as in several US cities and in Europe.

7.15 MERCE, 2011

Steve Jensen

Bronze; H 7 ft. × L 4 ft. 6 in.
Private commission
Intersection of Lenora Street, Denny Way, and Boren Avenue

Painter and sculptor Steve Jensen works in a variety of mediums, but one of his best known is uniquely carved wooden poles that are encircled with bold, deeply carved lines inspired by swirling wind, flowing water, and other natural forces. Those same lines are incorporated into this unusual bronze dance figure, which is a tribute to the American choreographer and dancer Merce Cunningham (1919–2009), a native of Centralia, Washington, who studied at Seattle's Cornish School from 1937 to 1939. In 1939 Cunningham joined the Martha Graham Dance Company and started a professional career that continued until his death, in New York at age ninety. Jensen's sculpture, which stands near Cornish College of the Arts (as the school is now known), was a gift to the school from Jack, Peg, Jill, Jody, and Grady Cunningham and their families.

7.16 THREE WOMEN, 2006

Akio Takamori

Fabricated and cast aluminum; H 6 ft. 10 in. to 7 ft. 4 in.
2200 Westlake (Whole Foods Market)
Private commission

University of Washington art professor Akio Takamori was internationally known for his unique (usually clay) figurative sculptures of subjects that often arose from memories of

7.16   *Three Women*, Akio Takamori

his childhood in Japan or from photos showing people in Japan just after World War II. These figures are fine examples of Takamori's glazing technique. He began with unadorned sculptural surfaces and painted on details, including hair, hands and feet, shoes, and pleated and creased clothes. *Three Women* is typical of the small groupings the artist created. They stand apart from one another, going about their daily business, often averting their eyes (the artist's nod to the Asian stereotype of resisting eye contact) but perhaps quickly glancing at someone. *Three Women* was commissioned by real estate developer Vulcan Real Estate.

7.17 UNIVERSAL ADAPTOR, 2009

Cris Bruch

Cast bronze; H 6 ft. 6 in. × L 16 ft. 3 in. × W 6 ft. 6 in.
Private commission
2201 Westlake Avenue

Cris Bruch's sculptures are good for the imagination. His *Universal Adaptor* has been likened to a prop from a fantasy movie. The tapered, telescoped west end could suggest to futuristic architecture or power generation.

The other end may be a bronze throne for planetary royalty. In fact, the form is based on an ordinary object—a piece of discarded plastic packaging—transformed into a monumental sculpture. By placing it below grade and in concrete, the artist suggests that this strange, settled form was perhaps too heavy to move and had to be accommodated—an object more permanent than the architecture and urban design surrounding it. Cris Bruch says that

7.17 *Universal Adaptor,* Cris Bruch

7.18 Chief Seattle, *James Wehn*

with *Universal Adaptor* he considers what is transient and throwaway compared to what is enduring. Bruch's sculpture was commissioned by real estate developer Vulcan Real Estate.

> The nearby weathered steel planters in the shape of lapstrake boat hulls were designed by landscape architects at the Berger Partnership. They refer to the location's proximity to the Lake Union shoreline.

7.18 CHIEF SEATTLE, 1912

James Wehn

Cast bronze; H 7 ft. 2 in.
City of Seattle collection
Tilikum Place, Fifth Avenue and Denny Street

James Wehn's statue of Seattle (ca. 1790–1867), chief of the Duwamish tribe, is the city's first commissioned statue and stands at Tilikum Place, the historic juncture of the original land claims of three Seattle pioneers: Carson Boren, William Bell, and Arthur Denny. In the early 1900s the first stage of the Denny Hill regrade was being funded, and the street improvement budget included funds to commission a statue to mark this site. *Tilikum* is Chinook Jargon (a trade language based on American Indian and European languages) for "everyone" (friends, relatives, fellow nations) except chiefs. Wehn posed the chief looking out toward Puget Sound with his arm raised in greeting. The chief's likeness is based on a studio photo taken by E. M. Sammis in 1864, when Chief Seattle was in his late seventies.

Wehn also sculpted the works on the granite base: two bronze bear heads that serve as waterspouts and two bronze plaques depicting historical events. One shows Chief Kitsap watching Capt. George Vancouver's ship, the first in these waters, arriving in 1792. The other plaque, flanked by salmon, pays tribute to Seattle, "A firm friend of the Whites."

SEATTLE CENTER

8 SEATTLE CENTER AND ENVIRONS

Art is the objectification of feeling.

—Herman Melville (1819–1891)

THE SEATTLE CENTER WAS THE SITE OF the 1962 Century 21 Exposition, Seattle's

second world's fair (the first was the 1909 Alaska-Yukon-Pacific Exposition on the University

of Washington campus). The seventy-four-acre site is now one of Seattle's most popular

gathering places, drawing millions of visitors to fairs and events, including opera, ballet, and

music and theater performances. The center grounds and buildings contain a large collection

of art that is readily accessible for public viewing. The collection includes a group of major

sculptures that were placed on a nearly three-acre sculpture garden, referred to as the Broad

Street Green, which is located below the Space Needle on the center's southern edge.

8.1   *Olympic Iliad,* Alexander Liberman

8.1 OLYMPIC ILIAD, 1984

Alexander Liberman

Painted steel; H 45 ft. × L 60 ft.
Seattle 1 Percent for Art Program and private donors
Broad Street Green

The immense red *Olympic Iliad* is one of Seattle's most important public artworks and is the late Alexander Liberman's largest and most complex work. From the time he was a young boy Liberman was attracted to industrial landscapes. That and his memories of broken columns in Greek ruins are both evident in *Olympic Iliad.* Typical of his monumental abstract sculptures, it was created with recycled industrial materials—forty-foot-long cylinders that are forty-eight and sixty-four inches in diameter, all painted red. They appear to be light and delicately balanced and create a tenseness as the collection of forty-one elements appear to be in imminent danger of collapsing. Liberman liked the concept of creating lightness from great volume. He also wanted his sculptures to create a sense of awe. Art historian Thomas B. Hess called these assemblages "extraordinary levitations."

Liberman's original color choice for his large sculptures was black, but his wife, Tatiana, hated that color and convinced him to use red. Some say that she harkened back to their native Russia and pointed out the similarity between the Russian words for "red" and "beautiful." Liberman, who was famously devoted to his wife, said that he chose red because Tatiana's happiness was paramount.

8.2   *Moon Gates*, Doris Chase

8.2 MOON GATES, 1999

Doris Chase

Bronze; H 17 ft.
Gift to the city
Broad Street Green

Doris Chase's *Moon Gates* is not as well-known as her *Changing Form* on Queen Anne Hill, but it provides equal opportunities for viewers to interact with her placement of related spaces and forms. The tallest of this sculpture's three bronze shapes has an oval cutout, and that cutout appears to be standing nearby with a round hole cut out of it. The convex sides of both of those vertical elements are the opposite of the adjacent horizontal shape, the sides of which are concave. The shortest of the three

abstract forms has a round void at its center, with a removed solid form resting on its top and able to rotate. Chase said that her sculpture was intended to offer "interior-exterior experiences and the opportunity to interact on many levels: physically (including creative play), visually, and spiritually" and create "the joyous relationship between spaces, form, and human interaction." *Moon Gates* was given to the city by the Seattle Center Foundation.

8.3 BLACK LIGHTNING, 1981

Ronald Bladen

Painted steel; H 24 ft. × L 60 ft.
Seattle 1 Percent for Art Program and the National
   Endowment for the Arts
Broad Street Green

Ronald Bladen's *Black Lightning* is the second minimalist sculpture installed at Seattle Center. As with Tony Smith's *Moses* (8.5), Bladen's creation does not embody a message. The object itself is the art, but as he explained to critic Bill Berkson, Bladen sought to create "space, dramatic relationships, and excitement," with its thrusting lightning bolt shape and the play of light and shadow on its simple painted steel planes. Nothing more exists than what each viewer sees or experiences.

In an interview with the author at its dedication, Bladen recognized that many would not enjoy his work when first viewed, but he predicted that "things may start to happen later . . . . You have to be quite open when you see it and deal with the dignity of the form . . . . Trusting your own vision is what art is all about. . . . The viewing is really a learning process and for years *Black Lightning* may be totally alien. But

8.3   *Black Lightning*, Ronald Bladen

after it becomes familiar, people will grow to love it."

8.4 JOHN T. WILLIAMS HONOR TOTEM POLE, 2012

Rick L. Williams and others

Red cedar; H 34 ft.
Gift to the city
Broad Street Green

The *John T. Williams Honor Totem Pole* was created to honor a Native American carver whose unjustified killing by a Seattle police officer in 2010 caused an outcry by many in the Seattle community. His brother Rick was the designer, principal carver, and leading force to create a totem pole to inspire a peaceful response to the tragedy, promote healing, and serve as a symbol of peace and honor for the future. The pole

has three principal figures. Looking down from the top is an Eagle. Note that the front edge of his wings curve outward, a design reportedly created by Williams's father to signify that the eagle has not yet settled after just landing. The second figure is a master woodcarver, which represents John Williams. He holds a kingfisher, his favorite carving subject. The Mother Raven at the base represents the honored Native tradition of respecting and listening to one's ancestors and elders.

A collection of family members, friends, and volunteers carved this honor pole in the style typical of John Williams's work, which is a style that is more common in smaller carvings made for sale to tourists. Several hundred people helped to manually carry this thirty-five-hundred-pound pole from the Seattle waterfront to the Seattle Center. It was then raised manually in traditional Native fashion.

8.4 *John T. Williams Honor Totem Pole*, Rick L. Williams and others

The *John T. Williams Honor Totem Pole* was funded by private donations.

8.5 MOSES, 1975

Tony Smith

Welded steel; H 11 ft. 6 in. × W 7 ft. × L 15 ft.

Seattle 1 Percent for Art Program, the National Endowment for the Arts, and private donors

Broad Street Green, north side of the Space Needle

Like many of Tony Smith's sculptures, *Moses* is a combination of multifaceted polyhedral forms that seem to unfold as would a cardboard model, which is evidence of his first career as an architect. Smith told critic Nicholas Calas that he preferred polyhedral forms over rectangles because they allow "for greater flexibility and visual continuity of surface." Smith's intention here is to offer only a basic form without sculptural supplementation. There's no evidence of craftsmanship or detail, only planes of flat welded steel. He allows viewers to read his sculpture differently according to the angle of viewing, sunlight, and shadows. What initially seems basic becomes quite complex.

The parallel uprights suggest the horns in Michelangelo's famous sculpture of Moses. Smith explains that Michelangelo's peculiar representation of a horned Moses was the result of a mistranslation of the Hebrew word *shone*, derived from the word for *horn*, but also used figuratively to denote rays or flashes of light from a luminous object, for example, the head of Moses.

Although this fifty-five-hundred-pound sculpture was installed in the spring of 1975, Smith's original full-size plywood mock-up, purchased by the Seattle Art Museum's

8.5 *Moses,* Tony Smith

8.7 *Sonic Bloom,* Dan Corson

Contemporary Arts Council, had been displayed in Seattle since 1968. In the early 1970s that council, the Seattle Arts Commission, the National Endowment for the Arts, and the Virginia Wright Fund (a private foundation in Seattle) funded the creation of this permanent steel version. *Moses* was the first major expenditure of funds under the city's new 1 Percent for Art Program, and it is the first large work of sculpture placed at the center since the Seattle World's Fair of 1962. The same sculpture can be seen at Princeton University.

8.6 MIDDLE EAST PEACE, 2003

Sabah Al-Dhaher

Marble and basalt; H 8 ft.
Gift to the city
Peace Garden, northwest edge of Broad Street Green

Middle East Peace is a little-known sculpture nestled in the small Peace Garden, a grove at the northwest corner of the Broad Street Green. The white marble form consists of two joined shapes that twist up from the basalt column. The only difference between them is that the surface of one is polished and the other is rough, symbolic of the fact that we are much the same with minor differences. The principal engravings on the upper portion of the basalt column are the words for peace in English, Arabic (*salaam*), and Hebrew (*shalom*). The names etched below are those of local Jewish and Arab children who participated in the sculpture project and are from the Arab Center of Washington, the Kadima Community School, the Iraqi Community Center, and the Middle East Peace Camp. That camp was a joint venture launched in the summer of 2002 by Kadima (a progressive Jewish organization), the Arab Center of Washington, and Seattle philanthropist Kay Bullitt.

8.8   *Neototems Children's Garden*, Gloria Bornstein

8.7 SONIC BLOOM, 2013

Dan Corson

Steel, fiberglass, and electronic media; H up to 40 ft.
    × Dia 20 ft.
*Seattle 1 Percent for Art Program and the Pacific
    Science Center*
Outside the southwest corner of the Science Center

Those standing near Dan Corson's *Sonic Bloom* may wonder about the source of an ethereal chorus that is emanating from his five gigantic, solar-powered flowers. Each hums a unique series of harmonic notes as people pass sensors near its stalk and up to five individuals, operating their designated bloom, are able to compose music together. Those sounds, and the patterned nighttime LED lighting located in the flowers' red stamens, are powered by forty-eight solar cells atop each bloom. Corson added another technological element by

creating an actual bar graph for the plant stalks designs, making them a "supersized puzzle" that can be translated with a bar code reader.

Sonic Bloom was commissioned by the adjacent Pacific Science Center and Seattle City Light, who wanted an artwork that would showcase the use of solar power.

North of *Sonic Bloom* is Chihuly Garden and Glass, a museum that showcases the glass sculpture of Dale Chihuly, one of the world's foremost, and most successful, studio glass artists. Many works can be seen in its outside garden and the collection of exhibits within provide a look at some of the inspiration and influences in Chihuly's career.

8.8 NEOTOTEMS CHILDREN'S GARDEN, 2002

Gloria Bornstein

Bronze whale tail; H 5 ft. × W 8 ft.; others various dimensions
Seattle 1 Percent for Art Program
Across from the Pacific Science Center, next to the Seattle
    Children's Theatre

The baby whale's tale in Gloria Bornstein's *Neototems Children's Garden* is a later addition to the theme she used for her Neototem whale sculptures near the International Fountain (8.17). The submerging whale is a member of that same pod, and it refers to the local Salish Indian legend that whales swam underground from Elliott Bay to Lake Union. Bornstein included a water feature to add not only enjoyment for children visiting this site but to refer to the water that runs off of whale tails as

8.9 *Seattle Mural*, Paul Horiuchi

they flip up before descending into the waves. Bornstein thought the baby whale was lonely by itself, so she added seven smaller bronze sea creatures to capture children's imaginations: an octopus, a hermit crab, a seahorse, a trio of comical puffer fish, and a pig fish. Only the first two are found in Puget Sound waters.

Bornstein created a surrounding labyrinth garden design that includes low native plantings shaped to resemble tidal pools. Her overall approach was to inspire children to explore and take risks as they play in and around her creations.

8.9 SEATTLE MURAL, 1962

Paul Horiuchi

Glass tile mosaic; H 17 ft. × L 60 ft.
City of Seattle collection
West of Space Needle, south of the Armory

When the Mural Amphitheatre was designed for the Seattle World's Fair (by Seattle architect Paul Thiry), Paul Horiuchi was commissioned to create a mural for the sixty-foot-long cyclorama behind the stage. Horiuchi had become well-known for his innovative use of torn paper collages, which were initially inspired by seeing torn posters and notices on utility poles in Seattle's International District. His unique collages became his signature medium. The design for this mural was transferred by artisans in Venice, Italy, to fifty-four glass tile panels that incorporated 160 color variations. In a 1968 interview with *Seattle Magazine*, Horiuchi explained that his collages "are attempts to produce areas of peace and serenity with which to balance the sensationalism—the fast, hard tempo—of our time." His *Seattle Mural* has been doing just that for over half a century.

8.10 TOTEM POLE, 1970

Duane Pasco, with Victor Mowatt and Earl Muldon

Carved and painted cedar; H 30 ft.
City of Seattle collection
West of Space Needle, at southwest corner of the Armory

This totem pole is a fine example of the unique art form of totem pole carving practiced by the Indigenous peoples in the coast region north of Puget Sound. In this case, the four main figures are, from top to bottom, Hawk, Bear (holding a salmon), Raven, and Killer Whale. The pole is an early work by Duane Pasco, who is not Native, but is highly regarded as a carver in the Northwest Coast Native style and an important teacher and contributor to revising the art form. His collaborators on this pole, Victor Mowatt and Earl Muldon, were hereditary chiefs and master carvers with whom he worked during his time teaching at the Gitanmaax School of Northwest Coast Indian Art at 'Ksan Village at Hazelton, British Columbia.

8.11 CHARLOTTE MARTIN THEATRE ARTWORKS, 1993

Garth Edwards

Cut steel figures and ceramic murals; various sizes
Seattle 1 Percent for Art Program, local and state government funding
Charlotte Martin Theatre

The artworks incorporated into the exterior and interior of the Charlotte Martin Theatre are the result of a close collaboration between Seattle artist Garth Edwards and the building's architectural firm, Mahlum and Nordfors McKinley Gordon. Rather than tack art onto the building toward the end of the design process, Edwards worked with the architects and the Seattle Children's Theatre, which occupies the building, to incorporate art into the design. Painted steel cutouts of cartoonish creatures and people (nicknamed "Garthgoyles") can be seen along the outside at the second-floor level. Some of them serve as canopy support brackets. The arched entrance is flanked by murals of thick ceramic tiles that at first glance appear to consist of abstract images of nature. Closer inspection reveals a collection of humorous faces and creatures. Seattle ceramic artist Ray

8.10　Totem pole, Duane Pasco

8.12 *Birdsong Listening Station,* Doug Taylor

The three parts of this windmill sculpture are shaped like upside-down boat hulls with their steel frames partially covered in polyester. The kinetic work is part of a more involved whole. The windmill and solar panels supply electrical power to operate an adjacent, nine-foot-eight-inch high listening station that, with the push of a button under a listening dome, provides viewers with the recorded songs of finches, which are often seen feasting on the seeds of nearby London planetrees. Doug Taylor created *Birdsong Listening Station* to remind busy urban dwellers that nature surrounds them. In addition, the energy sources that power the station are reminders of the importance of alternate energy sources in powering the tools and toys we use every day.

8.13 ARMORY INTERIOR ARTWORKS

William Sildar, Rita Kepner, and Kelly McLain

Standing in a dark alcove inside the north entrance of the Armory is *Queue VI,* a largely forgotten and rare public sculpture by the late William Sildar. Sildar was artist in residence with the City of Seattle in 1975 when he carved the abstract assemblage of horizontal and vertical forms, ten feet long and six and a half feet high, that depicts fourteen people waiting in line. This seventeen-hundred-pound sculpture was carved out of laminated wood.

Just beyond the Sildar sculpture and into the hallway is a collection of tile murals created in 1984 by Seattle elementary school children and some high school apprentices, all of whom attended the Pacific Arts Center. The murals depict real and fantastic imagines of China. These were originally installed at the Pacific Arts Center, an institution that was

Serrano helped create the ceramic works. Edwards also created the unique cut steel railings, door frames, and ventilation grills inside the theater.

After the theater was completed, Garth Edwards was given a second commission to create the cast concrete heads on the east side of the building. The main element, in the center of the small plaza, has four faces and a round head in the middle. Edwards is pleased with the fact that these sculptures show wear from children sitting and climbing on them.

8.12 BIRDSONG LISTENING STATION, 2008

Doug Taylor

Steel and polyester; H 30 ft. × W 15 ft. × Dia 15 ft.
Seattle 1 Percent for Art Program
Fisher Pavilion Rooftop, southeast corner

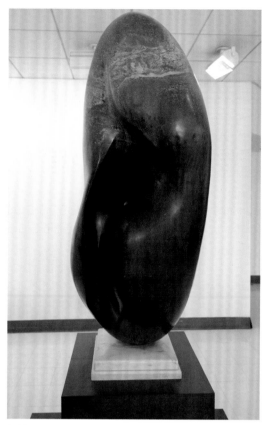

8.13　*Human Forms in Balance*, Rita Kepner

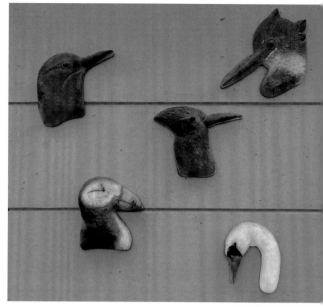

8.13　*Migrare*, Kelly McLain

8.13　*Queue VI*, William Sildar

once located at the Seattle Center and brought young people together with professional artists to explore visual, literary, and performing arts. In this case, the artwork was created under the guidance of Seattle artist Maggie Smith.

On the east side of the Armory, in the lobby of the Center Theatre, is Rita Kepner's five-foot-high sculpture, *Human Forms in Balance*. The artist says that the focus of her work has been introspection and a continual study of the human body. In this 1975 piece, Kepner carved an abstract form that she describes as "a collection of elegant male and female forms, almost in the Greek classical sense." It is designed to be seen from different angles with varying degrees of lighting to further emphasize the subtle curves and organic shapes she elicited from thirty-five hundred pounds of dark steatite. *Human Forms in Balance* was commissioned through the city's 1 Percent for Art Program.

The five cast-glass sculptures at the entrance of the Seattle Children's Museum, on the west side of Center House, depict birds that reside in the Pacific Northwest or visit the region during annual migrations. Titled *Migrare*, it is the Latin root of the word *migration*, which means to go from one place to another. Seattle artist Kelly McLain chose that name to also refer to the development of children as they move from one place or phase to another. In the center is a Steller's jay. Clockwise from the lower left is a puffin, a Bullock's oriole, a belted kingfisher, and a trumpeter swan. McLain created the colorful subjects in 1995 to pay homage to each and to arouse curiosity and imagination in visitors to the museum. There are additional heads inside the museum that children can more easily touch and explore.

8.14 POETRY GARDEN, 2007

John Hoge

Glacial red granite boulders; various sizes
Seattle 1 Percent for Art Program
West of the Armory

Seattle sculptor John Hoge's addition of sculpted red granite boulders to the small garden just west of Center House creates a natural setting to contemplate contemporary and traditional poems. Maya Angelou, Shu Ting, William Wordsworth, E. E. Cummings, Pablo Neruda, and Carl Sandburg are just a few of the poets whose words are engraved onto the red granite boulders. Some of the boulders provide opportunities to stand and read what is on them, while others are shaped to inspire sitting next to the poetic works.

8.15 BIOGRAPHY OF A BRANCH, 2002

Deborah Mersky

Glass tile and stone mosaic; H 8 ft. 8 in. × L 32 ft.
Seattle 1 Percent for Art Program
Exterior of Fisher Pavilion along east stairs

Deborah Mersky's *Biography of a Branch* is a glass tile and stone mosaic mural that extends along the concrete wall of the staircase on the east side of the Fisher Pavilion. In the vertical center portion, a branch consists of parts of different deciduous and evergreen trees and plants. Parts of other local fauna are included in the mural's horizontal portions. Mersky created the design as a metaphor for the many cultures and backgrounds that make up the Seattle population.

Mersky created a companion piece that extends along the far wall inside Fisher Pavilion's exhibition hall. Titled *Twine and Branch*, it consists of a twine and branch motif that refers to the interdependent relationship of humans and nature. Her design is sandblasted onto forty-two faux wood panels.

8.16 FOCUS, 2009

Perri Howard

Laminated glass and concrete
Seattle 1 Percent for Art Program
Seattle Center Skatepark

Perri Howard presents two innovative surprises in *Focus* at the Seattle Center Skatepark. The colorful images on the laminated safety glass panels along the Thomas Street side, the panel at the end of a skate ramp, and the

8.15 *Biography of a Branch*, Deborah Mersky

8.16 *Focus*, Perri Howard

vent shaft at the north end of the park are not painted; they are high-resolution photographs taken of the scrapes, patterns, and gouges on the bottom of used skateboards. She selected such imagery to emphasize the wear and tear and determination it takes to become skillful at skateboarding. The second surprise: the vertical glass panel at the end of the skate ramp is designed to be skated upon. Local blogger Matthew Lee Johnston reported that "Shaggy and . . . friend Justin tested out the glass wall and gave it the thumbs-up. 'It's like skating

8.17   *Neototems,* Gloria Bornstein

a dusty Masonite ramp. It's slippery, but it's doable.'"

8.17 NEOTOTEMS, 1995

Gloria Bornstein

Bronze and concrete; H 6 ft. × W 15 ft. × L 22 ft.; H 4 ft.
  × W 6 ft. × L 15 ft.
Seattle 1 Percent for Art Program
Southwest corner of the International Fountain

Rising out of the ground near the International Fountain are the almost life-size bronze backs of a mother whale and her calf. Note that they are not perpendicular to the surface but angled in a realistic pose inspired by Gloria Bornstein's observations while whale watching. Swirling water is represented by the texture of darker colored pavers, and the mother's tail (cast in concrete) rests at or just below the "water's" surface. *Neototems* refers to the local Salish Indian legend that whales swam underground from Elliott Bay to Lake Union. That legend is told in both English and Lushootseed (the Salish language) with bronze letters inlaid at the edges of the mother's tail. In the body of the tail is a map of the city, Lake Union, and Elliott Bay. Bornstein named her work *Neototems* to not only honor the Native American belief but to also give "symbolic form to western culture's renewed sense of humankind's connection to animals and the natural environment." See also 8.8, *Neototems Children's Garden.*

8.18 POOL, 1985

Randy Hayes

Oil on plywood; H 6 ft. 7 in. × L 50 ft.
Seattle 1 Percent for Art Program
On the building south of the Bagley Wright Theatre

Pool is a collection of nine figures standing around an imaginary swimming pool. Randy Hayes was commissioned to create an artwork for this location to replace an ugly concrete wall. The Seattle Center has no swimming pool, but the artist found that the site reminded him of a public pool in his

8.18 *Pool*, Randy Hayes

hometown of Jackson, Mississippi. Hayes painted the wall and installed behind large windows painted plywood figures seemingly going about their business with no knowledge that they are being watched. His use of colorful cutouts results from his training in both sculpture and painting, and the subjects seem three-dimensional and realistic from a distance, especially at night with the addition of green fluorescent underlighting.

8.19 FOUNTAIN OF CREATION, 1962/1992

Everett DuPen

Bronze, concrete and stone
City of Seattle collection
In the basin north of KeyArena

Seattle artist Everett DuPen created his *Fountain of Creation* with a philosophical theme in mind: the evolution of life on earth and the concept that water is the basis of all life. The three bronze sculptures placed in this large pool represent life-forms in the sea, in the

air, and on land. The two smaller elements are a group of four gulls and vertically growing seaweed. The more complicated central sculpture is *Tree of Life*, which shows the development of life from protozoans to fish, mammals, and humans. DuPen explained that the work "is not a specific evolutionary column. It is more a celebration of life. . . . The curving shapes outlining the central column represent forces of nature."

DuPen's original 1962 fountain, *Tree of Life*, stood on top of a cellular shape of colored concrete that was partially submerged. The shape was in keeping with his evolution theme, and its subtle earth colors—brick red, umber, and green—were chosen to harmonize with the bronze sculptures above. Wear and tear over the years required that the fountain be rebuilt. In 1992 design changes approved by DuPen were made that included the installation of boulders, changing the original rectangular pool to a curved design reminiscent of the cellular shapes that were replaced with a flat bottom better suited for its use as a wading pool in warmer months.

8.19 *Fountain of Creation*, Everett DuPen

In the level above and to the west of *Fountain of Creation* is what remains of a cast concrete fountain with inlaid glass tiles that was designed in 1962 by the office of Paul Thiry, the designers of what is now KeyArena. The rectangular fountain pool is now a garden, but you can still see the low-relief designs that were inspired by Northwest Coast Indian motifs. Other concrete reliefs in and around KeyArena were designed by the same firm.

8.20 THREE CRESCENTS, 2012

Austin Smith

Weathering steel; tallest H 6 ft. 1 in. × L 9 ft. 8 in.
Private commission
118 Republican Street, between First Avenue N and Warren Avenue N

To commemorate the fact that the Expo Building would be completed in the fiftieth anniversary year of the 1962 Seattle World's Fair, the building's developers asked artists to submit ideas for a sculpture inspired by

8.21 *August Wilson Way Portal*, Mindy Lehrman Cameron

8.21 AUGUST WILSON WAY PORTAL, 2009

Mindy Lehrman Cameron

Steel and glass; H 12 ft.
Private commission
South side of Bagley Wright Theatre

This portal was created to honor the late August Wilson (1945–2005), considered one of the finest playwrights in contemporary American theater. At the time of his death, the *Seattle Times* noted that Wilson's "monumental achievement was his decade-by-decade, ten-play cycle portraying the African-American experience in the 20th century." Those plays, known collectively as the Pittsburgh Cycle, were described by the *New York Times* as "a landmark in the history of black culture, of American literature and of Broadway theater." Wilson, who received two Pulitzer Prizes for Drama, spent the last fifteen years of his life creating works in Seattle, many of which were performed at the Seattle Repertory Theatre, which is housed next to this memorial on the south side of the Bagley Wright Theatre.

A large photo of Wilson is the principal feature of the portal, which also includes biographical facts and quotes from his plays. Artist Mindy Lehrman Cameron chose to create the portal out of steel, in recognition of Wilson's many connections to Pittsburgh where he was born and grew up. The red door refers to Aunt Ester, a spiritual healer and significant force in his cycle of plays. Lehrman Cameron put "stories" on the letterbox in recognition of Wilson's theme that people must understand their pasts to go healthfully into the future. The bronze

that event. The chosen artist, Austin Smith, had researched art and artists at the fair and became an avid admirer of the work of Doris Chase, not only from that period, but also her innovative subsequent work. *Three Crescents*, with their ovoid spaces and sweeping curves, are an homage to Chase, whose most famous sculpture is *Changing Form* in Kerry Park on Queen Anne Hill (see also 8.2, *Moon Gates*). As is true of many of Doris Chase's works, Smith's sculpture is designed to be experienced by moving around the elements and interacting with the positive and negative spaces.

plaque includes a quotation from a Wilson play that refers to those travels.

This portal, made possible by a grant from the Safeco Insurance Foundation, is the entryway to a planned promenade that may eventually extend to Fifth Avenue and include bronze art plaques, carved granite theater seats, and other artworks.

8.22 NEON FOR THE BAGLEY WRIGHT THEATRE, 1983

Stephen Antonakos

Red neon
Private commission
Seattle Center, Bagley Wright Theatre

8.22 *Neon for the Bagley Wright Theatre*, Stephen Antonakos

In 1979, during the design stage of the Bagley Wright Theatre (home of the Seattle Repertory Theatre), pioneer neon artist Stephen Antonakos was selected to design an artwork for the building's exterior. He worked with the Seattle-based architectural firm NBBJ and used neon to accentuate the building's curved green façade with a collection of straight lines, arcs, and squiggles that wraps around the building's corners and swoops above the roofline and outside of the inset horizontal lines on the walls. Antonakos described neon as "light arresting space" and in this case chose red neon, which he considered the most aggressive color. This is best viewed at night. In a 2013 obituary, the *New York Times* hailed Antonakos for his "abstract sculptures that illuminated indoor and outdoor spaces in cities around the globe, instantly recognizable for their vibrant colors and sinuous lines."

8.23 FOUNTAIN OF SESERAGI, 2000

Gerard Tsutakawa

Bronze; H 5 ft. 1 in. × L 11 ft. 8 in.
Gift to the city
South side of the Intiman Playhouse facing the
    International Fountain

Seseragi is a Japanese word that can be translated as "murmuring stream" or "babbling brook," and Gerard Tsutakawa's *Fountain of Seseragi* adds the soft sounds of babbling water to a quiet shaded section of the Seattle Center. Within each arm of the bronze sculpture, water cascades down five ledges and collects in a pool at the center of the piece. The scalloped edges of the metal troughs reference the curves of the waterfalls within. This fountain

exemplifies the inspiration Tsutakawa says he garners from the patterns and rhythms of the visual world. His resulting design is not literal or representational but creates a tranquil setting reminiscent of the natural environment. Tsutakawa explains that "whether in private settings or a public place, I want my works to be uplifting, to inspire feelings of happiness, and to be a gesture of gratitude to nature." *Fountain of Seseragi* was commissioned by the Seattle Center Foundation with additional assistance from a group of private donors.

8.24 ENCIRCLED STREAM, 1995

Ned Kahn

Carved granite and black anodized aluminum; H 5 ft. 1 in. ×
    Dia 9 ft.; Pool Dia 5 ft. 3 in.
Seattle 1 Percent for Art Program
Founder's Court, between Cornish Playhouse and Exhibition Hall

The spiral-shaped granite fountain on the west side of the Founder's Court may not seem particularly impressive if viewed at the wrong time. At one moment its basin has only a glassy, wet surface, but moments later water shoots out from the interior edges and creates a whirlpool that rhythmically fills and drains the basin. Different patterns are created as that process is repeated. The waves spiraling out of the center of the whirlpool create the illusion that the vortex has begun to spin in the opposite direction, which is a process of nature that artist Ned Kahn hopes will delight and inspire viewers. *Encircled Stream* shows Kahn's mastery of combining science and art to create controlled chaos in a confined space. This turbulent vortex refers to the history of the countless cycles of

8.23   *Fountain of Seseragi,* Gerard Tsutakawa

8.24   *Encircled Stream,* Ned Kahn (Courtesy Ned Kahn)

floods that have sculpted the terrain of eastern Washington over the eons. In 2011 Kahn used the same concept to create his elaborate, seventy-foot-diameter two-story *Rain Oculus* in Singapore.

Kahn's fountain is encircled by spiral-shaped granite elements that serve as benches for people to sit on and observe. That spiral motif is reflected in the paving patterns designed by Atelier Landscape Architects of Seattle that flow from the fountain into the surrounding plaza.

8.25 UNTITLED SCULPTURE, 1958

François Stahly

Carved stone; H 12 ft. 10 in. × W 2 ft. 8 in. × L 2 ft. 11 in.
Gift to the city
Founder's Court, between Cornish Playhouse and
   Exhibition Hall

This vertical stone sculpture was created by French artist François Stahly in the late 1950s. In 1961 Stahly was a visiting professor at the University of Washington when Seattle businessman Richard Lang purchased the sculpture from him and commissioned the artist to design a fountain in this courtyard that would incorporate the sculpture. Stahly's sculpture was the vertical element of that work, and it stood atop a collection of shallow rectangular concrete aggregate basins through which flowing water coursed. The column is a complex collection of rectangular forms and voids and is most interesting when viewed from different angles.

Courtyard renovations in 1995 necessitated the fountain's destruction and the sculpture, which is now sometimes incorrectly referred to as a *cairn*, was placed in its current location

8.25   Untitled sculpture, François Stahly

as the stand-alone work that Stahly originally created.

8.26 FOUNTAIN OF THE NORTHWEST, 1961

James FitzGerald

Bronze; H 20 ft. 6 in. × W 10 ft. 6 in. × L 11 ft.
Gift to the city
Cornish Playhouse courtyard

Fountain of the Northwest has been hailed by many as the finest example of James FitzGerald's fountain-sculptures. The water gushing and cascading from this fountain

8.26 *Fountain of the Northwest*, James FitzGerald

8.27 *Barbet*, James W. Washington Jr.

rushes through numerous channels within the bronze forms, and its welded bronze forms seem to have eroded naturally through time. The fountain was given to the city by Catherine Gould Chism in 1961 for the new playhouse and the world's fair. The same fountain can also be seen, although in a less attractive setting, at Princeton University.

8.27 BARBET, 1964

James W. Washington Jr.

Carved river boulder; H 1 ft. × W 2 ft. × L. 2 ft. 10 in.
Gift to the city
Cornish Playhouse courtyard

This stone sculpture by Seattle artist James W. Washington Jr. is typical of his works in the mid-1950s and early 1960s. Carved out of a local river boulder, it is a seemingly simple rendition of a bird, but it rests in a peaceful, some say spiritual, repose. In explaining his process of creating such sculptures, Washington told Seattle art critic Regina Hackett in *American Artist* that he waited "until intuition moves me,

and then I begin. I have to know the animal . . . before I can sculpt him. Not just know his features but feel them. I have to be him. Not until I get to the point where I am the animal can I release the spiritual force into the inanimate material and animate it. When this happens, I feel like I'm working with flesh rather than just stone" A barbet is a large-headed, stout-billed tropical bird that is related to the toucan.

8.28 GUARDIAN LIONS, 1962

Unknown Chinese artisans

Carved concrete; H 4 ft. 6 in. × W 2 ft. 5 in. × L 1 ft. 8 in.
Gift to the city
Phelps Center, 301 Mercer Street

The two four-foot-high Chinese guardian lions in front of the Phelps Center (home of the Pacific Northwest Ballet) were carved in ancient poses by Chinese artisans and given to the city by the government of Taiwan for the 1962 Seattle World's Fair. They are a male and a female, symbolic of yin and yang, and each has a paw resting on an embroidered ball. The female stands with a cub by her other paw, a symbol of female nurturing. The ball with each lion had ancient significance. In Chinese art it represents the sun, the egg symbol of the dual powers of nature, or a precious stone, and for imperial uses a symbol of supremacy over the world. It also refers to an ancient Chinese legend that the lion produces milk from its paws. Believing that legend, country people would leave hollow balls in the hills in the hope that lions would play with them and leave some of their milk with them.

Some refer to these sculptures as "Fu dogs," a term often used by Western curio collectors, but for over two thousand years in China, sculptures such as these have been called lions.

8.29 DREAMING IN COLOR AND KREIELSHEIMER PROMENADE, 2001

Leni Schwendinger, LMN Architects, Gustafson Guthrie Nichol Ltd., and Robert Israel

Seattle 1 Percent for Art Program
McCaw Hall, Kreielsheimer Promenade

As the plans for McCaw Hall evolved in the 1990s, the team at Seattle's LMN Architects (headed by Mark Reddington) wanted to design an outdoor space that would provide a unique experience for those attending events and for those stopping by or just walking through the space on their way to or from the Seattle Center. They considered hanging a series of huge sheets of finely woven material in the three-hundred-foot-long promenade. The hanging feature would relate to the landscaping designed by Gustafson Guthrie Nichol, and the experience would be richer with input from theater and opera designer Robert Israel. It was to become a "place to be" in its own right.

Internationally known light artist and designer Leni Schwendinger was commissioned to create the artwork for the space. The result was *Dreaming in Color*, nine scrims of woven metal mesh up to sixty feet long and thirty feet high, upon which are projected sequential programs of color. The scrims are twenty feet apart and twelve feet above the ground, and as people walk through the promenade, they progress through an ever-changing painting of five color compositions that are orchestrated much like a musical score. These "melodies for the eyes" are titled *White*

8.29   *Dreaming in Color*, Leni Schwendinger

on White; *Aquamarine, A Beguiling Song*; *Sleepwalk into Primary Red-Blue-Green*; *Within the Northern Lights*; and *Of Rothko, Section and Plane*. Light intensity is greatest from afar as the lighting on all scrims is visible, and it is best viewed at night. The lighting on each scrim disappears as a person passes beneath it.

For the promenade beneath *Dreaming in Color* the landscape design team created three large installations of greenish quartzite stone. Each forty-eight-foot-long section is slightly sloped to allow a film of water to gracefully flow. The water bubbles up from the higher edge, washes across the stones, and disappears into grates on the lower edge, all the while creating the pleasant sound of a gurgling stream that drowns out much of the nearby urban noises. Dark stone was selected to best reflect the colors at night and the sky during the day. Visitors can sit on the adjacent granite benches and enjoy the calming sounds of the water or increase their experience by walking through it. Those looking south should extend their view to the end of the promenade where the landscaping beyond is framed by the hard edges of the promenade and hanging scrims. All in all, it is a grand combination of architecture, art, and landscape design.

8.30 AN EQUAL AND OPPOSITE REACTION, 2005

Sarah Sze

Aluminum frame with assemblage of found parts; H 30 ft.
Seattle 1 Percent for Art Program
McCaw Hall lobby

Visible through the McCaw Hall lobby windows is Sarah Sze's 2005 sculpture, *An Equal and Opposite Reaction*, one of the most intriguing works of art in Seattle's public places. The suspended thirty-foot-tall vortex of lines, swirls, and found objects whirls up from the lobby and presents a myriad of sights and impressions from different angles and levels. The white lines are made of white aluminum bars. The rest of the work is composed of a wide collection of everyday objects, including ladders, rulers, industrial clamps, tape measures, electrical conduit and cords, carpenters' tools, electric fans, and water bottles. Arcs of ladders ascend past artificial plants, pots, and blue mesh crates. Electrical cords and conduit create slashes and swirls of lines. A carpenter's level becomes a yellow flash of a line from a different angle.

8.30   *An Equal and Opposite Reaction*, Sarah Sze

Sze explains that "on the one hand, the sculpture itself explores structures that are losing mass, stripped down and revealing skeletal structures, building-like foundations, or underlying support mechanisms that lie beneath. While on the other hand, they describe organic systems in growth, development, climbing, and accumulating. In this way the piece attempts to describe an entire organism still in the process of building or falling apart." The work's title is derived from Isaac Newton's Third Law of Motion: for every action, there is an equal and opposite reaction. Sze's sculpture was made possible through the city's 1 Percent for Art Program.

8.31   *Impatient Optimist*, Janet Echelman

8.31   IMPATIENT OPTIMIST, 2015

Janet Echelman

Spliced and braided fibers with colored LED lighting; H 40 ft.
   × W 80 ft. × L 120 ft.

Private commission

Bill & Melinda Gates Foundation buildings, 505 Fifth Avenue N

Massachusetts-based artist Janet Echelman has achieved worldwide recognition for using simple fiber to create complex, ethereal sculptures that hang above urban spaces. In the case of *Impatient Optimist*, she filled a space above the courtyard between two buildings at the Bill & Melinda Gates Foundation with a hovering collection of references to the natural colors of a day, the worldwide activities of the foundation, and the work of its employees. The origin of its form was a series of photographs Echelman took of the Seattle sky at frequent intervals over twenty-four hours. The color data from those photos was then analyzed to create a radial graph that was used to generate the multilayered shapes. The artist has described her aerial sculpture as a visual representation of the "shape of the day." Although most of the netting is white, some of the strands create bands of different shades of blue that interact with daytime lighting conditions.

Impatient Optimist comes alive at night, when it is best viewed. The colored lighting sequences in pinks, blues, and oranges that

8.32 *After All, Life is Change,* Dick Weiss

illuminate the form are coordinated with the appearance of dawn at the foundation's regional offices in India, Africa, China, the United Kingdom, and Washington, DC. The sky is a constant theme, but Echelman constructed the netting to also refer to those who work for the foundation throughout the world. The massive yet delicate floating nets were constructed (in Everson, Washington) using net-tying techniques common in the local fishing industry. Each knot represents an individual foundation employee. Those individual knots keep together a complex billowing whole and when one element moves, the others are affected, just as changes in the world can be caused by the work of a few.

The Gates Foundation commissioned this sculpture, and its title comes from the fact that Bill and Melinda Gates refer to themselves as "impatient optimists." That term is also the name of their foundation's blog.

8.32 AFTER ALL, LIFE IS CHANGE, 2008

Dick Weiss

Stained and clear glass; L 50 ft.
Gift to the City
Seattle Center's Fifth Avenue North Garage, Fifth Avenue N
    and Harrison Street

When Dick Weiss was commissioned to create a stained-glass assemblage for the Seattle Center's Fifth Avenue North Garage, he was asked to create a design that was "wild, playful, and crazy." In response he created this multi-hued biomorphic abstraction out of sheets of colored glass and portals of handblown clear glass. He describes the piece as a bit of a shape-shifter that mirrors life because it is composed of one-of-a-kind shapes that were presented to him. His title, *After All, Life Is Change,* refers to his philosophical approach to life: "You deal with a lot of strange things that you'll never

8.33 *Typewriter Eraser, Scale X*, Claes Oldenburg and Coosje van Bruggen

Pop artists Claes Oldenburg and his wife, Coosje van Bruggen, achieved artistic fame by fabricating colossal outdoor sculptures of mundane objects. When typewriters were essential office equipment, such erasers were an important tool that included a brush to clean off the corrected paper. The almost five-ton sculpture is placed at an angle as if falling over with the downward force thrusting up the brush bristles. Oldenburg's inspiration for this subject was his childhood memories of playing with a typewriter eraser in his father's office.

Typewriter Eraser, Scale X is owned by the Paul G. Allen family. Its "ancient" origin is one reason Microsoft cofounder Paul Allen was inspired to purchase it. "I have spent a lot of my life working with text and its function in computer programs," he told the *Seattle Times*. "I thought that a giant eraser was an interesting and brilliant conceptual piece." Another *Typewriter Eraser, Scale X* is in the National Gallery of Art Sculpture Garden in Washington, DC.

experience again. You put them all together and move forward."

The vibrant wall is a centerpiece of the garage and fits the artist's admiration for the place of stained glass in the history of Western architecture. "Stained glass has been a handmaiden to architecture for hundreds of years," Weiss says. "I like that. I like its traditional, hand-built quality. It feels very human."

After All, Life Is Change was a gift to the city from the Seattle Center with supportive funding by the Bill & Melinda Gates Foundation.

8.33 TYPEWRITER ERASER, SCALE X, 1999

Claes Oldenburg and Coosje van Bruggen

Painted stainless steel and resin; H 19 ft. 4 in.
Private collection
Harrison Street entrance to the Seattle Center

8.34 GRASS BLADES, 2003

John Fleming with Susan Zoccola

Painted steel; H 30 ft. × L 150 ft.
Seattle 1 Percent for Art Program
Harrison Street entrance to the Seattle Center

Grass Blades was created as part of a redesign of the Seattle Center's Harrison Street entrance and the center's desire to screen off an unattractive expanse of parking spaces. John Fleming created an abstract design of 110 thirty-foot-tall steel strips and worked with artist Susan Zoccola to paint them in a series of random bands of colors. The edge of each band

8.34　*Grass Blades*, John Fleming with Susan Zoccola

was left unpainted to rust and retain reference to the fact that steel is an essential part of the whole. The effect of these blades is further enhanced when wind causes the quarter-inch-thick steel to bend and sway.

Fleming is pleased that the sculpture often reminds people of gently swaying grass or bamboo, but he points out that it was created as an abstract work without intending to create any vision of waving grasses. He did not give the sculpture a title, but the management of the Seattle Center wanted one and called it *Grass Blades*.

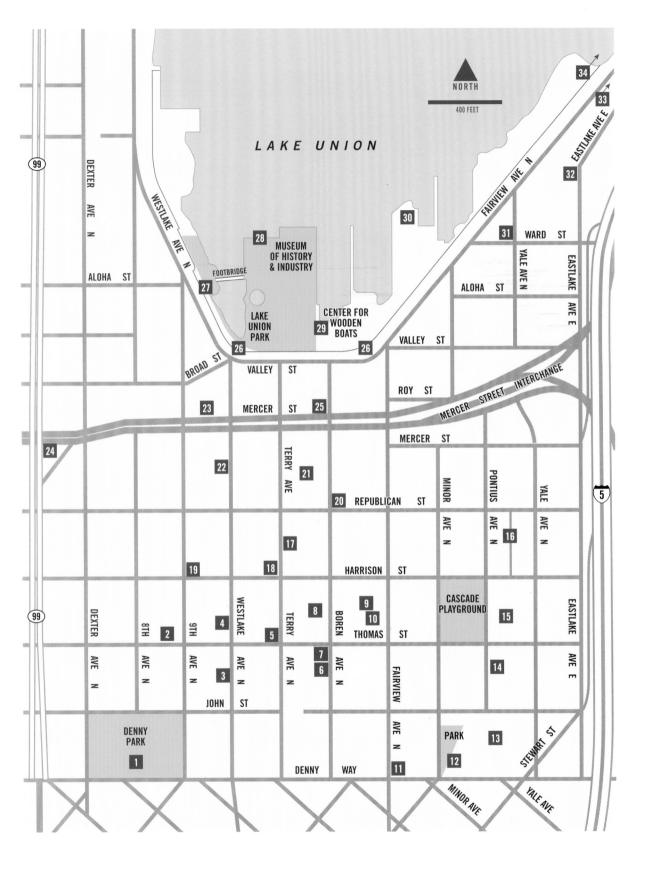

LAKE UNION

NORTH

400 FEET

99

DEXTER AVE N

WESTLAKE AVE N

ALOHA ST

FOOTBRIDGE

28

27

MUSEUM OF HISTORY & INDUSTRY

LAKE UNION PARK

29

CENTER FOR WOODEN BOATS

30

31

WARD ST

YALE AVE N

EASTLAKE

ALOHA ST

AVE E

FAIRVIEW AVE N

EASTLAKE AVE E

34

33

32

BROAD ST

26

VALLEY ST

26

VALLEY ST

ROY ST

MERCER STREET INTERCHANGE

23

MERCER ST

25

TERRY AVE

24

22

21

MINOR AVE N

PONTIUS AVE N

YALE AVE N

5

20

REPUBLICAN ST

16

17

HARRISON ST

19

18

CASCADE PLAYGROUND

8

9

10

THOMAS ST

15

EASTLAKE AVE E

WESTLAKE

TERRY AVE N

BOREN AVE N

DEXTER AVE N

8TH AVE N

9TH AVE N

2

4

5

7

6

14

3

JOHN ST

FAIRVIEW AVE N

DENNY PARK

1

PARK

13

12

DENNY WAY

11

STEWART ST

MINOR AVE

YALE AVE

9 SOUTH LAKE UNION

When you see a fish you don't think of its scales, do you? You think of its speed, its floating, flashing body seen through the water. . . . If I made fins and eyes and scales, I would arrest its movement, give a pattern or shape of reality. I want just the flash of its spirit.

—Constantin Brancusi (1876–1957)

NO PART OF SEATTLE HAS SEEN MORE DEVELOPMENT in the past decade than South Lake Union. This is due to the influx of technology and biomedical research enterprises, the major presence of Amazon, and the hyperactive construction undertaken by Vulcan Real Estate. Fortunately, Vulcan implemented an unparalleled program of commissioning artworks for many of its buildings. Add South Lake Union Park and improvements surrounding it, and an impressive collection of varied and interesting artworks is readily available for public view.

9.1 MARK A. MATTHEWS, 1941

Alonzo Victor Lewis

Cast bronze; H 3 ft. 6 in.
Gift to the city
Denny Park, facing Denny Way between Ninth Avenue N and
Dexter Avenue

This lesser-known sculpture was created the year after the death of Dr. Mark A. Matthews (1867–1940) and given to the city by friends and admirers of one of Seattle's most colorful and active ministers. Born in Calhoun, Georgia, Matthews came to Seattle in 1902 to become pastor of the First Presbyterian Church and was welcomed by a four-hundred-member congregation. When he died, that congregation, which included the downtown Seattle church plus branches—including what is now University Presbyterian Church—numbered ten thousand members. It was reportedly the largest Presbyterian congregation in the country.

Matthews's interests extended beyond church affairs. He crusaded against political and police corruption, started Seattle's first program to combat tuberculosis (which later developed into Firlands), and established the city's first kindergarten and nursery schools. Seattle's first juvenile court was created by his efforts, and as a practicing lawyer, he represented the underprivileged without charge. A committed foe of alcohol, he once said that "the saloon is the most fiendish, corrupt, hell-soaked institution that ever crawled out of the slime of the eternal pit. . . . It takes your sweet innocent daughter, robs her of her virtue, and transforms her into a brazen, wanton harlot. . . . It is the open sore of this land."

9.2 RE-STACK, 2015

Annie Han and Daniel Mihalyo (Lead Pencil Studio)

Stainless steel mesh; H 20 ft. × W 4 ft. × L 25 ft.
Private commission
Ninth and Thomas Streets

With their sculpture *Re-Stack*, Annie Han and Daniel Mihalyo refer to both the hard-edged architecture and stacked stone buildings (some with arched windows) that were common in the South Lake Union neighborhood before its modern redevelopment, and the stacking of containers common in today's online commerce. They were particularly inspired by photos of enormous piles of boxes stacked unevenly on pallets at an Amazon warehouse. They reviewed many early photos of the district and, in particular, the early twentieth century regrades and were inspired by the history of the place and the fact that everything is being upended. "We were thinking about incredible changes like the Denny Regrade," says Han. "We wanted to refer to what was there, what has been scraped away over time."

Han and Mihalyo wanted to "make stone out of welded steel" and *Re-Stack* is constructed of a custom-made, stainless steel wire fabric that has ten different gauges that decrease in size as the structure ascends. In addition to the predominant dark hues, green, blue, and earth-colored tones were added through a process that uses chromium oxide to change how the mesh reacts to light throughout the day. Daylight also creates a moving shadow pattern across the plaza, which the artists liken to the ghost of a building. As was true of many Seattle buildings in the late 1800s, this structure abuts the property line. The end result is what Mihalyo

9.2   *Re-Stack*, Annie Han and Daniel Mihalyo (Lead Pencil Studio)

has described as nonfunctional architecture as art. *Re-Stack* was commissioned by Vulcan Real Estate, the building's developer.

9.3 SELLEN CONSTRUCTION COMPANY OFFICES

Julie Speidel and Dennis Evans

Private commissions
227 Westlake Avenue N

Sellen Construction Company has two commissioned sculptures in its building lobby and welcomes visitors who want to see them. Both were created in 2001, and they relate to the company's business philosophy and the work it does. In *On Firm Ground*, a three-part sculpture of bronze elements on columnar basalt, Julie Speidel refers to the fact that the company works closely as a team with other parties involved in developing a building. The bronze swirl on the left represents the architect and the creative, sometimes artistic, force. The circle represents the owner and its needs, which connect the architect and the builder. The square represents the contractor, who often provides practical solutions to meet the architect's vision and the owner's desires.

In the building's elevator lobby is *The Anatomy of a Structure*, a three-part mixed-media work by Dennis Evans. Typical of his art, it consists of a varied collection of symbolic elements. Reading from left to right it refers to the essential elements in an architectural structure and includes nine themes—the three primary colors: red, yellow, and blue; the three primary building blocks of platonic solids: triangle, square, and circle; and the three attributes of structure: classical (including reference to Golden Section Proportions), practical, and conceptual.

9.4 LABYRINTH, 2004

Linda Beaumont

Laminated glass with photo process imagery, stainless steel;
H 7 ft. 7 in. × L 7 ft. 6 in.
Private commission
307 Westlake Avenue N

9.4 *Labyrinth,* Linda Beaumont

A focus of the work within the Center for Infectious Disease Research is the elimination of the world's most infectious diseases. Its research efforts cover four areas of infectious diseases: HIV/AIDS, malaria, tuberculosis, and what scientists refer to as emerging and neglected diseases, which include African sleeping sickness, leishmaniasis, Chagas disease, and toxoplasmosis. The images and colors of Linda Beaumont's *Labyrinth* arise from the work performed within the research center.

Labyrinth consists of two colorful panels of photo process imagery in laminated glass in stainless steel frames standing at the edge of the sidewalk. Beaumont says that the specific order of colors in this artwork is derived from a chronographic representation of the genetic sequence of the Leishmania parasite, which is one of the parasites studied at the center. It causes a disease called leishmaniasis, which affects twelve million people annually. Within the primary images are nodes of color and electron microscope images of disease-causing organisms. *Labyrinth* is designed to create a wash of color onto passing pedestrians in the daytime and to glow with lighting at night, which is the best time to view it. *Labyrinth* was commissioned by Vulcan Real Estate, Harbor Properties, and the Center for Infectious Disease Research.

9.5 PLACEHOLDERS: CLOUD, ROCK, TREE, 2007

Claudia Fitch

Painted steel; H 10 to 30 ft.
Private commission
Corner of Terry Avenue N and Thomas Street

9.5   *Placeholders: Cloud, Rock, Tree*, Claudia Fitch

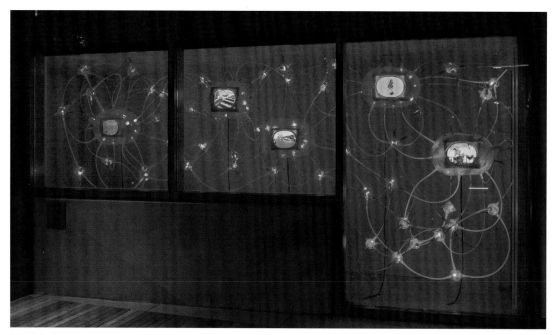

9.6 *Periscope*, Deborah Aschheim

In the early 1900s Terry Avenue was in an industrial use area in which a number of old growth trees still stood amid the urban grid of streets and buildings. Seattle artist Claudia Fitch refers to that short-lived circumstance and the contemporary environment and architecture with her tree-like painted steel sculptures at the Kaiser Permanente building. Each has a curved trunk with a crown consisting of an open oval grid. Two of them stand at the corner of Terry Avenue N and Thomas Street, while a third looms above on the roof. A fourth element is just beyond 950 Thomas Street halfway down the block from the corner.

Placeholders also includes the nearby landscape design. The trees are placed in curved concrete planters that relate to the shape of the tree crowns, as do the oval-shaped planting beds on both sides of the building. Note the inlaid brickwork shaped like the shadow of the sculpture above. The plantings include evergreen trees, common for the referenced historic landscape but not usually seen in contemporary urban design. These sculptures were commissioned by Vulcan Real Estate and Group Health Cooperative (now Kaiser Permanente).

9.6 PERISCOPE, 2012

Deborah Aschheim

Roto cast resin, solid core optical fiber, programmed LEDs, looping and dynamic video
Private commission
207 Boren Avenue N Boren Avenue N and Thomas Street

In a building window about fifty feet south of *Woodpile* (see 9.7) are the glowing blue synapses and video screens that make up Deborah Aschheim's *Periscope*, the artist's visualization of a fragment of the internet. She is interested in visualizing networks of information, memory, and thought and describes her creation as "giving a glimpse into other worlds, growing inside technology building complexes." The video, which changes daily, is comprised of surveillance and webcam images gathered from around the world. Joshua Pablo Rosenstock and Daragh Byrne collaborated with Aschheim to create this unique installation, which is best viewed at night. *Periscope* was commissioned by Vulcan Real Estate, the building's developer.

9.7 WOODPILE, 2012

Jenny Heishman

Stainless steel and bronze; H 8 ft. × L 19 ft.
Private commission
207 Boren Avenue N, at Thomas Street, southwest corner

With *Woodpile* (as with her nearby sculpture *Cabin Corners*, 9.20) Jenny Heishman brought a common rural element to the sleek, hard-edged architecture of its surroundings. Stainless steel

9.7   *Woodpile*, Jenny Heishman

9.8　*Articulated Start* (detail), Eric Eley

cylinders are stacked up like firewood against a vertical slab that seems to keep them from collapsing onto Thomas Street, and that wall appears to be precariously held in place by an angled, seemingly unanchored bronze plank. Hanging over that plank is a blue tarp of painted bronze, placed as if casually set aside to protect the pile from the elements. Heishman describes her design as "a playful response to the steep slope of Boren Avenue." *Woodpile* was commissioned by Vulcan Real Estate.

9.8　ARTICULATED START, 2011

Eric Eley

Steel, stainless steel, paint
Private commission
333 Boren Avenue N

Although the four elements of Eric Eley's *Articulated Start*—two rising out of the landscape on the Boren Avenue side of the plaza and two more hanging down from the ceiling above the stairs leading down to Terry Avenue N—refer to plant life, they are not organic forms. Eley has always been interested in how such things as mathematic diagramming and mapmaking create elegant ways to rationally describe something. Eley explains that the facets and angles of these folded and creased plantlike forms make it seem as if they are planned and controlled, but they are moving on their own. *Articulated Start* refers to the rapid development of South Lake Union and of Amazon.com, the building's owner. In both cases, Eley explains that those involved may think that growth will happen "according to algorithms or other calculations, but it isn't really controllable. Growth occurs on its own in unpredictable ways."

One of the artist's goals was to combine the expected with the unexpected, and the elements growing from the wood ceiling were positioned to be a surprise that draws people up the staircase from street level. The parts interact with those at ground level and reach for one another. Eley chose soft colors of the sky to relate *Articulated Start* to the sky, and to the Space Needle, which is visible looking up and out from the sculpture. It was commissioned by real estate developer Vulcan Real Estate.

9.9　TROY BLOCK

Annie Han and Daniel Mihalyo (Lead Pencil Studio)

Stainless steel mesh; H 20 ft. × W 4 ft. × L 25 ft.
Private commission
Troy Block, 307 Fairview Avenue N

In the center of the Troy Block's massive courtyard is a ghost of things past. Artists Annie

9.9 *Troy Block*, Annie Han and Daniel Mihalyo (Lead Pencil Studio)

Han and Daniel Mihalyo wanted to create a sculpture of something that existed before the South Lake Union neighborhood was developed, but they wanted it resemble a sketch. They created a replica of a parking lot ticket booth that once stood in this neighborhood. In selecting the form for *Troy Block*, they reviewed many historical photos of the area (as they did before creating *Re-Stack*, see 9.2) and observed tiny parking lot structures in the voids created by parking lots. The artists wanted to bring human scale into the complex of imposing buildings and "give people reason to pause in the current environment and reflect on its historic context—what was there before." Han and Mihalyo have been widely praised for their unique approaches to public art, which they describe as "architecture in reverse. . . . Our projects are everything about architecture with none of its function . . . spaces with no greater purpose than to be perceived and question the certainty posited by the man-made world." *Troy Block* was commissioned by Touchstone Development, the building's developer.

9.10 MECHANISM, 2017

Jim Blashfield

Epoxy-coated aluminum and electronics; approx. H 11 ft. ×
   L 13 ft.
Private commission
Troy Block, 307 Fairview Avenue N

Mechanism is located in the juncture of the east and north walls where the arcade and courtyard walkways intersect. Portland artist Jim Blashfield placed it there, under the Troy Laundry sign, to make it a focal point and

9.10   *Mechanism,* Jim Blashfield

present visual images to the many who will pass by each day. Its design is a combination of high-tech elements, with eleven high-definition monitors and recorded sounds in a structure that contains recovered remnants from the Troy Laundry facility that was demolished for this new complex. Blashfield explains that the rotating plates in his sculpture's screens suggest dampers for the control of airflow in old factory chimneys and refer to other valves, such as those that control the flow of electrical voltage and others present in biological organisms.

A central theme of *Mechanism* is the exploration of change over time, and many of the images arose from Blashfield's research into the cultural, technological, and natural histories of the South Lake Union area. Visible in the largest monitor, encircled by the frame of an antique industrial scale, is a photo of an old local scene, perhaps the digging of the Lake Washington Ship Canal or birdlife. All or portions of that photo are also visible behind rotating plates in the smaller screens to the right and left. Two other monitors with separate images can be seen on the floor behind. The artist explains that *Mechanism* does not have repeated presentations over a brief period. The monitors provide a wide range of complex, sporadic visual events, some of which will be immediately evident, while others will evolve over a period of days. *Mechanism* was commissioned by Touchstone Development, the building's developer.

9.11 SAILS AND MIRABELLA UMBRELLAS

Robert Foster

Aluminum
Private commissions
Mirabella Retirement Community, corner of Denny Way
  and N Fairview Avenue

Oregon artist Robert Foster created two commissioned sculptures for the Mirabella Retirement Community. The most prominent is the twenty-two-foot-high *Sails*, which stands at the corner of Denny Way and N Fairview Avenue. Its curved aluminum sheets, with swirls of texture, attached to two masts may remind viewers of sailboats on the Salish Sea or windy days in Seattle. Foster's other work, *Mirabella Umbrellas*, is the seventeen-foot-tall

sculpture north at the entrance to the Mirabella facility.

9.12 TRANSFOREST, 2018

Annie Han and Daniel Mihalyo (Lead Pencil Studio)

Mixed patinated metal; H 110 ft.
Seattle 1 Percent for Art Program
Seattle City Light Denny Substation, 1250 Denny Way

Hidden behind the angular sloped walls of Seattle City Light's Denny Substation is the usual array of cables, transformers, switch gears, and other equipment that distributes electricity to its customers from the utility's power-generating dams along the Skagit River in the Cascades. City Light's first dam of three in that project was completed in 1924, and

9.12   *Transforest*, Annie Han and Daniel Mihalyo (Lead Pencil Studio; Courtesy of the artists)

9.14 *Baladeuse,* James Harrison

large steel electrical towers were built to bring the power from the mountains to Seattle. Constructing those towers required extensive clear-cutting and refiguring of the landscape. To commemorate the completion of a tower, crews often temporarily topped it off with a tree.

Artists Annie Hahn and Daniel Mihalyo are intrigued by Seattle City Light and how it accomplishes its mission. *Transforest*, their 110-foot-tall metal tower on the southwest corner of this site arose out of their extensive research into the utility's history and how it operates. They also admire snag trees, remnants of great towering trees that are dead or dying and provide critical habitat for woodpeckers and other creatures before they decay and return to the soil. The lattice work on this sculpture refers both to the power grid and the immense reordering of the landscape needed to generate and supply electricity to the city. *Transforest* has the same height and girth and a shape similar to the artists' favorite snag tree in the Cascades.

9.13 SWITCHWALL, 2018

Ned Kahn

Stainless steel, anodized aluminum, and LED lights
Seattle 1 Percent for Art Program
Seattle City Light Denny Substation, 1250 Denny Way

Seattle City Light's Denny Substation was originally going to cover most of the block with vertical walls looming over passersby. After public meetings and community input, the design was refined and the edges of the walls were pulled in to reduce the building's mass and set at angles to create adjacent open, public-oriented spaces.

The sloped walls are clad in angular patters of stainless steel tiles except for four of the upper planes on the southeast and northeast sections. Those spaces make up *Switchwall*, another of Ned Kahn's innovative sculptures that enable viewers to observe and interact with natural processes.

Switchwall consists of thousands of thin anodized aluminum tiles that swing on posts and hang perpendicular to the walls. As wind causes them to swing back and forth, a neodymium magnet embedded in the base of each acts as a switch that turns off and on orange and blue LED lights. The tiles create rippling affects across the building planes that are regulated by wind velocity and direction, creating what Kahn describes as patterns of behavior that are recurring themes in nature. At night the tiles are less visible and varying patterns of colored light enliven the spaces and on windless evenings the walls rest. A similar but more subtle affect can be observed in Kahn's *Tholian Web* in in the Denny Triangle (7.8).

Kahn explains that the inspiration for *Switchwall* came from looking at downtown Seattle at night and thinking that each of the lights of the city is connected to a switch controlled by people. This led to the thought of an array of switches controlled by nature not humans.

9.14 BALADEUSE, 2006

James Harrison

Art glass and stainless steel; H. 20 ft.
Private commission
223 Yale Avenue N

In the center of the four-part building complex at Yale Avenue N and Pontius Avenue N, which is divided by pedestrian alleys, is James Harrison's *Baladeuse,* a tower of lush green art glass on stainless steel plates, all held together by an external stainless steel skeleton. Its 217 panels extend up from a seventeen-sided polygonal base, and the work appears to twist as it tapers up to a squared-off pinnacle. During the day the subtly patterned glass reflects light, but this is a sculpture best appreciated at night when its interior lighting creates a glowing urban beacon. *Baladeuse* is French for "lantern" or "wanderer." Harrison named it in honor of early twentieth-century aviation pioneer Alberto Santos-Dumont (1873–1932). His small dirigible, Baladeuse #9—very high-tech in its day—was famous in 1903 Paris because its creator flew at very low altitudes over the city center, occasionally landing on a boulevard in front of a favorite café for a bite of lunch. *Baladeuse* was commissioned by Vulcan Real Estate and PEMCO Insurance.

9.15 ISLAND TREEHOUSE, 2018

Annie Han and Daniel Mihalyo (Lead Pencil Studio)

Miscellaneous materials; H 15 ft. on 24 ft. high plinth
Private commission
1522 Harrison Street

This new building has a large, open courtyard that the developer, Vulcan Real Estate, thought was a perfect place for a tree house. Lead Pencil Studio designed the resulting structure to float in the open space high above the plaza and serve as an enclosure (complete with working fireplace) where people can retreat. It sits atop

9.16 *Laundry Strike,* Whiting Tennis

a twenty-four-foot-high plinth and is accessible via a small bridge connected to the office building. Han and Mihalyo emphasize that *Island Treehouse* is not a work of architecture, "but a place you can be."

9.16 LAUNDRY STRIKE, 2014

Whiting Tennis

Painted bronze; H 12 ft.
Private commission
Alley off of Republican Street between Pontius Avenue N and
  Yale Avenue N

Laundry Strike stands in a quiet spot in a developed alley amid Vulcan Real Estate's Stack

House Mixed-Use Project and is located across from the smokestack of the 1906 Supply Laundry Building. Seattle artist Whiting Tennis chose to memorialize the Seattle Laundry Strike of 1917 with this, his first commissioned public artwork. The strike was organized by a group of female unionized laundry workers who were required to work long, arduous hours for less than the minimum wage at that time. On June 14, many of them walked out on strike, and they were quickly supported by other unions and many members of the general public. The number of those on strike increased to fifteen hundred and within a month management agreed to an eight-hour day with weekly pay of ten dollars, one dollar more than the minimum wage at the time.

Wicker hampers were used throughout laundry operations, and Tennis chose them as symbols of the strike. He studied designs of the period, learned how to weave rattan, and, with help from members of the local Northwest Basket Weavers guild, created this twelve-foot-tall tower of hampers and hamper tops.

9.17 *Convergence*, Ann Gardner

Its elements were individually cast in bronze, welded together, and painted white. The artist's intent to unambiguously memorialize the strikers is further evidenced by the woven "1917" on the tower's west side. At several points in the sculpture, Tennis created spaces for plants—envisioning a flowering tree in the center and flowers growing in the perimeter—so that the sculpture and its surroundings would take on the look of an overgrown Victorian garden. Tennis was never able to complete that aspect and, although surrounding vegetation has grown around and in *Laundry Strike*, it's not what the artist had in mind. This sculpture was commissioned by Vulcan Real Estate.

9.17 CONVERGENCE, 2009

Ann Gardner

Glass tile mosaic; H 12 ft. × L 50 ft.
Private commission
426 Terry Avenue N

Ann Gardner's *Convergence* consists of two undulating golden arcs whose tips converge at a central spot on a curved concrete plaza wall. The surfaces are composed of thousands of smalti, or tiles, in yellow and golden hues. Smalti are created by a process that was developed during the Byzantine Empire (330–1453 CE) in which molten glass is mixed with metal oxides and formed into slabs that are then hand broken into individual pieces. In some cases the process includes topping the tile with gold leaf, which is then covered with a layer of thin glass. The iridescence of *Convergence* is due in part to such gold leaf, and the color of the tiles intensifies as the convergent point is

reached. It is well worth the time to look closely at the surface of these arcs. As with many fine paintings, what appears to be a single or a small range of color is a complicated collection of many. Gardner's artwork was commissioned by Vulcan Real Estate and Schnitzer West.

9.18 PING PONG PLAZA, 2004

Buster Simpson

Bronze, stainless steel, Ping Pong paddles, catenary lighting
Private commission
West side of Harrison Street between Terry Avenue N and
    Westlake Avenue N

Buster Simpson's *Ping Pong Plaza* is designed as an outdoor room with a three-sided planter and a scored concrete "rug." Within the space is a bronze, regulation-size Ping Pong table on ball feet with a stainless steel net and line

9.18   *Ping Pong Plaza,* Buster Simpson

inlays and a suspended catenary light fixture. The shape of each table leg includes profiles of great thinkers: physicists Max Planck and Albert Einstein; molecular biologist, geneticist, and zoologist James Watson and biophysicist Rosalind Franklin; biologists Stephen Jay Gould and Edward O. Wilson; French naturalist Jean Baptiste Lamarck and English naturalist Charles Darwin. Simpson explains that the "paired individuals represent a metaphysical ping pong match, bouncing ideas and concepts back and forth, each in pursuit of validating a hypothesis. Perhaps in some future match between contemporary scientists having a discussion in this room, a distracting thought will occur during a volley, a synapse will occur, and a 'fifth leg' will begin to form." *Ping Pong Plaza* was commissioned by Vulcan Real Estate and Schnitzer West.

9.19 NEBULOUS, 2015

Dan Corson

Glass, transparent conducting film, aluminum, photovoltaics, LEDs, and electronics; left: H 12 ft. × W 10 ft. × L 25 ft.; right: H 9 ft. × W 7 ft. × L 15 ft.
Private commission
400 Ninth Avenue N

With *Nebulous*, Dan Corson refers to Seattle's cloudy weather and its role in computer innovation and the fact that both the environmental and technological climates are changing. "We are currently shifting from our analog hard copy world and local computer storage to cloud-based systems," he says. "The intricacy of these systems eludes most software users and yet clouds of electrons constantly transport information all around us." The

cloud-inspired sculptures that float above the plaza are made up of more than 350 glass disks, some of which electronically change levels of opacity and pulsate at varying rhythms. Corson describes the effect as "a digital dance resembling old school calculating computers or perhaps pulsing lightning within clouds on a stormy day." Embedded in the plaza pavement are lights that outline the forms above. *Nebulous* was commissioned by Vulcan Real Estate, the building's developer.

9.20 CABIN CORNERS, 2010

Jenny Heishman

Painted aluminum; each unit approx. H 5 ft. 5 in. × L 6 ft. 6 in.
Private commission
500 Boren Avenue N at Republican Street

Jenny Heishman's *Cabin Corners* uses artificial logs of hand-painted aluminum to create three corners of intersecting units. She refers to the region's history of logging as the sculpture intersects with the architecture of the adjacent building and the planter beds in this pocket park. Heishman says that she chose to create a "fabricated reality" that arose from her experiences as a child in Florida where she created seasonal changes "with plastic autumn leaves, artificial snow, and unspoken agreements." In this case she was also interested in seeing "how the three components of the sculpture enclose an imaginary room, creating a space within a space and how the invented history embodied in the work might send its audience back in time." As with her nearby *Woodpile* (9.7), Heishman has placed an unexpected rural element in the hard edges of an urban setting.

9.19 *Nebulous,* Dan Corson

9.20 *Cabin Corners* (detail), Jenny Heishman

9.21 *Beacon,* Jamie Walker

Vulcan Real Estate, the building's developer, commissioned this sculpture.

9.21 BEACON, CLOUD, TOTO, 2010

Jamie Walker

Painted aluminum; *Beacon* H 11 ft. 3 in. × W 7 ft. × L 7 ft.;
  Cloud: H 6 ft. × W 5 ft. × L 10 ft.; *Toto:* H 3 ft. 6 in. ×
  W 2 ft. 3 in. × L 2 ft. 8 in.
Private commission
550 Terry Avenue N

Vulcan Real Estate commissioned University of Washington professor and artist Jamie Walker to create art that would be provocative and add interest to its Terry Avenue building and plaza. The artist responded with three unique sculptures composed of clusters of fabricated aluminum spheres. The largest is *Beacon*, which stands at the Terry Avenue entrance. Walker created this vertical collection of pewter-colored spheres to evoke the geological forces that create mountains. Some may envision subterranean forces bubbling to the earth's surface. Its finely incised parallel lines on the surface of each form create an illusion of independently spinning orbs.

Cloud hangs on the northeast corner of the south building, twenty feet up. It is a mass of bright white spheres that may appear to be an

9.21   *Cloud*, Jamie Walker

9.22 *There is Another Sky,* Spencer Finch

ever-changing cloud formation or one that has descended with the weight of collected moisture. On bright days the painted surfaces facing the building reflect a pink glow onto its walls. The blue zoomorphic *Toto* sits at the edge of a landscape island near the Boren Street entrance. It is intended to evoke a playful pet and at first glance some may think of a teddy bear. He is named after Dorothy's little dog in *The Wizard of Oz*.

9.22 THERE IS ANOTHER SKY, 2014

Spencer Finch

Stained glass canopy
Private commission
515 Westlake Avenue N

Artist Spencer Finch is known for his unusual conceptual public works that use color and light to create unique experiences. *There Is Another Sky* is a complicated rendition of a forest canopy with overlapping green, yellow, and orange disks in different hues that are placed as if they are overlapping leaves. Light filters through the canopy at different levels of intensity, sometimes creating a greenish glow below. Finch points out that, oddly enough, when looking up through the canopy, the best visual effects are produced on cloudy days when neutral light shines through the open spaces. The blue of a clear sky reduces the contrast between the leaves and the voids. One effect that Finch did not anticipate, but is pleased to see, is the extension of his abstract natural canopy by means of reflections in the adjoining glass walls. To create further natural references to this urban setting, Finch added a collection of tiny LED lights to the landscaping, which create a variety of choreographed patterns as if the floor is populated with fireflies.

Spencer Finch often draws inspiration from the poetry of Emily Dickinson and the title of this artwork is that of the following Dickinson poem.

> There is another sky,
> Ever serene and fair,
> And there is another sunshine,
> Though it be darkness there;
> Never mind faded forests,
> Austin, never mind silent fields—
> Here is a little forest,
> Whose leaf is ever green;
> Here is a brighter garden
> Where not a frost has been;
> In its unfading flowers
> I hear the bright bee hum:
> Prithee, my brother,
> Into my garden come!

There Is Another Sky was commissioned by real estate developer Vulcan Real Estate.

9.23 MIRALL, 2012

Jaume Plensa

Painted stainless steel; H 12 ft. 3 in. × W 7 ft. 6 in.
 × L 7 ft. 4 in.
Private collection
Allen Institute for Brain Science, 615 Westlake Avenue N

Jaume Plensa's *Mirall* (Catalan for "mirror") is one of his many sculptures, in various forms, that focuses on internal dialogue and interpersonal communications (see also 3.18). "Every

9.23 *Mirall*, Jaume Plensa

one of my projects," he says, "pretends . . . to create a certain quietness, a place where you can listen to your own words, your own heart." The lack of opportunity to do so in the modern world troubles Plensa. In this case, two identical figures of white painted steel latticework sit holding their shins and face each other. They have no faces and their torsos are open and hollow. Plensa views the human figure as a container for thoughts and emotions, and he made these figures hollow to allow viewers to enter within and think quiet thoughts.

Mirall is constructed of letters from eight alphabets: Hebrew, Arabic, Chinese, Japanese, Greek, Cyrillic, Hindi, and Latin. Plensa explained in a 2011 TED talk that no words are spelled out on these sculptures. He likens each to a single cell in biology, which standing alone may accomplish little but when associated with others can create text and do a myriad of things. "Our bodies are like a text," he

said, ". . . a place where you invite others to come in."

9.24 ATMOSPHERIC FLURRY, 2018

Catherine Wagner

Powder-coated panels with integrated LED lighting; each
    section L 120 ft. × H 4 ft. 6 in.
Seattle 1 Percent for Art Program
Mercer Street underpass at Aurora Avenue N

For decades the Mercer Street underpass at Aurora Avenue N had barren and boring concrete walls. The City of Seattle commissioned California artist Catherine Wagner to liven things up with *Atmospheric Flurry,* two 120-foot sections of abstract, interactive electronic imagery created with forty-seven powder-coated panels that have integrated LED lighting. The sections are the north and south sides of the underpass and each consists of moving moiré patterns that were inspired by rainstorms. Wagner explains that the moiré patterning is designed to create the experience of the ever-changing weather patterns of Seattle.

9.25 ORIGAMI TESSELLATION 324.3.4 (FRACTURED), 2012

Ellen Sollod

Stainless steel; H 28 ft.
Seattle 1 Percent for Art Program
Mercer Street at Boren Avenue N

This gray column at the north edge of the South Lake Union business district is a tessellation, which is an arrangement of shapes placed side-by-side to produce a pattern without gaps. Artist Ellen Sollod chose this form because she wanted a technology-oriented work for this multifaceted neighborhood of biotech and technical research. The tessellation she selected is one used by engineers to study buckling patterns of cylinders, and the design began as a drawing, which was then scored and folded like origami, the Japanese art of folding paper into shapes. To add additional interest, Sollod incorporated interior white lighting to emphasize the folding patterns and the lines between the geometric shapes and included exterior blue and white lighting to illuminate the piece at night.

The numbers in the sculpture's title are those used in the title of the engineers' tessellation, and they refer to the specific folding pattern and the number of sides of each polygon. Sollod says that her tessellation also refers to an additional characteristic of the neighborhood. A pattern of individual parts that repeats

9.25 *Origami Tessellation 324.3.4 (Fractured),* Ellen Sollod

itself is a fractal, and she was inspired by the fact that fractal forms are seen throughout science, art, and nature. While her artwork relates principally to the highly technological space to the south, it also refers to natural features at South Lake Union Park to the north.

9.26 MERCER CORRIDOR STREETSCAPE ART, 2013–14

Ellen Sollod

Mixed media
Seattle 1 Percent for Art Program
Valley Street at Westlake and Fairview; Fairview Avenue and
  Mercer Street

9.26 *Lost in Thought,* Ellen Sollod

In addition to *Origami Tessellation 324.3.4 (Fractured)* (9.25), Ellen Sollod created three sidewalk features to help invigorate the pedestrian environment in the area north of her sculpture with the hope that some might pause for a moment and engage with streetscape art. At the west end of Valley Street at Westlake Avenue, she placed two black granite benches that relate to the history of nearby Lake Union. The designs of their curved sides were influenced by boat forms on the lake, and the rough-hewn ridges of stone that rise above the polished surfaces refer to the coal and lumber that was transported on the lake long ago.

Sollod used mosaic tiles to create *Lost in Thought*, which consists of three seven-foot-diameter sidewalk inserts that may engage some to contemplate the thoughts of characters depicted in each. The circle at Valley Street and Fairview Avenue features the silhouette of a man against a blue sky with a speech bubble containing a question mark. His thoughts are open to interpretation and completion by passersby. The same approach is taken with two mosaic circles at Valley Street and Westlake Avenue with a woman's silhouette in one and a dog and a cat in another.

Sollod's third design, located on metal hatch-covers at both the northwest and southwest corners of Fairview Avenue and Mercer Street is called *The Web*, and it features a large spider in its web. This work refers to the world-wide web, which has had such a tremendous impact on the rapid growth of technology and to the web of life that is the focus of so much of the work performed by people in South Lake Union biotech companies. The word *electric* on the cover refers to the interconnectedness of city's electrical grid and the fiber optic network.

9.27 JEWELBOATS, 2017

Jen Dixon

Glass mosaic, steel, and stamped concrete; dimensions
   variable
Seattle 1 Percent for Art Program
Westlake Cycle Track, Westlake Avenue N, southwest end of
   Lake Union

Jen Dixon's *Jewel Boats* is a three-part work that begins at the southwest corner of Lake Union and ends near the Aurora Bridge. Her design for each element was inspired by sparkling reflections off of Lake Union and her desire to bring that luminous nature ashore. Each also refers to the changing character of Lake Union over the years. The first part is *Glacial Canoes*, which stands at the south end of the Westlake Cycle Track just south of the Kenmore Air terminal. The track is a 1.25-mile path that extends along the west side of Lake Union from South Lake Union Park to Fremont. Dixon placed *Glacial Canoes* to serve as a bicycle gateway to the track and it refers to the Vashon Glacier that created Lake Union (and other regional bodies of

9.27 *Glacial Canoes*, Jennifer Dixon

water) more than sixteen thousand years ago. The swirling lines on the faceted blue sides of its two seven-and-a-half-foot tall elements are inspired by topographical maps and refer to the lake and its surroundings. The mirror mosaics that make up the flat faces of each section refer to sparkling water reflections.

At the foot of the Galer Street Bridge are *Stone Dinghy*, *Crystal Kayak*, and *Diamond Speedboat*. Dixon created this work with pedestrians in mind, and the boats are three multi-faceted inlaid stainless steel designs that are inspired by cut diamonds. They are inlaid along a forty-five-foot stretch of the path that includes thirty-three stainless steel rings inlaid with sparkling glass tile mosaics of multiple blue tones. Those sparkling bubbles relate to the embossed forms in the nearby concrete, which Dixon also designed. *Stone Dinghy*, *Crystal Kayak*, and *Diamond Speedboat* serve as

transitional pieces in which the stone dinghy refers to ancient canoes while the other two forms relate to contemporary times.

At the north end of the track, at the edge of Westlake Avenue N just south of the Aurora Bridge is another *Diamond Speedboat*, but this one is sixteen feet tall and consists of a multi-faceted frame of stainless steel that rests atop a bright blue post. It is the three-dimensional version of the designs in the Galer Street installation. With this aerodynamic shape at the edge of a busy street, Dixon focuses more on cars and speed. The form refers not only to fast cars and streamlined speedboats but also to overhead seaplanes that land on the lake and plane assembly at Boeing's Lake Union facility in the early 1900s.

9.28 BLANCHE, 2010

Peter Richards, with Sue Richards

Wood, steel, stainless steel, aluminum, and PVC pipe; H 12 ft. × W 20 ft. × L 30 ft.
Seattle 1 Percent for Art Program, 2000 Parks Levy
North end of South Lake Union Park

The name of this sculpture is derived from the Blanchard Junior Knockabout, a twenty-foot sailboat design built by the Blanchard Boat Company during its sixty years of operating on Lake Union. The sculpture's focal point is an upside-down hull of one of those vessels, which was provided by the nearby Center for Wooden Boats (where Knockabouts can still be rented to sail). The entire artwork consists of the boat, the float upon which it rests, and sound chambers created by PVC pipes through which the sound of lapping waves rises up into small listening ports on two of the columns. The boat hull is described as an acoustic chamber for water sounds, but whatever sound is audible can be heard only from the PVC pipes. It's best to put one's ear right next to a pipe to hear eerie vibrations that have been likened to Australian didgeridoo music.

Richards created *Blanche* to connect people to the surrounding environment and local history and he did so after researching the area in which it was to be placed. Boating is ever present on Lake Union and boatbuilding is an important part of the area's history. Looking up into the hull from the boat-shaped bench, you can see the craftsmanship of the hand-made boat. The outside of the hull and its keel are covered in stainless steel, a reference to a more technological era.

9.29 HONOR POLE, 2007

Noelle Demmert, Eric Robertson, Spencer Walker, Jess Isaacs, and Sean Hall, under the direction of Jon Rowan

Carved cedar; H 28 ft.
Center for Wooden Boats, 1010 Valley Street, next to South
  Lake Union Park

This twenty-eight-foot-high cedar totem pole was carved by students at Klawock High School, in the city of Klawock, on Prince of Wales Island in southeastern Alaska, under the guidance of master carver Jon Rowan, a Native arts teacher. It was a gift of the Tlingit people of the City of Klawock and the Klawock community in recognition of a gift in 2005 to that city of *Spirit of Peace*, a thirty-six-foot-long cedar canoe that was carved at the Center for Wooden Boats by Sáadúúts (pronounced sa-doots), the

9.28   *Blanche*, Peter Richards, with Sue Richards

Tsimshian-Haida artist in residence at the center, and his students.

Standing at the top of the pole are Eagle and Raven, prominent figures in Pacific Northwest Native culture and two principal crests of the Tlingit nation. They stand on a bentwood box that represents the box of knowledge. The box's design depicts Gonakadate, a wolf-like undersea monster who bestows wealth. The male figure below the box represents the boys of Klawock. He holds three coppers, shield-like symbols that were the ultimate sign of wealth and prestige in many Northwest Coast Native societies. Next in line is a female figure—with her pierced lower lip accentuated by a labret, a plug worn by noble women of the northern tribes—who holds a model of the *Spirit of Peace*. She represents the girls

Inside the Museum of History & Industry (MOHAI), are two important artworks, John Grade's monumental, sixty-five-foot-tall sculpture *Wawona*, created in 2012, and Kenneth Callahan's 1936 oil painting, *Engine Room*. MOHAI has an admission charge, but touring this highly regarded museum is well worth it.

Wawona, which hangs from the ceiling and extends to the museum's ground floor, is made of planks from the hull of a historic 1896 schooner. Its wood is stained by fish oils accumulated during decades of cod fishing in Alaska and by corroded iron used in its construction. The inspiration for the exterior of this eleven-thousand-pound sculpture is an old-growth Douglas fir and, similar to a hollowed-out tree, *Wawona* has two vertical sections, one inside the other. Its interior design recalls the inside of the schooner's hull. A small section of the sculpture extends underneath the museum and is visible through a window on the floor, while another sits on the roof. Those exterior elements will eventually weather away, offering a comparison between the effects of change and the efforts of preservation.

The wood protrusions and concave depressions extending up the sculpture refer to a type of phytoplankton that swirl in great masses just below and on the surface of the world's oceans. The masses diminish in length as they travel upward, which Grade likens to the movement of waves and the condensation of moisture as it rises to form clouds.

Callahan's painting, on the east wall of MOHAI's mezzanine level, depicts men tending to boilers, fittings, and valves in the engine room of a ship. It is one in a series of eleven paintings which were commissioned for the Marine Hospital (now Pacific Tower) on Beacon Hill under the Depression-era Works Progress Administration program. Seven others are on view in Pacific Tower at 1200 Twelfth Avenue.

Engine Room, Kenneth Callahan

Wawona, John Grade

of Klawock and stands on the curved tale of a killer whale, the second to the last figure. Killer whale is described on the accompanying plaque as "the most powerful being in the ocean which represents the ocean nations." The face at the bottom of this pole represents the people of Klawock.

9.30 FOUNTAIN, 1988

John Geise

Welded silicon bronze; H 7 ft. 6 in. × W 6 ft.
Private commission
901 Fairview Avenue N, in front of Chandler's Crabhouse
  restaurant

This untitled work is John Geise's fourteenth fountain, and although he had many issues in mind when he created it, the principal form is two hearts. He has described it as "a sensual piece about love, that pulsates with water." In the center is an umbrella of water that flares out and over the edges of the silicon bronze forms. Geise was raised in Seattle, and he thought an umbrella was an appropriate reference to this region. This fountain was commissioned by real estate developer Trace and Associates.

9.31 VESSEL, 2008

Ed Carpenter

Aluminum, stainless steel, glass, concrete; H. 60 ft. × Dia 39 ft.
Private commission
Fred Hutchinson Cancer Research Center, 1100 Fairview
  Avenue N (turn off Fairview at either Ward Street or Yale
  Avenue N)

9.31   *Vessel,* Ed Carpenter

Ed Carpenter's massive and intricate *Vessel* rises out of a landscaped circular island with its lattice work accentuated with strips of laminated dichroic glass and beveled clear glass that create a multicolored glow. Carpenter says that this "basket of light" represents the optimistic spirit and the dynamism of the world-renowned cancer research center. In addition, its interwoven structure represents the interconnected and collaborative nature of the center and refers to the optimistic nature of the many center staff members that he worked with in the years he created *Vessel.* Native plants were chosen to grow in, up, and around the structure to create a "lush sanctuary" filled with color from the sculpture and dappled sunlight shining through the vegetation. The visual experience will change not only as seasons change but also throughout the day as colors created by the sun through the glass create images on the ground, and shadows are created by the frame itself. In *Vessel*, Carpenter intends to suggest "a variety of dualistic metaphors: natural and technological, intuitive and rational, transparent and opaque, formal and informal." A group of anonymous donors gave *Vessel* to the research center.

On the edge of the traffic circle across from *Vessel* is a thirty-one-inch-tall bronze bust of Dr. Robert W. Day, created in 1999 by Oregon sculptor Robert W. Bane. Dr. Day was president and director of the research center from 1981 to 1997 and is credited with establishing the present research campus. From 1972 to 1982, he was the dean of the University of Washington School of Public Health and Community Medicine.

9.32 TUAREG SUN AND HOLDING THE INTANGIBLE

James Kelsey

Painted stainless steel

Private collection

Fred Hutchinson Cancer Research Center, 1100 Fairview Avenue N, stairs between Fairview and Eastlake Avenues, and 1100 Eastlake Avenue

Two sculptures by Seattle artist James Kelsey can be seen on the grounds of the Fred Hutchinson Cancer Research Center. On the stair landing between Fairview and Eastlake is *Tuareg Sun*, an eight-foot-high sculpture of three stacked and tilted stainless steel rings with their outside edges painted bright orange.

9.32   *Holding the Intangible*, James Kelsey

9.32   *Tuareg Sun*, James Kelsey

It was inspired by the Tuareg people, who are nomadic inhabitants of the Sahara Desert where Kelsey once traveled. He was taken by the fact that whatever buildings exist in the stark, desolate environments in which the Tuareg live are the same color as the surrounding sand. The harsh sun looming over all is referenced with the sculpture's color.

Up the hill at 1100 Eastlake Avenue is Kelsey's *Holding the Intangible*, in which a highly reflective stainless steel sphere is held by the ends of a curved painted and burnished steel swirl shape with its inside edge painted blue. With this six-and-a-half-foot-high sculpture Kelsey refers to the fact that scientists at the Fred Hutchinson Cancer Research Center are always "looking to grasp something that they can't see or hold onto. Something they may not even understand, yet through perseverance, creativity, and even failure they come to understand and discover the answers."

9.33   *Sheardraft*, Thomas Lindsey

9.33 SHEARDRAFT, 1995

Thomas Lindsey

Painted steel; H 12 ft. × L 26 ft.
*Funded by the City of Seattle Department of Neighborhoods
and private donors*
Intersection of Fairview and Eastlake Avenues

The late Thomas Lindsey, an artist and architect, said that his welded steel sculpture *Sheardraft* was influenced by both aircraft and shipbuilding and reflects the centuries-old legacy of water transportation and industry on Lake Union. The composition suggests the lines of a sailboat under construction with one hull laid bare to expose the long and graceful forms of a work in progress. A plaque adjacent to the sculpture shows naval architectural line drawings of a hull broadside, another hull perpendicular to the first, and below them a line drawing of a hull upside down. *Sheardraft* marks the southern gateway to the Eastlake community and its placement was the result of a five-year project undertaken by the Eastlake Community Council's Gateways Project, which involved a large collection of residents and business people in the community. Sculpture fabrication was provided at Lake Union Drydock, which has been located on Lake Union (just west of the sculpture) since 1919.

9.34 BY WATER ON LAND, 2013

Carolyn Law

Aluminum, steel, and stainless steel
Seattle and King County 1 Percent for Art programs
Fairview Avenue N and Eastlake Avenue E

9.34   *By Water on Land,* Carolyn Law

The close proximity of Carolyn Law's *By Water on Land* to Lake Union and the lake's long history of use by sailing vessels is symbolized by the seven white masts and shrouds at the top of the sculpture. Four of them move with the breeze. Rising up through the clutter of utility wires are recycled utility poles, which join other reused parts of an earlier work by Law that was placed south of this location but was removed because of a trolley system redesign. Law explains that this 2013 creation stands as if the components of the original have been swept north and combined with the newer elements to refer to the urban infrastructure and "to shifting light and oyster skies at the water's edge."

ARTIST BIOGRAPHIES

Adams, Alice (b. 1930)   Alice Adams was born in New York City and now resides in the Bronx, New York. She earned a BFA from Columbia University in 1953, after which she received a French Government Fellowship and a Fulbright Travel Grant and studied at the École Nationale d'Art Decoratif in Aubusson, France. She has since received numerous other grants and fellowships. Adams has exhibited her work primarily in New York, including several group showings at the Whitney Museum of American Art. Since 1977 much of her work has been devoted to sculpture for public places. (1.14)

Aitken, Doug (b. 1968)   Doug Aitken was born in Redondo Beach, California, and earned a BFA in 1991 from the Art Center College of Design in Pasadena. He has become internationally known for his innovative, often complex, art installations that use a variety of mediums, including photography, sculpture, architecture, sound installation, multichannel video installation, and performance. A few examples are *Mirror*, a permanent work at the Seattle Art Museum (6.14), his 2007 *Sleepwalkers* exhibition in which he covered the exterior walls of the Museum of Modern Art in New York with projections, and *Station to Station* a 2013 creation in which a train designed as a moving light sculpture traveled for three weeks from New York to San Francisco, stopping along the way to create happenings by artists and performers. Aitken has received several important awards for his work, and his creations have been featured at important museums in the United States and Europe. He currently lives and works in Los Angeles and New York.

Al-Dhaher, Sabah (b. 1967)   Sculptor and painter Sabah Al-Dhaher was born in Nasriyah, Iraq, and is a 1989 graduate of the Institute of Fine Arts in Basra, Iraq. He came to the United States in 1993 as a political refugee and now lives in Seattle, where he currently teaches stone carving at the Pratt Fine Arts Center. Al-Dhaher has exhibited his work in numerous solo and group exhibitions at venues in western Washington and has created public artwork for the cities of Puyallup and Longview, Washington. (8.6)

Anderson, Parks (b. 1942)   Parks Anderson was born in Seattle and was educated at the University of Washington, where he earned a BA in microbiology in 1966 and an MFA in sculpture in 1973. He has exhibited his sculpture throughout the region and has worked in a variety of sculptural mediums. In 1990 he created a large kinetic sculpture in downtown Seattle (5.15). His only other readily accessible public sculpture in Seattle is outside of Lakeside School. In addition to creating three-dimensional works, Anderson is a published photographer, and he has made biological models for use in hospital study and has illustrated a microbiology textbook.

Antonakos, Stephen (1926–2013)   Born in Greece, Stephen Antonakos's family moved to the United States in 1930, and he lived in this country for the rest of his life. He was known for his abstract sculptures and became one of the early artists who used neon as an art form. He began exhibiting neon sculpture in 1967, and

7.16 *Three Women* (detail), Akio Takamori

his works have been included in exhibits throughout the United States and Europe. In addition to his work at the Bagley Wright Theatre (8.22), Antonakos created many commissioned public sculptures throughout the United States, including a neon work at the Tacoma Dome in Tacoma, Washington.

Aschheim, Deborah (b. 1964) Boston native Deborah Aschheim is an American new media artist who lives and works in Pasadena, California. She is a graduate of Brown University (BA, anthropology and studio art, 1986) and the University of Washington (MFA, ceramic sculpture, 1990). Her innovative work often includes video sculptures that visualize memory, thought, and place. An example of that approach is *Periscope*, located in the South Lake Union neighborhood (9.6). Aschheim has created a number of commissioned public works in the United States, as well as installations for group and solo exhibitions across the United States and in Europe.

Askman, Tom (b. 1941) Tom Askman was born in Leadville, Colorado, and is a graduate of the California College of Arts and Crafts in Oakland, where he earned a BA in education in 1965 and a BFA in 1966. He received an MFA from the University of Colorado at Boulder in 1968. Since 1966 Askman has exhibited his work in numerous solo and group exhibitions in museums and galleries throughout the United States, including the Whitney Museum of American Art in New York. Askman has also spent considerable time teaching throughout his career and is currently an art professor at Eastern Washington University at Cheney. (See sidebar following 1.6)

Balazs, Harold (1928–2017) Born in Westlake, Ohio, Harold Balazs lived in and around Spokane, Washington, most of his life. He was a graduate of Washington State University (BA, 1951) and immediately after graduation began his life as a successful artist and craftsman. He worked in almost every sculptural material and completed numerous sculptures and architectural design commissions throughout the northwestern United States, focusing on abstract

sculptures and enamel on steel panels. Examples of both can be seen in downtown Seattle (4.3, 5.2, 5.14).

Beaumont, Linda (b. 1950) Linda Beaumont was born in Renton, Washington, and earned BFAs in painting (1972) and ceramics (1974) from the University of Washington. Her artistic mediums include painting, drawing, and sculpture, and her works have been shown in solo and group exhibitions in the Pacific Northwest since 1992. Beaumont is best known for her many installations in public places in the region, created in a variety of mediums including mosaic and photoprocess imagery (5.1, 9.4). Some have been created as part of an artistic team (1.27). When not pursuing such endeavors, she is a freelance window designer.

Bell, Bill (b. 1928) Bill Bell is a native of Pittsburgh, Pennsylvania, and resides in Brookline, Massachusetts. After earning a BA in physics from Princeton University in 1949, he served in the army and then worked as a computer engineer and later as an aircraft pilot. He is now a full-time creator of high-tech artworks. Two local examples of his public works include his collection of sequential light bars in Metro's University Street Station (6.11) and a 2015 installation at the Beacon Hill light rail tunnel. Bell has placed commissioned works and has exhibited throughout the United States and at several international locations.

Bender, James (b. 1951) James Bender was born in Summit, New Jersey, raised in Honolulu, and received his college education at the University of Puget Sound (1969–71) and the University of Washington (BFA, 1975). He began working in Northwest Coast Indian art at the University of Washington in 1975 and has studied under master carvers Bill Holm, Tony Hunt, and Duane Pasco. Bender's works have been exhibited primarily in the Pacific Northwest and are included in several prominent collections of Pacific Northwest Indian art. (6.21)

Ben Zvi, Gedalia (b. 1925) Born in Czechoslovakia, Gedalia Ben Zvi is an Israeli artist who in 1953 cofounded Ein Hod, a Jewish artists colony in the Carmel Mountains near Haifa. Largely self-taught, he studied art for a short time in Bratislava, but studies stopped after Nazi occupation and his imprisonment in a concentration camp from 1942 until his escape in 1945. He moved to Israel in 1948 and has lived in Ein Hod ever since, having taught painting and handicraft before devoting his time to his own art in 1965. Ben Zvi has exhibited in the United States as well as in Europe and Israel. *Fusion* is his only work in a Seattle public place (3.31).

Beyer, Richard (1925–2012) Richard Beyer was born in Washington, DC. He attended Columbia University (BA, English and history, 1950) and then received an MS in education from the Putney-Antioch School of Teacher Education in Vermont. He later returned to Columbia University and pursued graduate studies in economics, which he continued at the University of Washington after moving to Seattle in 1957. A former Boeing employee, in 1966 Beyer began devoting all of his time to sculpture and has many pieces in Seattle's public places as well as in other parts of the United State, although principally Washington, Oregon, and Alaska. Beyer's most famous work is *Waiting for the Interurban* in Seattle's Fremont neighborhood. (2.2, 6.20, 7.4)

Beyette, Pam (b. 1945) Pam Beyette was born in Stockton, California, and is a longtime Seattle-based artist and art planner. She graduated from the University of Washington in 1970 with a BFA in painting and printmaking. Beyette has created a number of site-specific public artworks, primarily in Washington State, and has participated in many collaborative design teams to create art in urban settings. She was a member of the team that created art for the Seattle Justice Center and the Municipal Court Building (5.11, 5.12).

Bishop, Jeffrey (b. 1949) Jeffrey Bishop was born in Berkeley, California, and received his BFA from Tufts University in 1973 and his MFA from the University of Washington in 1977. Bishop resided in Seattle for many years and was the subject of gallery exhibits in Seattle and elsewhere in the country. He now lives in Brooklyn, New York, and exhibits primarily in New York as well as in other East Coast venues. Bishop's paintings are included in many of the region's major collections. (6.3)

Bladen, Ronald (1918–88) Ronald Bladen was a native of Vancouver, British Columbia, who moved to the United States in 1939 and became an American citizen in 1956. He received his art education at both the Vancouver School of Art and the California School of Fine Arts in San Francisco. In 1960 he began exhibiting monumental minimalist sculptures and established himself as one of the important artists in that artistic style. Because of the size of his works, he received relatively few public commissions until the early 1980s. Seattle's *Black Lightning* (8.3) was the first of four commissions he received in 1981. In the later part of his career Bladen was a lecturer at several institutions, including Yale and the Parsons School of Design in New York City.

Blashfield, Jim (b. 1944) Jim Blashfield is known primarily as a filmmaker and media artist and has created award winning short films and music videos for notable musicians, including Talking Heads, Michael Jackson, Joni Mitchell, Paul Simon, and Peter Gabriel. His awards in that realm include a Grammy and several MTV Music Awards. Blashfield has also created several multi-image sculpture installations, the most recent of which is *Mechanism* in South Lake Union (9.10). Born in Seattle, he resides in Portland, Oregon, and reports that studies pertinent to his work occurred in the early 1970s at Portland State University's Center for the Moving Image.

Bornstein, Gloria (b.1937) Gloria Bornstein was born in the Bronx, New York, graduated in 1958 from Hunter College in New York City (BA, art and education), and studied printmaking with S. W. Hayter at his Atelier 17 studio in Paris in 1962. In 1976 she studied visual arts at the University of California, San Diego, and in 1979 earned a master's degree in psychology from Antioch University in Seattle. Bornstein has exhibited widely and has created a large collection of public works throughout Washington State as well as in New York and Tokyo. Bornstein has several works in Seattle public places.

Borofsky, Jonathan (b. 1942) Jonathan Borofsky was born in Boston, Massachusetts, and received his artistic education at Carnegie Mellon University (BFA, 1964), after which he studied at École de Fontainebleau in Paris. He earned an MFA from Yale in 1966. Borofsky has worked in a wide range of mediums, from sculpture and painting to video and installation art. He has exhibited his work throughout the United States and in Europe and Japan, and he is included in major private collections and museum collections, the latter including the Whitney Museum of American Art and the Museum of Modern Art in New York. Borofsky's *Hammering Man* (6.15) is one of his many large public installations that have been placed throughout the world.

Botero, Fernando (b. 1932) Born in Medellín, Colombia, Fernando Botero is an internationally known sculptor and painter who is largely self-taught through extensive personal studies in Paris, Barcelona, and Florence. He is known for depicting exaggerated, bloated figures of people, animals, and nature, first in paintings then also as a sculptor after he moved from Bogotá to Paris in 1973. Since the 1990s Botero sculptures have been collected, exhibited, and installed in public places throughout the world. His only work in a Seattle public place is *Adam* (4.8).

Bourgeois, Louise (1911–2010) Born in Paris, Louise Bourgeois began studying mathematics at the Sorbonne in 1932 but left the next year to study art at several schools, including the École des Beaux-Arts in Paris. After moving to New York in 1938, Bourgeois studied at the Art Students League. She began exhibiting in 1945 and was a prolific sculptor, painter, and printmaker whose abstract works focused on highly personal psychological themes, including pain, sexual desire, and the body. Bourgeois became prominent late in life and was one of

the rare women of her generation to establish an international reputation. In 1982 she was the subject of a major retrospective at the Museum of Modern Art in New York. Her only works in a Seattle public place are at the Olympic Sculpture Park (3.16, 3.17).

Brodax, Laura (b.1953) Detroit native Laura Brodax is a Seattle-based ceramic tile artist, photographer, and serigrapher who earned a BFA in ceramic art from the University of Washington in 1977. She is known for her photographic images transferred onto ceramic tile. Such works, along with architectural tile murals, have been placed in public and private collections throughout the Northwest and elsewhere on the West Coast. Three have been placed in downtown Seattle public places (1.17, sidebar following 1.21, 7.3).

Brooks, Richard (1865–1919) Sculptor Richard Brooks was born in Braintree, Massachusetts, and studied in Boston with T. H. Bartlett and in Paris with Jean-Paul Aubé and Jean-Antoine Injalbert at the Académie Colarossi. He had a notable career as a classical sculptor and exhibited in Paris, including an award-winning statue at the Paris Exposition of 1900. He also had an award-winning sculpture displayed at the 1901 Pan-American Exposition at Buffalo, New York. Brooks created major works in Washington, DC, as well as in Boston and Hartford, Connecticut. His statues of John Harte McGraw in downtown Seattle (6.24) and William Seward in Volunteer Park are his only works on the West Coast.

Brother, Beliz Seattle artist Beliz Brother earned a BFA from Prescott College in Prescott, Arizona. Her education included an apprenticeship with eminent photographer Frederick Sommer. Brother first began exhibiting her art in Seattle in 1986, and in addition to exhibiting her work, for over twenty years she has been involved in many public art installations and design team projects throughout the United States. Four of her commissioned works can be seen in downtown Seattle, three of which are at Seattle City Hall (1.26, 5.13).

Brown, Cecily (b. 1969) New York–based artist Cecily Brown was born in London and graduated from the Epsom School of Art in Surrey, England (B-TEC, art and design, 1987) and the Slade School of Art in London (BFA, 1993). Brown is highly regarded for her combination of abstract expressionism and figurative painting, the latter often incorporating erotic images described as explorations of sexuality from the feminine perspective. *Bring Me the Sunset in a Cup*, in the lobby of the Hyatt Regency Hotel (6.27), is a fine example of Brown's bold and animated brushwork. Cecily Brown has been the subject of solo exhibitions in prominent venues in the US and Europe, and her works have been collected by major museums, including the Museum of Modern Art, the Guggenheim, and the Whitney Museum of American Art in New York, Boston's Museum of Fine Arts, and the Tate Gallery in London.

Bruch, Cris (b. 1957) Cris Bruch is a native of Sugarcreek, Missouri, and a graduate of the University of Kansas (BFA, 1980) and the University of Wisconsin (MA, 1985; MFA, 1986). Bruch has spent his career in Seattle and has exhibited widely throughout the region as well as in Germany where he had art residencies in 1999 and 2001. His works are included in major public and private collections, as well as those of the Seattle, Tacoma, and Frye Art Museums, the University of Washington's Henry Gallery, and the Yale University Art Gallery. Bruch has several sculptures in Seattle public places, including *Universal Adaptor* in the South Lake Union neighborhood (7.17).

Burke, Leo (b. 1973) Seattle artist Leo Burke was born in Bury St. Edmonds, UK, and received a BFA from the University of Illinois at Urbana-Champaign in 1997, and an MFA from the University of Washington in 1999. He has exhibited his innovative artworks primarily in Washington and on the West Coast, and his works are included in the collections of the Seattle, Tacoma, and Frye Art Museums as well as the University of Washington's Henry Gallery. Burke has several commissioned works in Seattle public places, the most recent of which was commissioned for the new passenger ferry terminal on Seattle's waterfront ("Six Artworks Scheduled for Installation," chapter 2). Some sources refer to this artist as Leo Saul Burke, but he explains that using his full name was an agent's idea long ago. Burke is content to use only his first and last names.

Butterfield, Deborah (b. 1949) Sculptor Deborah Butterfield was born in San Diego and is a graduate of the University of California, Davis (BA, 1972; MFA, 1973). Her education included study with artists Manuel Neri (4.10) and Robert Arneson. Butterfield is well-known for her unique abstract sculptures of horses rendered in wood, bronze, and found materials, a fine example of which can be seen in downtown Seattle (6.25). Her works have been shown in solo and group gallery and museum exhibitions throughout the United States, and they are included in the collections of many major US museums, including the Smithsonian's Hirshhorn Sculpture Garden, the Metropolitan Museum of Art in New York, the Museum of Contemporary Art in Los Angeles, the H. M. de Young Museum in San Francisco, and the Seattle Art Museum. Butterfield lives and works in studios in Hawaii and Montana.

Calder, Alexander (1898–1976) Alexander Calder was born in Lawton (now part of Philadelphia), Pennsylvania. His mother was an accomplished painter, and his father and grandfather were both sculptors (his grandfather created the famous statue of William Penn on the top of Philadelphia's City Hall). In the early 1920s Calder studied at the Art Students League in New York with the group of American painters that became known as "The Eight" or the "Ashcan School." In 1926 Calder began his career as a sculptor in Paris by carving wood and creating wire structures resembling three-dimensional drawings. He was soon befriended by the avant-garde artists and writers of the time and came under the influence of artists such as Joan Miro, Piet Mondrian, and Naum Gabo. Calder's works are included in public spaces and museum collections throughout the world. His best-known creations are his kinetic mobile sculptures and his earthbound stabiles, an example of which is *Eagle* at the Olympic Sculpture Park (3.11).

Caldwell, Judith Judith Caldwell was born in Seattle and earned her BFA from the University of Washington in 1990. Since 1997 she has been creating art with her husband, Daniel, out of the Caldwell Sculpture Studio in Seattle. The duo has created fabricated metal artwork for private, public, and commercial projects, including many works in public places in Seattle and elsewhere in Washington State. Although the Caldwell team has no work in a downtown Seattle public place, an early work by Judith Caldwell can be seen on Western Avenue (3.24).

Callahan, Kenneth (1905–86) Kenneth Callahan was born in Spokane, Washington, and spent his youth in Glasgow, Montana. A self-taught artist, at the age of twenty-one he had his first one-man show in San Francisco and thereafter exhibited regularly until his death in Seattle in 1986. In the 1960s Callahan gained national recognition, with contemporaries Mark Tobey, Morris Graves, and Guy Anderson, as part of the art movement known as the Northwest School. His work has been included in exhibits and collections of many of the nation's most prominent museums, including the Metropolitan Museum of Art and the Guggenheim Museum in New York. During his long career, Callahan had visiting teaching posts and artist-in-residence positions at several American universities and museums. (6.18, sidebar following 9.27)

Cameron, Mindy Lehrman (b. 1955) Mindy Lehrman Cameron is an artist-architect and the principal at the Seattle-based Lehrman Cameron Studio, which she founded in 1988. A native of Newark, New Jersey, Cameron earned a BFA in painting from Boston University in 1977, then a master's of architecture from the Massachusetts Institute of Technology in 1982. Cameron describes herself as an artist who uses architecture as a medium for the expression of ideas, and she has worked with many architects to develop unique aspects of interior design, including

interpretive museum exhibits. A local example of her combination of art and architecture is the *August Wilson Way Portal* at the Seattle Center (8.21).

Carpenter, Ed (b. 1946) Portland-based artist Ed Carpenter was born in Los Angeles and is a 1971 graduate of the University of California, Berkeley. He subsequently studied architectural glass with Ludwig Schaffrath in Germany and Patrick Reyntiens in England. Since 1973 Carpenter has been creating large-scale commissioned sculpture and infrastructure design for public places, commercial locations, and churches. His works have been placed at locations throughout the United States, as well as in Taiwan and Japan. Ed Carpenter has two major works in downtown Seattle (7.13, 9.31), and he created the monumental screen and rose window at St. Mark's Cathedral on Capitol Hill.

Carpenter, James (b. 1948) James Carpenter is an American light artist and designer and a principal of James Carpenter Design Associates in New York City. His firm, which is recognized for its distinctive use of natural light, describes itself as one engaged in cross-disciplinary design that intersects art, engineering, and the built environment. An example of that approach is Carpenter's *Blue Glass Passage* at Seattle's City Hall (5.13). James Carpenter is a 1972 graduate of the Rhode Island School of Design (BFA, sculpture) and early in his career was a student of Dale Chihuly. Carpenter and his firm have earned numerous awards for their work. James Carpenter is also a 2004 MacArthur Foundation Fellow.

Cella, Lou (b.1963) Lou Cella is a sculptor known for his many depictions of prominent sport figures, primarily through his association with the Fine Art Studio of Rotblatt-Amrany in Highwood, Illinois. Cella was born in Chicago and graduated from Illinois State University in 1985 where he majored in fine arts and graphic design. He joined the studio ten years later. He has sculpted works on public display throughout the country, including the statue of Ken Griffey Jr. outside of Seattle's Safeco Field (1.27), the statue of longtime Mariner's sports announcer Dave Niehaus on the stadium's Main Concourse level, and the Don James statue at Husky Stadium.

Chase, Doris (1923–2008) Born in Seattle in 1923, Doris Chase studied architecture, and some interior design, at the University of Washington for two years. Although she studied under Jacob Elshin and Mark Tobey, Chase was by and large a self-taught artist. She began sculpting in 1960, and her first large sculptural commission was *Changing Form,* placed in Kerry Park on Queen Anne Hill in 1971 (see also 6.1, 8.2). Later in her career, Chase gained wide recognition for her work with video art. Paintings, sculpture, and video artworks by Doris Chase are included in private and museum collections throughout the region as well as in the Museum of Modern Art in New York, the Art Institute of Chicago, the Smithsonian American Art Museum, and the Pompidou in Paris.

Chew, Nancy See Metz & Chew

Chihuly, Dale (b. 1941) Dale Chihuly was born in Tacoma, Washington, and earned a BA in interior design from the University of Washington in 1965. Chihuly is a founder of the renowned Pilchuck Glass School in Stanwood, Washington, and he is a significant figure in the international studio glass movement, which underwent a resurgence in the 1970s. His artistic experimentation with glass began during his years at the university and continued with studies at the University of Wisconsin–Madison (MS, 1967) and then at the Rhode Island School of Design (MFA, 1968). Chihuly's career has included studies in Europe and teaching positions at various American institutions. He was an artist in residence at the Rhode Island School of Design and is past director of that school's sculpture department. Chihuly works have been exhibited throughout the United States and the rest of the world and are included in museum collections worldwide. He has several works in downtown Seattle public places (1.11, 6.3, 6.4) and his art is featured in Chihuly Garden at the Seattle Center.

Choi, Sung-ho (b. 1954) Born in Seoul, South Korea, Sung-ho Choi is a Korean American mixed-media artist. He earned a BFA from Hongik University in 1980 and an MFA degree from Pratt Institute in 1984. Choi has lived in the United States since 1981 and has been exhibiting his work, which often focuses on Korean American cultural issues. He is the founder of the SEORO Korean Cultural Network, a collective of Korean American artists. His only work in a Seattle public place is *Quiltroad* in the US Courthouse (7.13).

Cooper, Douglas (b. 1946) A native of White Plains, New York, Douglas Cooper is an architect and artist who, since 1976, has been a professor of architecture at Carnegie Mellon University, his alma mater (B Arch, 1970). Since 1990 Cooper has become increasingly well-known for his elaborate and detailed panoramic murals of cities. A large example, executed in charcoal and graphite, can be seen at the King County Courthouse (5.1). Cooper is the author of two books on drawing, *Steel Shadows* and *Drawing and Perceiving.*

Corson, Dan (b. 1964) Born in Glendale, California, Dan Corson received a BA in theatrical design from San Diego State University in 1986 and subsequently studied theater design in London for two years. In 1992 he earned an MFA in sculpture from the University of Washington and then spent three years at the Pilchuck Glass School studying glassblowing and neon fabrication. Corson has created a number of public artworks and has received much recognition for his individual creations and for collaborative work with architects and landscape architects. Two large Corson sculptures have been installed in Seattle public places (8.7, 9.19). Corson now lives in Hawaii.

D'Agostino, Fernanda Since 1986, Portland artist Fernanda D'Agostino has been exhibiting her art in solo exhibits, principally in Washington and Oregon, and in group exhibitions in the United States and internationally. D'Agostino has also created numerous commissioned public artworks in the western

United States, including *Bridge Between Cultures*, a 1999 work on the Weller Street pedestrian bridge in downtown Seattle, which she made in collaboration with Valerie Otani (1.25).

Davis, Michael (b. 1948) A native of Los Angeles, Michael Davis earned an MFA from California State University, Fullerton, in 1971. His work has been the subject of numerous solo exhibitions and included in group exhibitions, and he has created a wide variety of public artworks in cities throughout California as well as several major cities elsewhere in the United States. Davis was a member of the team that created art for the Municipal Court building and the Seattle Justice Center in downtown Seattle (5.11, 5.12).

Dimopoulos, Konstantin (b. 1954) Born in Port Said, Egypt, Konstantin Dimopoulos emigrated to Wellington, New Zealand, and then moved to the United States and now lives in New York City. He earned a BA in sociology from Victoria University in Wellington in 1976 and then studied at the Chelsea School of Art in London. Dimopoulos has created a number of multidisciplinary artworks and installations in the United States, Canada, Australia, and New Zealand that address issues relating to ecology and the human condition. His only work in a Seattle public place is *Red Stix* (1.28). In 2012 Dimopoulos created *The Blue Trees*, a temporary work in Seattle and Kenmore and part of a series of art installations around the world, in which he painted trunks of trees a vivid blue to draw attention to deforestation.

Dion, Mark (b. 1961) New York–based Mark Dion is an American conceptual artist who has been recognized for works that incorporate art and scientific presentations, one of the best-known examples of which his *Neukom Vivarium*, an installation in Olympic Sculpture Park (3.1). Other well-recognized public commissions have been installed on the Los Angeles waterfront and at Johns Hopkins University. Dion earned a BFA in 1986 from the University of Hartford. He is currently a mentor at Columbia University in New York and co-director of Mildred's Lane, a visual art education and residency program in Beach Lake, Pennsylvania.

di Suvero, Mark (b. 1933) Marco Polo "Mark" di Suvero was born in Shanghai, China, and lived in that country until his Italian family immigrated to the United States in 1941. Di Suvero is a 1957 graduate of the University of California, Berkeley (BA, philosophy), after earlier studies at San Francisco City College (1953–54) and the University of California, Santa Barbara (1954–55). He began creating sculptures while at the latter institution. In 1957 di Suvero moved to New York to pursue a career in sculpture and over the years established himself as a leading abstract expressionist. His early large outdoor sculptures incorporated such elements as used timbers and steel beams (3.10); however, he is best known for his steel sculptures (3.19). Mark di Suvero has received numerous important awards for his career achievements, including the Smithsonian Institution Archives of American Art Medal (2010) and the National Medal of Arts, awarded by President Barack Obama in 2010.

Dixon, Jen (b. 1958) Jen Dixon is a native of Roswell, New Mexico. In 1987 she earned a painting and drawing certificate from the Marchutz School in Aix-en-Provence, France, and then in 1991 earned a BFA in painting and drawing from the Minneapolis College of Art and Design. In 1997 she earned an MFA in sculpture from the University of Washington. Her art has been widely shown in group and solo exhibitions in Seattle, and she has created numerous works in Seattle's public places, the most recent of which is the three-part *JewelBoats* along the west side of Lake Union (9.27).

Dohna, Clare (b.1956) Clare Dohna is a Vashon Island–based artist who specializes in handmade custom tiles and mosaic art for external and interior applications. Born in Old Saybrook, Connecticut, she is a 1978 graduate of the Maryland Institute of Art (BFA, sculpture/ceramics). Early in her career Dohna sold her mosaic artworks in Seattle's Pike Place Market. In 2017 she created her largest work for the new wing of the market (6.20). She has also placed works in public places in Tacoma and Everett and on Vashon Island.

Drugan, Tom See Haddad/Drugan

DuPen, Everett (1912–2005) Born in San Francisco, Everett DuPen received much of his art education at the University of Southern California and at the Chouinard Art School in Los Angeles. He then earned a BFA from Yale University in 1937. Afterward he spent several years assisting sculptors in New York with works for the 1939 New York World's Fair. In 1945 DuPen became the chairman of the University of Washington Sculpture Department and remained at that post until 1980. Before retiring in 1982, DuPen headed the university's Division of Sculpture. One of Everett DuPen's largest works is his *Fountain of Creation* at the Seattle Center (8.19). He also created the large bronze fountain in front of the Washington State Library in Olympia. (See also sidebar following 4.10 and 5.14, 5.21)

Echelman, Janet (b. 1966) Born in Tampa, Florida, Janet Echelman is a 1987 graduate of Harvard University. She began her career as a painter but has become better known as a sculptor and fiber artist who has created large, lighted, aerial net sculptures that have been exhibited or permanently installed at locations around the world. Her unique creations respond to wind and elements in the environment and project a theme of interconnectedness. A typical example is her *Impatient Optimist*, which was commissioned for the Bill & Melinda Gates Foundation building in Seattle (8.31). In 2012 Echelman was named an *Architectural Digest* Innovator for "changing the very essence of urban spaces."

Edwards, Garth (b. 1950) A native of Stockton, California, Garth Edwards was raised in Portland, Oregon, and studied at the University of Oregon and Portland State University, as well as the Pilchuck Glass School in Stanwood, Washington. He is largely a self-taught artist and works in a variety of mediums, with emphasis on stained glass, enamel on steel, and cut steel. He used cut steel for his six-panel gate for the entrance to Metro's Pioneer Square Station (1.1) and for artwork at the Charlotte Martin Theatre at the Seattle Center (8.11). Edwards's works have been included in group exhibitions at the Smithsonian and the Museum of Arts and Design in New York, and he has several commissioned public works in the Pacific Northwest and Alaska. He is one of several artists who designed imaginative manhole covers that have been placed in downtown Seattle.

Eley, Eric (b. 1978) A native of Dubuque, Iowa, Eric Eley earned a BFA from Syracuse University in 1999 and then in 2005 earned an MFA from the University of Washington. Between degrees, Eley spent two years as an artist in residence at the Archie Bray Foundation for the Ceramic Arts. Since 1999 Ely's art has been the subject of several solo exhibitions and has been included in a number of group shows, primarily in Seattle and in Texas, as well as other locations in the United States and in Germany. He has created commissioned public artworks in Seattle (9.8) and Fort Worth and Austin, Texas. Eley has had a variety of teaching experience focusing on ceramics, sculpture, and three-dimensional design and, as of 2017, was on the faculty of Eastfield College in Mesquite, Texas.

Ericson, Kate (1955–95) A native of New York City, Kate Ericson earned a BFA from the Kansas City Art Institute (1978) and an MFA from the California Institute of the Arts (1982). She attended both of those institutions with fellow artist Mel Ziegler (who she later married) and worked and exhibited with him in the United States (including in a 1988 exhibit at the Museum of Modern Art in New York) and abroad from 1980 until her death in 1995. Ericson was one of the five original design team artists of the Metro Downtown Seattle Transit Project and was the lead artist for the Pioneer Square Station (1.1). Her *New York Times* obituary reported that the indoor and outdoor installations that she created with Ziegler were "noted for their beauty, complexity and social awareness."

Etrog, Sorel (1933–2014) Sorel Etrog was a well-known Canadian sculptor who was born in Laşi, Romania. After World War II, he and his family moved to Israel where he studied drawing, painting, sculpture, graphic design, and theater set design at the Tel Aviv Art Institute. In 1958 he won a scholarship that allowed him to study at the Brooklyn Museum of Art, after which he moved to Toronto and became a Canadian citizen in 1963. Etrog's works can be found in the collections of the National Gallery of Canada, the Museum of Modern Art and the Guggenheim Museum in New York, the Hirshhorn Museum and Sculpture Garden in Washington, DC, and the Tate Gallery in London, among others. His only work in a Seattle public place is in the Selig sculpture plaza (3.31).

Evans, Dennis (b. 1946) Dennis Evans was born in Yakima and graduated from the University of Washington (BS, chemistry, 1969; BFA, ceramics, 1973; MFA, design, 1975). Evans is highly regarded for his skillfully designed and constructed assemblages of found objects, antiquities, oil and encaustic paints, and a wide variety of other materials that delve into the relationship between language, science, and art. His scholarly artworks have been included in solo and group exhibitions throughout the United States. Museum collections that include his works include the Museum of Modern Art in New York and the art museums in Seattle, Tacoma, and Portland. Works by Evans can be seen in numerous public places in Seattle (6.3, 9.3), including two in each of Seattle's five Carnegie libraries.

Fajans, Michael (1947–2006) Michael Fajans was born in Philadelphia and in 1970 earned a BA in art and dance from Antioch College in Yellow Springs, Ohio. He subsequently taught art and dance at Antioch and then mural techniques at the University of Illinois before moving to Seattle in 1977, where he spent the rest of his career. Fajans preferred not to paint "for the enjoyment of only a select few" and most of his work was created for public display. He had numerous public art commissions in Ohio and Illinois and created murals throughout Washington

State beginning in 1975. In 1980 he began creating highly realistic, finely crafted paintings in airbrushed acrylics, an outstanding example of which is *Three Sets of Twelve* at the federal courthouse in Seattle (7.13).

Fay, Ming (b. 1943) Ming Fay is a Shanghai-born, New York–based sculptor and art professor who immigrated to the United States from Hong Kong in 1961 to study at the Columbus College of Art and Design. He subsequently studied at the Kansas City Institute of Art and in 1975 earned a graduate degree in sculpture at the University of California, Santa Barbara. He currently teaches sculpture at William Paterson University in Wayne, New Jersey. Fay is best known for his large sculptures and installations that focus on plants and other elements of nature as symbolic of Utopia, and on the relationship between people and nature. An example of his unique approach is *Pillar Arc* at the federal courthouse in downtown Seattle (7.12). Fay has exhibited his work in solo and group exhibits throughout the world, including the Whitney Museum of American Art at Phillip Morris, the National Academy Museum in New York, and the Museum of Contemporary Art in Shanghai.

Fernandes, Roger (b. 1951) Roger Fernandes is a Native American artist, storyteller, and educator who was born in Seattle. He has spent over twenty years engaging in teaching the art and culture of the Coast Salish tribes of the Puget Sound region. He is a member of the Lower Elwha S'Klallam Tribe, which is based in Port Angeles. Fernandes graduated from Evergreen State College in 1974 with a degree in Native American studies and in 2014 obtained a master's degree in whole systems design from Antioch University. Fernandes has also studied graphic design at the University of Washington. His sculpture *Snoqual/Moon the Transformer* is an example of the artist's combination of graphic art, sculpture, and cultural representation (3.28).

Fernández, Teresita (b. 1968) Brooklyn-based artist Teresita Fernández is a graduate of Florida International University (BFA, 1990) and Virginia Commonwealth University (MFA, 1992). She is known for her large-scale, site-specific public art installations, such as *Seattle Cloud Cover* at Seattle's Olympic Sculpture Park (3.15). Artworks by Fernández are included in many prominent collections and have been exhibited extensively both nationally and internationally, including exhibits at the Museum of Modern Art in New York, the San Francisco Museum of Modern Art, and the Smithsonian Museum of American Art, Washington, DC. Fernández is a 2005 MacArthur Foundation Fellow.

Finch, Spencer (b. 1962) Spencer Finch graduated from Hamilton College in 1985 with a BA in comparative literature and then earned an MFA in sculpture from the Rhode Island School of Design in 1989. He began exhibiting his art in 1988 and has since worked in a variety of mediums, often depicting natural affects through innovative reconstructions that sometimes also refer to literature and poetry (9.22). Finch has exhibited widely throughout the United States and internationally, and he created the only commissioned artwork for the National September 11 Memorial and Museum in New York City. Titled, *Trying to Remember the Color of the Sky on That September Morning*, it consists of 2,983 squares of paper, each of which he hand-painted in a unique shade of blue for every person killed in the September 11 attacks on the World Trade Center in 2001.

Fischer, R. M. (b. 1947) New York–based artist R. M. Fischer became well-known in the 1980s for his sleek, futuristic sculptures and anthropomorphic light sculptures. His exterior public works include several major commissions in Battery Park and the Holland Tunnel in New York City, as well as the Kansas City Convention Center. He has exhibited extensively, and museums that include his work in their collections include the Museum of Modern Art and the Whitney Museum of American Art in New York and the Dallas Museum of Fine Arts. Seattle's *Bell Harbor Beacon* is a largely forgotten work by R. M. Fischer (2.5).

Fitch, Claudia (b. 1952) Seattle artist Claudia Fitch was born in Palo Alto and is a graduate of the University of Washington (BFA, painting, 1975) and the Tyler School of Art in Philadelphia (MFA, 1979). She has exhibited her sculptures regularly in Seattle galleries as well as in group and solo exhibitions in New York and elsewhere in the United States. Her art is part of several museum collections, including those of the Seattle, Tacoma, and Portland Art Museums. As is true of her exhibited work, Fitch's many public commissions combine popular culture and art and local history. Two examples of that approach are her *Colossal Heads* at CenturyLink Field (1.26) and *Placeholders: Cloud, Rock, Tree* in the South Lake Union neighborhood (9.5).

FitzGerald, James (1910–73) A Seattle native, James FitzGerald was an active sculptor, painter, craftsman, and designer in the Pacific Northwest. He earned a degree in architecture from the University of Washington in 1935 and began his artistic career as a painter. In the late 1930s he worked in Kansas City as an assistant to Thomas Hart Benton. Afterward he taught at the University of Washington and served as director of the Spokane Arts Center. After World War II, FitzGerald focused on sculpture, and it is in that medium that he is best known. In addition to his works in Seattle (2.3, 5.21, 5.25, 8.26), James FitzGerald created the *Centennial Fountain* at Kirkland's Marina Park; *Rain Forest*, a fountain at Western Washington State University; and fountains at Princeton University and the US Courthouse in Ogden, Utah.

Fleming, John (b. 1956) Seattle-based artist-architect John Fleming graduated from Fort Lewis College in Durango, Colorado, in 1975 and studied ceramics at the Sun Valley Center for the Arts in 1977. In 1978 he earned a BFA in ceramics from Northern Arizona University, followed by a master's in architecture from the University of New Mexico in 1983. An architect who has been creating and exhibiting art, including art in public places, primarily in Washington and Colorado since 2002, he has two works in Seattle's downtown public places (6.20, 8.34).

Foster, Robert A native of Woodstock, New York, Robert Foster is a painter and sculptor based in Lake Oswego, Oregon. He primarily exhibits his work in Oregon and has created a few sculptures for public places, two of which are at the Mirabella Retirement Community (9.11).

Gardner, Ann (b. 1947) Born in Eugene, Oregon, Ann Gardner studied ceramics and painting at the University of Oregon and Portland State University from 1967 to 1974. In 1984 she studied under a residency at the Koehler Art Center in Sheboygan, Wisconsin. She is largely a self-taught artist who has exhibited her glass and ceramic work in Seattle, Portland, San Francisco, and other locations on the West Coast. Gardner has achieved considerable recognition for her glass mosaic works, several of which can be seen in Seattle downtown public places (2.6, 6.1, 6.25, 9.17).

Geise, John (b. 1936) Born in Wenatchee, Washington, John Geise is a self-taught artist who began his career as a sculptor in 1963. Before then, he spent five years as an apprentice architect with Seattle architect Stephen Richardson and what is now the NBBJ architectural firm. Earlier in his career he exhibited regularly in the Pacific Northwest and in Seattle. Geise has had commissioned works placed in Seattle and Bothell, Washington; Eugene, Oregon; and Anchorage, Alaska. (9.30)

Gerber, Georgia (b. 1955) Georgia Gerber was born in East Orange, New Jersey, and obtained her undergraduate education at Bucknell University in Lewisburg, Pennsylvania. She earned her MFA from the University of Washington in 1981. Gerber lives on Whidbey Island, where she creates bronze sculptures, primarily of animals, that are regularly exhibited and have been placed in many public places throughout the region. Several of her works are on display at the Woodland Park Zoo and at the University Village Shopping Center, to name a few. Her best-known work is *Rachel the Pig*, which has become the iconic symbol of Seattle's Pike Place Market (6.20).

Gilkey, Richard (1925–97) Richard Gilkey was born in Bellingham, Washington, and lived in the Northwest most of his life. Although always interested in drawing, he did not become an artist until after World War II, when he returned to Seattle and fell under the influence of Morris Graves, Mark Tobey, and Guy Anderson, major figures in what many refer to as the Northwest School. Largely self-taught, Gilkey traveled extensively throughout Europe to study paintings by the masters. In 1958 he was awarded a Guggenheim Fellowship and painted landscapes in Ireland for six months, followed by further travel and study in Europe. His work was exhibited widely and collected throughout the Northwest and was included in numerous exhibits of artists from this region. (6.1, 7.13)

Govedare, David (b. 1950) David Govedare is a long-time Spokane-area resident who created one of downtown Spokane's best-known sculptures, *The Joy of Running Together*, a 1985 work that shows forty figures jogging. A similar, much smaller work can be seen in downtown Seattle (3.25). In 1990 he created *Grandfather Cuts Loose the Ponies* which is an often-seen artwork of fifteen life-size horse galloping across a ridge above the Columbia River near Vantage, Washington. Govedare moved to Washington State in the early 1970s after studying architecture at California Polytechnic State University at San Luis Obispo. He is a self-taught artist who has been a full-time sculptor since 1975.

Grade, John (b. 1970) A native of Minneapolis, Seattle artist John Grade earned a BFA from the Pratt Institute in Brooklyn, New York, in 1992. Grade is primarily a sculptor whose works often arise from extensive research about the environments in which they were created or placed, or to which they relate, oftentimes including their gradual deterioration by natural forces. The recipient of numerous national and regional awards for his unique work, Grade has been described as an artist who explores sculpture as a presence both created and destroyed through landscape. His first permanent commissioned sculpture in a Seattle public place is *Wawona* at the Museum of History & Industry (MOHAI) (sidebar following 9.27).

Graham, Lois (b. 1930–2007) A native of Kewanee, Illinois, Lois Graham earned her BA from Knox College in 1952 and subsequently studied with Paul Burlin at Washington University in St. Louis. She also studied under Nathan Oliveira and Lothar Schall, followed in the late 1970s with master classes taught by abstract expressionist painter Jack Tworkov. Graham is regarded as one of the region's important abstract expressionist painters of her time. Her works were the subject of a retrospective exhibit in 1984 at the Bellevue Art Museum, and she exhibited throughout the Pacific Northwest and in Los Angeles, Chicago, and Houston. Her only work displayed in a Seattle public place is *Sargasso Stir* in Seattle's City Hall (5.13).

Greer, Mandy (b. 1973) Mandy Greer is a Seattle-based mixed-media installation and multidisciplinary artist who is best known for her distinctive, critically acclaimed fiber artworks, three of which can be seen in Seattle's downtown public library (5.21). Greer was born in Landstuhl, Germany, and is a 1996 graduate of the University of Georgia, where she earned a BA in English and a BFA in ceramics. In 1999 she earned an MFA in ceramics from the University of Washington. Mandy Greer has exhibited regularly in solo and group shows throughout the Pacific Northwest and elsewhere in the United States as well as in Europe.

Haddad/Drugan Haddad/Drugan is the Seattle-based studio composed of Laura Haddad and Tom Drugan, two artists who have collaborated together since 2001 in creating site-specific public artworks and art master plans for local governments. They have created artworks in a wide variety of mediums in cities throughout the United States as well as in Canada, the designs of which are inspired by the physical, functional, natural, social, and historical aspects of each site (3.21). Laura Haddad was born in Cambridge, Massachusetts, in 1966 and attended Bowdoin College (AB, history, 1988) and the University of California, Berkeley (master of landscape architecture, 1993). Tom Drugan was born in Biloxi, Mississippi, in 1964 and is a graduate of the University of Colorado (BA, architecture, 1986). In 1990 he earned a master's degree in landscape architecture from Harvard University.

Hamilton, Ann (b. 1956) Born in Lima, Ohio, Ann Hamilton earned a BFA in textile design from the University of Kansas in 1979 and in 1985 earned an MFA in sculpture from the Yale School of Art. She was on the faculty of the University of California, Santa Barbara, from 1985 to 1991 and since 2001 has taught at Ohio State University, where she is a distinguished professor in the Department of Art. She has exhibited extensively and has placed major commissioned works around the world. One of her important artworks is *LEW Wood Floor* at the downtown Seattle Public Library (5.21). Hamilton's art is included in the collections of many prominent American museums, as well as the Tate in London and museums in Japan and throughout Europe. Her many honors include a 1993 MacArthur Foundation Fellowship.

Hamrol, Lloyd (b. 1937) Lloyd Hamrol was born in San Francisco and earned his BA in art at the University of California, Los Angeles, in 1959, where he also earned his MA in 1963. The artist lives and works in Los Angeles and was for many years a professor of art at the University of California, San Diego. Hamrol has placed numerous public art pieces throughout the country, and his work is included in the collections of many museums, including the Los Angeles County Museum of Art and the Hirshhorn Museum and Sculpture Garden in Washington, DC. His only work in a Seattle public place is in downtown Seattle (7.4).

Han, Annie See Lead Pencil Studio

Haozous, Robert (b. 1943) Robert Haozous is a Chiricahua Apache (enrolled in the Fort Sill Apache

Tribe) artist who lives and works in Santa Fe, New Mexico. Born in Los Angeles, Haozous studied at Utah State University and later, after serving in the US Navy, attended the California College of Arts and Crafts in Oakland, where he earned a BFA in sculpture in 1971. Haozous is a multimedia artist whose primary focus is sculpture, especially monumental public works such as his *Earth Dialogue* at CenturyLink Field (1.26), which have political references that relate to his Apache heritage and the environment. His work has been exhibited and collected throughout the United States and in Europe.

Harrison, James (b. 1967) James Harrison is the Portland, Oregon, artist and designer who created the sculpture *Baladeuse* in the South Lake Union neighborhood (9.14). Harrison was born in Anaheim, California, and holds degrees from the Cooper Union (architecture, 1990), the University of Florida (BA, design/architecture, 1992), and Bennington College (BFA, sculpture and architecture, 1995). At the age of fifty, Harrison decided to change careers and he is now a practicing hypnotist in Portland.

Hassinger, Maren (b. 1947) Born in Los Angeles, Maren Hassinger is a graduate of Bennington College (BA, visual art, 1969) and the University of California, Los Angeles (MFA, fiber structure, 1973). For over forty years she has been exhibiting her art and creating public sculptures, primarily in Los Angeles and the greater New York City area. Hassinger has taught art at Hunter College in New York City and is currently the director of the Rinehart School of Sculpture at the Maryland Institute College of Art. She is also a recognized performance artist. In 1990 Maren Hassinger created tree grates for Metro's Pioneer Square Station (1.1).

Hayes, Randy (b. 1944) Randy Hayes was born in Jackson, Mississippi, and received his BFA degree from the Memphis Academy of Arts in 1968 and did postgraduate work at the University of Oregon in 1969. He moved to Seattle in 1976 and had a successful career that spanned more than thirty years

during which he was recognized as one of the foremost artists of his generation in Seattle. A typical example of his painting style can be seen at the Seattle Center (8.18). Hayes has regularly exhibited his work in Seattle and his works have been included in exhibits at the Los Angeles County Museum of Art and the New Museum of Contemporary Art in New York, among many others. Hayes has resided in Mississippi since 2013.

Heap of Birds, Edgar (Hock E Aye Vi) (b. 1954) Edgar Heap of Birds is an art educator and multidisciplinary artist who earned a BFA from the University of Kansas in 1976 and in 1979 earned an MFA from Temple University. From 1976 to 1977 he studied painting at the Royal College of Art in London. He is Southern Cheyenne, and his given Cheyenne name is Hock E Aye Vi, not "Hachivi" as some sources report. Works by Heap of Birds—which range from drawings and paintings, works in glass, and monumental enamel on steel sculpture—have been exhibited and installed throughout the United States and internationally, including at the Museum of Modern Art and the Whitney Museum of American Art in New York, the Smithsonian, and the National Gallery of Canada. *Day/Night* (1.4) is the artist's first permanent public artwork. Edgar Heap of Birds has been a faculty member at the University of Oklahoma for over twenty years.

Heishman, Jenny (b. 1971) Jenny Heishman was born in Gainesville, Florida, and graduated in 1995 from the University of Florida with a BS in geology and spent the following year in concentrated study at the Penland School of Crafts in Penland, North Carolina. In 1998 she earned her MFA from Ohio University. Heishman lives and works on Bainbridge Island, and her work has been included in solo and group exhibits principally in Seattle, but also in Nevada, Texas, and British Columbia. Her sculptures have been commissioned for public places in Seattle and King County, as well as two prominent works in the South Lake Union neighborhood (9.7, 9.20).

Heizer, Michael (b. 1944) Born in Berkeley, California, Michael Heizer is considered a leader of the school of art that uses nature itself, with little or no embellishment, as the medium for sculpture. In the early 1960s he studied painting at the San Francisco Art Institute, followed by a move to New York, where he continued to paint. In 1967 he directed his attention to earth-art sculptures, which were deep trenches, shallow cuts, and depressions in remote desert areas of Nevada. His reputation was based on such creations until 1976, when he broadened his sculptural subject matter to include works such as Seattle's *Adjacent, Against, Upon* (3.22). After creating that work, he gained many other commissions throughout the country, including, *Levitated Mass*, a 340-ton boulder installed in 2012 above a concrete trench outside of the Los Angeles County Museum of Art. Heizer lives and works in Nevada, where he is creating *City*, a monumental creation over a mile long, which he began in 1972.

Henry, John (b. 1943) Sculptor John Henry was born in Lexington, Kentucky, and is a graduate of the University of Chicago (BFA, 1969). Throughout his career Henry has produced a number of monumental welded-steel sculptures for public places in the United States as well as commissioned works in Germany and Korea. He creates his sculptures in his studio in Chattanooga, Tennessee. Henry is a professor of art at Chattanooga State College. His only work in the Pacific Northwest is *Songbird* in downtown Seattle (5.6).

Hepworth, Barbara (1903–75) Barbara Hepworth, a 1924 graduate of the Royal College of Art in London, is one of two English sculptors (with Henry Moore) and one of the few women of her generation who achieved an international reputation before World War II. She and her husband, British painter Ben Nicholson, were leaders of the abstract movement of the time. Hepworth was known for her abstract-organic sculptures, which arose from the influence of modernist sculptor Constantin Brancusi. Her career stretched across many decades, during which she became perhaps best known for "pierced" sculptures, a late example of which can be seen in the Selig sculpture plaza in Seattle (3.31). Hepworth was widely recognized for her achievements as a sculptor and in 1965 was made a Dame Commander of the Order of the British Empire by Queen Elizabeth II.

Hoge, John (b.1953) Seattle-based sculptor John Hoge was born in Manitowoc, Wisconsin, and in 1978 earned a BA in landscape architecture from the University of Wisconsin–Madison. Hoge has spent three decades creating sculpted stone installations, often including water features, that have been placed throughout the Puget Sound region for commercial and civic projects as well as residential gardens and estates. His two works in Seattle's downtown public places are the multipart *Cascadia* at the edge of the International District (1.16) and *Poetry Garden* at the Seattle Center (8.14). Hoge is now creating fewer large landscape-related works and is concentrating on smaller sculptures.

Horiuchi, Paul (1906–99) Born in Kawaguchi, Japan, Paul Horiuchi moved to the United States in 1922 and became an American citizen six years later. He moved to Seattle in 1946 and lived here for the rest of his life, establishing a unique and well-respected niche in Pacific Northwest art history. Horiuchi studied sumi-brush techniques as a youth and began painting watercolors in the early 1950s, but by 1956 he had become inspired by the beauty of outdoor posters in Seattle's International District that had been frayed by wind and rain. As a result, he began working with collages as his principal art medium. He was the subject of a one-man exhibition at the Seattle Art Museum two years later. Horiuchi's work has been exhibited and collected throughout the world. His many honors include an award of the Sacred Treasure Fourth Class from Emperor Hirohito of Japan in 1976. Works on paper by Horiuchi can be seen at the Washington State Convention Center (6.1), the Sheraton Hotel (6.3), and the Four Seasons Hotel (6.18). In 1962 he created his iconic *Seattle Mural* at the Seattle Center (8.9).

Howard, Perri (b. 1971) Perri Howard was born in Marblehead, Massachusetts. She is a graduate of the Evergreen State College (BA, 1994), the University of Washington (BFA, 1996), and Cranbrook Academy of Art (MFA, 2001). Her career has included work on location as a Fulbright Scholar in South India; Covas do Rio, Portugal; the Mamori region of Amazonia; and Civita di Bagnoregio, Italy. Now a resident of Twisp, Washington, Howard's work includes painting, drawing, sculpture, and sound, and she has worked on arts integration master planning for local governments. Howard has exhibited her works throughout western Washington, where she has also created numerous works of art for public places. Her 2009 installation, *Focus*, can be seen at the Seattle Center (8.16).

Ishii, Sonya (b. 1952) A native of Honolulu, Hawaii, Sonya Ishii received a BFA from the University of Oregon in 1978 and pursued graduate studies at the College of Architecture and Urban Planning at the University of Washington from 1981 through 1984. She has spent most of her career creating commissioned public artworks throughout the United States, much of it in collaboration with the artist Jim Hirschfield. Ishii was one of five artists who served on the design team for the Metro tunnel project in downtown Seattle and has designed some of the artwork for the International District Station (1.14). She resides in Chapel Hill, North Carolina.

Jensen, Steve (b. 1955) Seattle artist Steve Jensen graduated from the University of Washington in 1976 and in 1982 earned a BFA from the Cornish College of the Arts in Seattle. Although perhaps best known for his carved wood sculptures, Jensen creates both sculptures and paintings from wood, metal, glass, and found and recycled items, which are inspired by different cultures and influences from the natural environment. He has been exhibiting his work regularly since 1990 and has shown in solo and group exhibitions primarily in western Washington and Idaho but also in several other states and Canada. He has placed sculptures in public places throughout western Washington (7.15) as well as in Oregon, Colorado, Florida, China, and Japan.

Jones, Fay (b. 1936) A Seattle resident, Fay Jones was born in Boston, Massachusetts, and earned her BFA from the Rhode Island School of Design in 1957. Her unique style, an example of which can be seen in the Metro station at Westlake Mall (6.23), has earned her a considerable following in the Seattle area, where a great deal of her work is exhibited and collected. Her paintings were the subject of a retrospective exhibit at the Boise, Seattle, and Washington State University art museums, and have also been included in group and solo exhibitions elsewhere in Washington, as well as in Oregon and California.

Kahn, Ned (b. 1960) California artist Ned Kahn was born in New York City and is a graduate of the University of Connecticut (BA, environment studies, 1982). He is known for using elements of atmospheric physics, geology, astronomy, and fluid motion to create innovative artworks that allow viewers to interact and observe natural processes. In the 1980s, early in his career, Kahn received critical praise for creating such interactive sculptures at the Exploratorium Museum in San Francisco. Since then he has completed more than forty public art projects in the United States and throughout the world. Three Ned Kahn works in downtown Seattle provide viewers with ever-changing wind- or water-generated patterns (7.8, 8.24, 9.13). Kahn, a 2003 recipient of a MacArthur Foundation Fellowship, has said that he is not interested in creating an alternate reality with his art. He wants his art to capture "the mysteriousness of the world around us."

Keeler, Stuart (b.1973) Stuart Keeler is an artist, art curator, writer, and critic who was most recently chief curator and manager of museums for the City of Mississauga. Ontario. He is a graduate of the University of London (BFA, art history, 1989) and the School of the Art Institute of Chicago (MFA, 2005). Keeler is a studio and public artist who has placed works in public places in Seattle, Tacoma, Federal Way, and throughout the United States. He was a member of the art team that created *The Tempest* at

Safeco Field (1.27). Keeler is currently working on a PhD with an emphasis on community engagement and the role of the artist.

Kelly, Ellsworth (1923–2015) Ellsworth Kelly was an American painter, sculptor, and printmaker who is regarded as one of America's great twentieth-century abstract artists. He was born in Newburgh, New York, and grew up in northern New Jersey. He studied at the Pratt Institute in New York from 1941 to 1942, served in World War II, and then studied at the School of the Museum of Fine Arts in Boston (1946–47) and at the École Nationale Supérieure des Beaux-Arts in Paris (1948–49). During his studies and travels in and around Paris, Kelly developed his unique approach of combining forms and colors common in European abstract art with shapes from everyday observations, such as the space and shadows under an arched bridge (3.3). Kelly's distinctive style using solid shapes and bright colors doesn't fit into any artistic movement, but his approach is credited with influencing the development of hard-edge painting, pop art, Color Field painting, and minimalism. In 2013 President Barack Obama awarded Kelly the National Medal of Arts for artistic excellence.

Kelly, Lee (b. 1932) Lee Kelly was born in McCall, Idaho, and has lived and worked in Portland, Oregon, since 1945. He received his art education at Vanport College in that city (1949–51) and at the Portland Art Museum (1954–59). Although he has been a visiting professor of art at Reed College in Portland and an instructor at Mount Angel College in Mount Angel, Oregon, most of Kelly's career has been spent as a full-time sculptor. He has exhibited regularly in the Northwest and is one of the most widely represented artists in the region's public places. Kelly has also created sculptures in numerous locations in the United States. (6.5)

Kelsey, James (b. 1964) James Kelsey was born in Milwaukee, Wisconsin. He is largely a self-taught artist who began sculpting as a full-time occupation in 1998 when he started a two-year welding program at Olympic College in Bremerton. Kelsey has placed several works in public places in the Pacific Northwest, including two on the campus of the Fred Hutchinson Cancer Research Center (9.32). He lives in Centralia, Washington.

Kepner, Rita (b. 1944) Rita Kepner was born in Binghamton, New York, and in 1966 earned a BA in fine art at Harpur College of the State University of New York at Binghamton. A sculptor, she has exhibited and installed works in public spaces primarily in the Pacific Northwest, and also elsewhere in the US and Europe. In 1975, the year she served as a City of Seattle artist-in-residence, Kepner created *Human Forms in Balance*, the granite sculpture located in the Center Theatre at Seattle Center (8.13). Kepner had a successful career in management and communications with various US government agencies and is currently a reservist with the Federal Emergency Management Agency (FEMA), and helps people after catastrophic events.

Law, Carolyn (b. 1951) Carolyn Law was born in Morgantown, West Virginia, and earned her BA from Georgetown University in 1972. She spent the following year working extensively with intaglio and lithography at the metal plate lithography workshop at Kalamazoo Art Center in Kalamazoo, Michigan. Law then received an MFA from the University of Washington in 1974. A printmaker and sculptor, Law has exhibited in regional and national solo and group exhibits, and her works on paper are in many private and public collections. During her career she has been involved in creating commissioned art for public places, as well as creating local art plans and serving on design team projects for public art. Her most recent work in a Seattle public space is *By Water on Land* (9.34).

Lawrence, Jacob (1917–2000) Jacob Lawrence was born in Atlantic City, New Jersey. At the age of thirteen he moved to Harlem, which at that time was at its height as a thriving and culturally rich community. Throughout the 1930s he studied with many of the major black artists of the time, including Charles Alston at the Harlem Art Workshop,

Alston and Henry Bannarn at a WPA Harlem Art Workshop, and with Anton Refregier, Sol Wilson, Philip Reisman, and Eugene Moreley at the American Artists School. Lawrence is one of this country's leading African American artists. Some of his most acclaimed works focused on the struggles in African American history, including The Migration series, a group of sixty paintings chronicling the migration of blacks from the Deep South to the North. Some of those works were the subject of his first major solo exhibition, at the age of twenty-six, at the Museum of Modern Art in New York.

Lawrence taught at the Pratt Institute and the Art Students League in New York, and he was a highly regarded and influential professor of art at the University of Washington from 1971 until 1986, when he became professor emeritus. Works by Jacob Lawrence have been widely exhibited and are included in the collections of major museums around the world, including the Museum of Modern Art, the Whitney Museum of American Art, and the Metropolitan Museum of Art in New York; the Philadelphia Museum of Art; and the Philips Collection in Washington, DC. (6.1)

Lead Pencil Studio Lead Pencil Studio is the working name of the Seattle art and architecture collaborative founded in 1997 by Annie Han and Daniel Mihalyo in order to cooperatively pursue installation art, site-specific art, and functional architecture. Annie Han was born in Pusan, South Korea, in 1967 and is a naturalized US citizen. In 1993 she earned an accredited master's equivalent in architecture (five-year B Arch) from the University of Oregon and in 1993 studied sculpture for a year at Portland State University. Daniel Mihalyo was born in Bellevue, Washington, in 1970 and studied fine art at Western Washington University before attaining an accredited master's equivalent in architecture (five-year B Arch) from the University of Oregon in 1994. Han and Mihalyo have been widely praised for their unique approach to public art, which they describe as "everything about architecture with none of its function." Those qualities are evident in their works in Seattle public places (9.2, 9.9, 9.12, 9.15).

Legrady, George (b. 1950) George Legrady is a native of Budapest, Hungary, who moved to Canada as a youth and is dual Canadian-US citizen. During his undergraduate studies he became interested in photography as an art form and in 1973 graduated from Goddard College in Vermont with a degree in photography and visual anthropology. In 1976 he earned an MFA in photography from the San Francisco Art Institute, and in the early 1980s he worked with Harold Cohen, a pioneer of computer-generated art, at the University of California, San Diego. Legrady is an important figure in the medium of combining art and data processing into interactive media installations. One of his most significant works to date is *Making Visible the Invisible* at Seattle's Central Library (5.21). Installations by Legrady have been exhibited at important venues in North America, Europe, and Asia, including the National Gallery of Canada, Centre Pompidou in Paris, and the San Francisco Museum of Art. His work can be found in the collections of many museums, including the San Francisco Museum of Modern Art, the Whitney Museum of American Art in New York, the Smithsonian's American Art Museum, and the National Gallery of Canada. Legrady is currently professor of interactive media and the University of California, Santa Barbara.

Lentelli, Leo (1879–1961) A native of Bologna, Italy, Leo Lentelli studied art in Italy before immigrating to the United States in 1903. For fifty-two years he created a wide range of freestanding and architectural sculptures throughout the country. He is perhaps best known for his work in San Francisco and New York, beginning with sculptures at the Panama-Pacific International Exposition of 1914 and sculptural works created during his involvement in the artistic renewal that took place after the 1906 San Francisco earthquake. Lentelli spent most of his career working in New York, where he taught at the Art Students League and the Cooper Union, and created a wide range of sculpture in that city, including bas reliefs at Rockefeller Center and sculptures for the 1939 New York World's Fair. Commissioned memorial and commemorative plaques by Leo Lentelli can be seen throughout the country, including his D. E. Skinner bas relief in downtown Seattle (6.7).

Levine, Phillip (b. 1931) Born in Chicago, Phillip Levine attended the University of Colorado where he took art courses and then moved to New York where he pursued painting and sculpture. He moved to Seattle in 1959 and attended the University of Washington where he earned an MFA in 1961. Except for various temporary teaching and lecturing positions in the Pacific Northwest, he has devoted his career to sculpture and is known primarily for his figurative bronze works. Levine has many works in public places throughout the state, including a major work in downtown Seattle (3.29). One of his best-known works is *Dancer with a Flat Hat* at the University of Washington. Levine's artwork is included in many public and private collections, and his work has been exhibited in many individual and group shows throughout the United States.

Lewis, Alonzo Victor (1886–1946) Alonzo Victor Lewis was born in Logan, Utah. His artistic education began in Butte, Montana, where he studied for a short time with western artist E. S. Paxson. He later attended what is now the Art Institute of Chicago. Lewis came to Seattle in 1919 (after living and working as a sculptor in Tacoma) to work as an art lecturer for the University of Washington and to pursue his career as a sculptor. His first public commissions in Seattle were terra-cotta figures created in 1920 for Miller and Savery Halls at the university, where he also taught sculpture. Although Lewis became a well-known sculptor in this state, his reputation did not spread far beyond the Pacific Northwest. His best-known work in Seattle is *American Doughboy Bringing Home Victory* at Evergreen Washelli Cemetery. Another major Lewis sculpture in Washington is *Winged Victory Monument* (1938), the World War I memorial on the grounds of the state capitol in Olympia. After the latter was dedicated, the Washington State Legislature named him Washington Sculptor Laureate (6.7, 9.1).

Liberman, Alexander (1912–99) Alexander Liberman was born in Kiev, Russia. After the 1917 Russian Revolution, his family moved to England and then Paris. He was educated in Paris. In 1930 he graduated from the Sorbonne, where he studied philosophy and mathematics, and then he studied architecture at the École Spéciale d'Architecture (1931–32) and the École des Beaux-Arts (1932–33). Liberman was a recognized painter and photographer, but he is primarily known in the art world as a sculptor, with major works included in the Metropolitan Museum of Art, the Guggenheim, and the Tate Gallery. Liberman's principal career was in publishing, and for thirty-two years he held influential senior director positions at Condé Nast Publications in New York. His only public work in this region is *Olympic Iliad* at the Seattle Center (8.1).

Lindsey, Thomas (1942–2017) Artist and architect Thomas Lindsey earned a BFA from the Kansas City Art Institute in 1967, followed by a year of study at Carnegie Mellon University. After graduating, Lindsey worked at a number of jobs in construction, as a welder, and as a teacher and then began working for architects as a designer/draftsman. In 1994, after twelve years in the latter occupation, he became a licensed architect. Lindsey had several public artworks placed in Washington State as well as installations in Alaska, Japan, and Slovenia. His only work in a Seattle public place in *Sheardraft* (9.33).

Loomis, Charles M. (b. 1945) Charles Loomis is the founder and president of Kirkland-based Charles Loomis Lighting, which is known for its unique, high-end lighting designs. Loomis was born in Worcester, Massachusetts, but raised in Bellevue, Washington. After attending Central Washington University and Olympic College, he graduated from what is now the Art Institute of Seattle (BA 1966). Loomis founded his company in 1968 and has since created lighting designs and sculptures for a wide range of commercial, government, and private clients throughout the United States and internationally. (6.13)

Lyle, Nick. See Whitesavage & Lyle

Machnic, Michael (b. 1973) Michael Machnic earned a BA in architecture from Syracuse University in 1987. He was a member of the art team that created *The Tempest* at Safeco Field (1.27).

Mackie, Jack (b. 1946) One of Seattle's more active public (rather than studio) artists, Jack Mackie is a native of Princeton, New Jersey. In 1969, after studying sociology and psychology for three years at Western Washington University, Mackie left college and embarked on a career in art, much of it related to art in the urban environment. He has created commissioned artworks, served on art design teams, and written public art plans for communities and organizations around the country. Jack Mackie was one of the five artists on the design team for the Metro tunnel in downtown Seattle (6.23). Perhaps his most widely known work is his series of dance steps embedded in sidewalks along Broadway Avenue on Capitol Hill. His most recent work in a Seattle public place is *The Plaza* (1.12).

Mason, Alden (1919–2013) Alden Mason was born in Everett, Washington, and earned his MFA from the University of Washington in 1947. Mason is considered one of the region's important artists and exhibited regularly in the Pacific Northwest beginning in 1958 with a solo exhibition at the Seattle Art Museum. His paintings were also shown throughout the United States during a long and active career that extended well into his old age. In 1949 he joined the art faculty of the University of Washington and taught painting until retiring in 1981. He inspired and mentored a large number of artists, including Roger Shimomura, Gene Gentry McMahon, and Chuck Close. Mason's paintings are included in major West Coast private and museum collections, as well as in the collections of the San Francisco Museum of Modern Art and the Milwaukee Art Museum. There are several works by Alden Mason available for view in Seattle's downtown public places (5.3, 6.1, 6.3, 6.18).

Mason, Jimilu (b. 1930) A native of Las Cruces, New Mexico, Jimilu Mason grew up in Washington, DC, and earned a BFA from George Washington University, where she studied sculpture and fine arts. She has been a self-employed sculptor ever since. Her works are included in a wide variety of public and private collections. Mason has many works on display in Washington, DC, the best known of which may be the busts of President Lyndon Johnson in the US Senate, and Chief Justice Frederick M. Vinson in the US Supreme Court. Her only work in a Seattle public place is *Servant Christ* (7.14).

Mayer, Catherine (b. 1950) Seattle-based artist Catherine Mayer is a native of New Orleans and a graduate of Newcomb College Institute of Tulane University (BFA, 1972). For many years she has been creating commissioned paintings and murals for corporate and private clients and has shown her work in galleries both in the United States and internationally. She has also created sculptures, two of which are in downtown Seattle (3.30, 7.7).

McCracken, Philip (b. 1928) Philip McCracken was born in Bellingham, Washington, and has spent most of his life in the rural environment of nearby Guemes Island. He is a graduate of the University of Washington (BA, sculpture, 1954), where he studied under George Tsutakawa, Everett DuPen, and Charles Smith. In the summer of 1973, he worked as an assistant to noted British sculptor Henry Moore. McCracken has exhibited widely throughout the United States, primarily in New York and Seattle, and his work is included in many prominent private and museum collections, including the Whitney Museum of American Art in New York and the Phillips Collection in Washington, DC. Two of his sculptures can be seen in downtown Seattle public places (4.2, 4.4).

McDonnell, Joseph (b. 1936) A native of Detroit, Joseph McDonnell received his BA and MFA degrees in 1958 and 1959 from the University of Notre Dame, followed by studies at the Accademia di Belle Arti in Florence (1959–61) and a year studying design at Harvard University (1987). During his long career he has created more than 150 major commissions for institutions, corporations, and individuals, and he has exhibited and is included in collections throughout the United States and Europe. McDonnell resides in Seattle and has works in the downtown area (6.25) as well as major sculptures at the University of Washington and Seattle University.

McLain, Kelly (b. 1958) Kelly McLain was born in Carson City, Michigan, and in 1979 graduated from Rocky Mountain College in Billings, Montana (BA, art and philosophy). McLain lived in the Seattle area for many years and exhibited her work and created a number of public artworks (8.13). Her works are included in the collections of the City of Seattle and Washington State, among others. Due to health issues in 2006, McLain retired from being a professional artist. She now lives in Baldwin, Michigan.

McMahon, Gene Gentry (b. 1941) A native of Jacksonville, Florida, Gene Gentry McMahon earned a BA in English (1967) as well as a BFA (1976) and an MFA (1978) in painting from the University of Washington. Her paintings have been included regularly in group and individual exhibits in the Northwest since 1976 and have also been part of group exhibitions in several western states. McMahon's works are included in many private and public collections, including the Seattle and Bellevue Art Museums and the Henry Gallery at the University of Washington. She has created numerous works in public places, the best known of which is her grand mural at Metro's Westlake Station (6.23).

McMakin, Roy (b. 1956) Roy McMakin is a Seattle-based artist, designer, furniture maker, and architect who was born in Lander, Wyoming. After initial studies at the Museum Art School in Portland, he attended the University of California, San Diego (BA, 1979; MA, 1982). For many years he operated Domestic Furniture, a showroom in Los Angeles (now online) in which he produced furniture that has been described as bridging the gap between art and design. McMakin has been the subject of exhi-

bitions at the Museum of Contemporary Art in Los Angeles and the Portland Art Museum and in 2005 a twenty-year retrospective exhibit at the University of Washington's Henry Art Gallery. Two examples of McMakin's work can be seen at the Olympic Sculpture Park (3.12, 3.20).

Mee, Nancy (b.1951) Born in Oakland, California, Nancy Mee earned a BFA in printmaking from the University of Washington in 1974. She also studied for a year at Atelier 17, the Paris studio of S. W. Hayter, where she studied his technique of multicolored etching. Throughout the 1970s her career was centered on printmaking, and her work was included in numerous group exhibits in the Pacific Northwest, as well as exhibits in California, New York, and Philadelphia. In the 1980s, after a residency at the Pilchuck Glass School, Mee changed her focus to sculptures in which fused and slumped glass are the sole or principal medium. Her creations have gained her considerable recognition as an innovative artist, and her works are included in many public and private collections, nationally and internationally. She has a number of works in Seattle public places, (6.1, 6.3).

Meisel, Squeak (b. 1977) Born in Hays, Kansas, Squeak Meisel earned a BFA in sculpture and drawing from Kansas State University (2000) and an MFA in sculpture and installation from Washington State University in 2002. Since 2006 he has been an art professor at Washington State University. Meisel is principally known in the Pacific Northwest, but he has exhibited elsewhere in the United States. His unique sculpture *cloud haiku*, was placed in downtown Seattle in 2011 (7.11).

Mersky, Deborah (b. 1955) A native of Austin, Texas, Deborah Mersky is a mixed-media artist who lived in Seattle for many years and now lives in Johnson City, Texas. She is a graduate of Evergreen State College (BA, anthropology and art, 1980), and the University of Washington (MFA, painting, 1988). Since 1980 Mersky has been exhibiting her prints and collages in the Pacific Northwest, Texas, and elsewhere in the

United States. In those works, as well as her public works, she incorporates images, remnants, or references to the natural world. Since 1996 she has been creating glass, porcelain enamel, and metal artworks that are often incorporated into buildings. (8.15)

Metz & Chew Metz & Chew is the collaborative art practice of Jacqueline Metz and Nancy Chew in Vancouver British Columbia, through which the artists have been creating art, principally in the public realm, since 1997. Jacqueline Metz was born in 1960 in Dawson Creek, British Columbia, and is a graduate of the University of British Columbia (BA, 1982 economics; architecture degree 1989). Nancy Chew was born in Duncan, British Columbia, in 1962 and is also a graduate of the University of British Columbia (BA, fine arts, 1985; architecture degree, 1989). Metz and Chew have created a large collection of art in public places throughout western Canada, as well as in Washington and Oregon. They emphasize that a thread running through their body of work is a "meditation on landscape and culture." An example of that approach is their downtown Seattle sculpture, *bamboo, luminous* (1.9).

Mihalyo, Daniel See Lead Pencil Studio

Millett, Peter (b. 1949) Longtime Seattle resident Peter Millett was born in Evanston, Illinois. In 1971 he earned his BFA in sculpture from the Rhode Island School of Design and from 1973 to 1975 studied at the University of Washington. Millett has been exhibiting his highly regarded paintings and geometric sculptures on a regular basis since 1980, primarily in Seattle and elsewhere in Washington State, but also in California, Colorado, Idaho, and New Mexico. His works are included in the collections of the Museum of Modern Art in New York, San Francisco's Museum of Modern Art, the University of Washington's Henry Gallery, and the Seattle and Tacoma Art Museums, as well as a number of corporate art collections and the City of Seattle's collection. (5.16, 6.3)

Moore, Henry (1898–1986) Henry Moore studied at the Royal College of Art in London and eventually taught there in the 1920s. He first began exhibiting his sculpture in 1926, and by the mid-1930s had become an innovative leader of modern British sculpture. He also achieved considerable fame with his drawings, especially those of civilians living in London bomb shelters during the German bombardment of that city in 1940. From midcentury until his death in 1986, Henry Moore was the acknowledged dean of British sculpture and a prominent figure in the history of modern art. His many works are included in collections throughout the world. His only work in a Seattle public place is *Three-Piece Sculpture: Vertebrae* (5.18).

Morris, Carl A. (1911–93) Born in Yorba Linda, California, Carl Morris studied at the Chicago Art Institute and then in Paris and Vienna. He came to the Pacific Northwest during the Depression to open the Spokane Art Center. Although he spent most of his career in Portland, Oregon, his list of friends included Mark Rothko, Robert Motherwell, and Barnett Newman in New York and, closer to home, Guy Anderson, Clifford Still, and Mark Tobey. Morris was a leading abstract impressionist painter in the Pacific Northwest whose work was widely exhibited, including at the Whitney Museum of American Art and the Guggenheim Museum in New York City, the Art Institute of Chicago, and the Seattle Art Museum. His paintings are included in private and public collections throughout the region as well as those of the Denver Art Museum, the Metropolitan Museum of Art, and the San Francisco Museum of Modern Art. (6.13, 6.18)

Morris, Hilda (1911–91) Hilda Morris was born in New York and studied in New York City at both the Cooper Union School of Art and Architecture and the Art Students League. In the late 1930s she moved to Spokane, Washington, and worked at the Works Progress Administration Art Project at the Spokane Art Center. The project's director was painter Carl Morris, whom she later married. She moved to Portland, Oregon, with her husband in

1941 and lived there for the rest of her life. Hilda Morris exhibited both sculptures and paintings regularly throughout the West Coast, and her works are included in major West Coast collections. She has several large commissioned sculptures in Oregon, as well as one at the Memorial Art Galleries in Rochester, New York. One of her larger abstract expressionist sculptures is on display at the Washington State Convention Center (6.1, 6.18).

Morris, William (b. 1957) William Morris has achieved international recognition as an innovative sculptor of glass. He was born in Carmel, California, in 1957 and was educated at California State University, Chico, and at Central Washington University in Ellensburg. He took art classes in college, but his introduction to glass was at the Pilchuck Glass School where he began working as a driver. He later started working with the school's founder, Dale Chihuly, and eventually became his chief gaffer and then chief glassblower, a relationship that lasted almost a decade. Morris subsequently embarked on a solo career and for more than twenty-five years created a range of unique glass forms—inspired by ancient artifacts and cultures from around the world—that have been described as visually stunning and evocative. (6.4)

Works by William Morris are included in public and private collections throughout the United States and the world, including those of the Metropolitan Museum of Art in New York, the Musée des Arts Décoratifs in Paris, and the Victoria and Albert Museum in London. Morris retired in good health in 2007 and maintains an online gallery.

Murase, Robert (1938–2005) Robert Murase, a third-generation Japanese American, was born in San Francisco and graduated from the University of California, Berkeley, with a BA in landscape architecture. Before establishing his own landscape architecture firm in Portland in 1982, Murase apprenticed at the office of Robert Royston and Lawrence Halprin (5.26), practiced in Japan for almost ten years, and taught landscape architecture at the University of Oregon. His Portland-based firm, Murase Associates, specializes in urban design planning and landscape architecture services, and Murase was known internationally for his creative approach to landscape design. One of his most notable projects is *Garden of Remembrance* in downtown Seattle (6.12). Other well-known local projects are the Japanese-style Yao Garden addition to the Bellevue Botanical Garden and a large rock and water sculpture at Sea-Tac Airport.

Murch, Anna Valentina (1949–2014) Born in Scotland, Anna Murch grew up in London and graduated from the University of Leicester with an art degree and then in 1973 earned an MA in sculpture from the Royal College of Art in London. A year later she received a graduate degree from London's Responsive Environment Architectural Association. Murch came to the United States in 1976 and began teaching at the San Francisco Art Institute. She later had teaching positions at the University of California, Berkeley, and at Mills College, where she was widely admired by her students and colleagues. Murch was highly regarded for her ability to create art that turned public spaces into contemplative, multisensory oases, three examples of which are in Seattle public places (5.5, 6.10). Anna Murch also collaborated on a number of large public artworks in the United States with her husband, artist Douglas Hollis.

Nagasawa, Nobuho (b. 1960) A native of Japan, Nobuho Nagasawa studied at the State Academy of Fine Arts in the Netherlands and the Hochschule der Künste Berlin, where she received her MFA in 1986. She also attended the California Institute of the Arts in Valencia, California. She is based in New York City where, in addition to an active career as a conceptual artist, she is a professor at State University of New York Stony Brook. Nagasawa's work ranges from site-specific projects to gallery and museum installations that are often interactive and relate to the culture and other aspects of the greater environments in which they reside. In addition to her unique sculpture, *Water Weaving Light Cycle*, at

Seattle's City Hall (5.13), Nobuho Nagasawa has created commissioned works in major cities in California and elsewhere in the United States.

Nakamura, Stuart (b. 1953) Seattle artist Stuart Nakamura was born in Hawaii and is a graduate of the California College of the Arts (BFA, 1977). In college he focused on painting and drawing, which he continues to do, but his principal medium is public sculptures that arise from his studies of the cultural history, character, function, and purpose of their location. Two examples can be seen in downtown Seattle (1.9, 1.22). Nakamura has also created a number of artworks in other communities throughout Washington, as well as in several locations elsewhere in the country.

Neri, Manuel (b. 1930) Manuel Neri was born in Sanger, California, and studied at the California College of the Arts in Oakland and the San Francisco Art Institute. Early in his career Neri studied with prominent names in the Bay Area figurative movement such as Richard Diebenkorn, Elmer Bischoff, and Frank Lobdell. Neri is a painter and a printmaker, but his principal place in art history is as an important figurative sculptor. Since 1955 he has focused on expressionist renditions of the classical female figure (4.10), which in many cases are accented with surface paint. Sculptures by Manuel Neri are included in major art museums and collections throughout the United States.

Nevelson, Louise (1899–1988) Born in Kiev, Ukraine, Louise Nevelson began seriously studying art at the age of thirty-two when she took art classes at the Art Students League of New York. She later studied with artists Hans Hofmann and Chaim Gross. Nevelson first sold a work (to someone other than a friend) in her late forties. Ten years later she began experimenting with creating sculptures from discarded wooden objects found lying about. She called her creations "assemblages," and by the late 1950s she had successfully established herself as a major talent. Nevelson was one of relatively few internationally known woman artists of her time and was a major figure

in the history of modern sculpture. Her works are included in major museum and corporate collections throughout the world. *Sky Landscape* at the Olympic Sculpture Park (3.5) is her only work in a Seattle public place. Her 1973 sculpture, *Night Flight I*, is displayed at Sea-Tac Airport.

Nielsen, Max P. (1864–1917) During the ten years Max P. Nielsen resided in Seattle, he was an active and highly respected sculptor in the city. He came to the United States in 1905, arriving in New York from Copenhagen, and moved to Portland that same year to create plaster ornamentation on buildings at Portland's Lewis and Clark Centennial Exposition. He moved to Seattle in 1907 to perform similar work for Seattle's Alaska-Yukon-Pacific Exposition. Nielsen created a number of bronze portrait medallions and busts of local and national figures during his career (6.7). His 1915 *Sherwood Gillespie Memorial* at Jefferson Park Public Golf Course received wide local praise. His last significant creation was the 1916 bas relief plaque of Henry Yesler at the King County Courthouse (5.1).

Niemi, Ries (b. 1955) A Seattle native, Ries Niemi is a graduate of the Evergreen State College who describes himself as an "industrial artist." He has been creating metal sculptures since the late 1970s, and in 1979 he was a member of the artist-architect collaborative team that created artworks for Seattle City Light's Creston Nelson Substation in south Seattle. That unique project received national attention. Since then Niemi has shown his work in solo and group exhibitions and has created numerous public artworks throughout western Washington and elsewhere in the United States. One of his well-known creations is the collection of metal cut baseball figures on the exterior walls of Safeco Field (1.27).

Noguchi, Isamu (1904–88) Isamu Noguchi was born in Los Angeles of a Japanese father and an American mother, and his work was influenced by a combination of his parents' cultures and his cosmopolitan education. Between the ages of two and fourteen, he lived with his parents in Japan. He later studied at Columbia University and subsequently worked with American realist sculptor Gutzon Borglum (who carved Mount Rushmore). By 1927 Noguchi had moved to Paris, where he became the assistant to sculptor Constantin Brancusi and was exposed to that artist's contemporaries, notably Alberto Giacometti and Alexander Calder.

Noguchi returned to the United States in the 1930s and continued his artistic endeavors while earning income through furniture and product design. His reputation as an innovative sculptor grew dramatically from the late 1940s, and he was still actively working when he died in New York at the age of eighty-four. Many critics saluted him as the greatest American sculptor of the twentieth century. Two major Noguchi works can be seen in Seattle's public places: *Landscape of Time* in downtown Seattle (4.5) and *Black Sun* in Volunteer Park.

Okada, Frank (1931–2000) Frank Okada was born in Seattle and earned a BFA from the Cranbrook Academy of Art in Michigan in 1957. Following graduation he studied in New York on a John Hay Whitney Fellowship, in Japan on a Fulbright Fellowship, and in France on a Guggenheim Fellowship. Okada was a professor of art at the University of Oregon for many years and was regarded as an important abstract expressionist painter. He was principally known in the Pacific Northwest but exhibited regularly throughout the western United States and his paintings were included in group exhibitions elsewhere in this country and in France and Japan. An example of Okada's work is on display at the downtown Seattle Public Library (5.21).

Oldenburg, Claes (b. 1929) Claes Oldenburg was born in Stockholm, Sweden, but grew up in Chicago and became an American citizen in 1953. During his four years at Yale University (1946–50), he studied literature and art history. He subsequently took classes at the Art Institute of Chicago. In 1956 he moved to New York to pursue a career as an artist, and he has lived and worked there ever since. Oldenburg is considered one of this country's leading pop artists and achieved international fame for his large-scale outdoor sculptures of everyday objects, which have been placed in major urban areas and at important museums. Many of them were created in collaboration with his wife of thirty-two years, artist Coosje van Bruggen (1942–2009). A typical example of their work is *Typewriter Eraser, Scale X* at the Seattle Center (8.33).

Oliver, Marvin (b. 1947) Marvin Oliver is a Native American of Quinault and Isleta Pueblo heritage. He was born in Seattle and holds a BA from San Francisco State University (1970) and an MFA from the University of Washington (1973). He is currently professor of American Indian studies and art at the University of Washington and serves as adjunct curator of Contemporary Native American Art at the Burke Museum. Marvin Oliver has been a well-known and respected contemporary Native American artist in the Pacific Northwest for decades. His prints and sculptures are widely collected, and he has exhibited frequently in Seattle and New York. Oliver has created a number of monumental public artworks throughout the United States, and in Canada, Japan, and Italy. His public artworks in Seattle include his early totem pole in Steinbrueck Park (6.21).

Otani, Valerie (b. 1947) Valerie Otani was born in Berkeley, California, and is a 1968 graduate of Antioch College (BA, philosophy, 1968) and San Francisco State University (MA, creative, experimental, and interdisciplinary arts, 1983). She has focused her career on creating public art and public art master plans for cities and neighborhoods, including those in Seattle, Portland, and Vancouver, British Columbia. Otani is responsible for a number of commissioned public artworks in Seattle, Portland, Oakland, and Phoenix. In 1999 she and Fernanda D'Agostino created *Bridge Between Cultures* on the Weller Street pedestrian bridge in downtown Seattle (1.25). Otani is currently the supervisor of the public art program for the City of Hillsboro, California.

Otterness, Tom (b. 1952) Brooklyn-based sculptor Tom Otterness is a native of Wichita, Kansas. In 1970 he studied at the Art Students League in New York and in 1973 did an independent study program at the Whitney Museum of American Art. Otterness is known for his simple, cartoonish figural sculptures that often have political undertones that may allude to wealth, social class, and sex. He is best known for works in public places, which can be seen in dozens of locations in the United States and elsewhere in the world. Otterness sculptures are also included in the collections of the Museum of Modern Art, the Whitney Museum of American Art, the Guggenheim Museum, the Museo Tamayo in Mexico City, and the Israel Museum in Jerusalem, among others. His only work in a Seattle public place is *The Sculptor* (6.26).

Oursler, Tony (b. 1957) Tony Oursler was born in New York City and in 1979 earned a BFA from the California Institute for the Arts, in Valencia, California. The longtime New York resident has become a well-known multimedia and installation artist whose mediums include video, sculpture, performance, and painting. His most famous installations, an example of which is *Braincast* at Seattle's downtown public library (5.21), use videotaped moving faces that are eerily projected on heads, immobile bodies, walls, or floors.

Padelford, Morgan (1902–94) Morgan Padelford was born in Seattle and earned both his BA (1924) and his MFA (1925) from the University of Washington (where his father, Frederick, the namesake of the university's Padelford Hall, taught English for forty-one years and served as dean of the graduate school). Padelford's short career as an artist in Seattle was devoted to painting, primarily portraiture. He taught art for a few years at the University of Washington and moved to California where he spent the rest of his life. He taught at Scripps College in Claremont, California, from 1929 to 1935, then began a long career in Los Angeles as a color consultant in the motion picture industry. (4.1)

Paine, Roxy (b. 1966) Roxy Paine was born in New York City and was educated at both the Santa Fe University of Art and Design in New Mexico and the Pratt Institute in New York. He is known for his unique sculptures of stainless steel trees and other natural forms or environments, a typical example of which is *Split* at Seattle's Olympic Sculpture Park (3.2). In creating his industrial sculptures of organic forms, Paine refers to humankind's continual attempts to control nature. Paine's sculptures have been widely exhibited and collected throughout the world and are in the collections of major museums, including the Smithsonian's Hirshhorn Museum and Sculpture Garden, the Museum of Modern Art and the Whitney Museum of American Art in New York, the San Francisco Museum of Modern Art, and the Israel Museum in Jerusalem.

Pasco, Duane (b. 1932) Duane Pasco was born in Seattle but raised in Alaska, where he was heavily influenced by regional Native American art and culture. A resident of Poulsbo, Washington, he has been a full-time artist and teacher since 1966. In the late 1960s, before regional Native arts and culture had experienced their resurgence, Pasco began painting and carving in the traditional Pacific Northwest native 'Ksan style. Although not a Native American, he became a leading master artist and influential teacher of Native art and culture of the Northwest. He is also a speaker and teacher of Chinook Jargon.

Pasco has exhibited regularly since 1969, and his works are included in major private and public collections throughout the country. He has several large commissioned works in Seattle's downtown public places (1.5, 8.10). Commissioned works by Pasco can also be found in many locations throughout the United States and around the world.

Pepper, Beverly (b. 1924) Beverly Pepper was born in New York City. In 1942, at the age of eighteen, she earned her BA in advertising and design from the Pratt Institute in New York. Between 1946 and 1949 she studied at the Art Students League in New York City and then in Paris with André Lhote and Fernand Léger. A strong influence in her artistic approach was the work of Constantin Brancusi, who worked in Paris during her years there. Pepper was a painter from 1949 until 1960, when she turned to sculpture, which has been her predominant medium since.

Pepper has lived in Italy and New York since 1951 and exhibits regularly in Europe and the United States. She is regarded by many as one of the most important sculptors of the day, and her works have been included in major European and North American exhibitions as well as in museum collections on both continents and elsewhere. (3.6, 3.7, 4.6).

Peterson, Shaun (Qwalsius) (b. 1975) Shaun Peterson is a Native American of Puyallup and Tulalip tribal ancestry whose Native name is Qwalsius. He is a painter, printmaker, and sculptor who learned traditional styles and techniques of southern Coast Salish art by apprenticing with master Native artist Steve Brown and mentoring with Greg Colfax, George David, and Loren White. Peterson is an important figure in reviving Coast Salish art and culture. His work has ranged from traditional forms to more contemporary works combining wood with glass and metal. He is both a studio artist and a creator of public works, and his art has been exhibited in the Pacific Northwest as well as in New York, Europe, and Japan. Shaun Peterson has also created a number of commissioned works of art for public places. He is one of the artists commissioned to create a sculpture for Seattle's redeveloped waterfront ("Six Artworks Scheduled for Installation," chapter 2).

Petty, Ron (b.1939) Ron Petty was born in Casa Grande, Arizona, and received his formal artistic education at the Arizona State University School of Art from 1959 to 1961. During his career he has worked as a carpenter and sculptor in Alaska, the Pacific Northwest and the Southwest. Petty has created several works in Seattle's public places, the best known of which is *Seattle Fishermen's Memorial* at Fishermen's Terminal. He also created *Salmon Dance*, a quartet of fish sculptures in downtown Seattle (6.6).

Plensa, Jaume (b. 1955) Catalonian artist Jaume Plensa was born in Barcelona, where he continues to live and work. He studied art at the Escola de la Llotja and the Escola Superior de Belles Arts de Sant Jordi, both in Barcelona. Plensa has received wide recognition for his unique sculptures in public places that combine conventional sculptural materials with water, light, sound, and video and often incorporate text. In each he seeks to engage viewers and stimulate intellectual engagements. Many of his works deal with human communication, and two examples of that approach can be seen in Seattle (3.18, 9.23). Plensa has placed sculptures in public places throughout the world, including London, Nice, Tokyo, Dubai, and Chicago, and he has had solo exhibitions in the United States, Europe, and Asia.

Point, Susan (b. 1952) Susan Point is a Coast Salish artist raised on the Musqueam Reserve on Vancouver Island, British Columbia. She is primarily a self-taught artist, who has intensively studied Coast Salish art and design and has been hailed for bringing scholarly attention to Salish culture. Point is a leading figure in contemporary Coast Salish Art and, in addition to sculpture, is well-known for her paintings, prints, and silver and gold engraving. Susan Point has two works in Seattle's downtown public places (1.1, 1.26) as well as several important works in public places throughout British Columbia (including Vancouver's international airport and Stanley Park). Her works are also included in the Smithsonian's National Museum of the American Indian and in the University of British Columbia Museum of Anthropology.

Poirier, Anne and Patrick (b. 1942) Anne and Patrick Poirier were both born in 1942. She in Marseille; he in Nantes. They attended school together and have been creating art as a team ever since. From 1963 to 1966 they studied at the École Nationale Supérieure des Arts Décoratifs in Paris. After winning the Prix de Rome, they lived in Rome from 1969 to 1971 as fellows of the Académie de France à Rome. During their forty-plus-year career, the Poiriers have worked in photography, drawing, installation, and monumental public sculpture, which often delve into ancient civilizations and cultural memory and loss. Their works have been exhibited in and included in the collections of major museums in Europe and the United States. Their only work in a Seattle public place is the monumental *New Archetypes* in downtown Seattle (4.11).

Pridgeon, Jim (b. 1948) Seattle artist Jim Pridgeon was born in Nashville, Tennessee, and is a graduate of Stanford University (BA, English, 1970). Pridgeon has been involved in proposing and creating art for public places since 1982 and has created a number of commissioned works in western Washington. His art has also been exhibited at several venues, including the Seattle Art Museum, the Portland Center for the Visual Arts, and the Exploratorium in San Francisco. His only work in a downtown Seattle public place is *Angie's Umbrella* (7.1). Pridgeon is currently on the faculty of the University of Washington School of Medicine as a teaching associate in neurological surgery, where he also holds the title artist in residence.

Purcell, John Wallace (1901–74) Born in New Rochelle, New York, John Wallace Purcell spent most of his professional career in the Chicago area and was a sculptor, craftsperson, teacher, and writer who showed his works principally in the Chicago and Evanston, Illinois, area. He graduated from Cornell University and engaged in further study at the Art Institute of Chicago. He taught art at the art institute from 1925 to 1944 and then was an instructor at the Evanston Art Center (1944–46). Purcell exhibited his work from 1925 to 1946 and may have created the bronze bas relief plaque of John Hoge in downtown Seattle (6.7). After 1946 he pursued a career in the Chicago area as a child psychologist.

Radoczy, Maya (b. 1948) Seattle artist Maya Radoczy was born in New York. From 1974 to 1984 she studied glass art at a number of locations, including the New England School of Art and Design, the Pilchuck Glass School, Cornish College of the Arts, and Pratt Fine Arts Center. She also studied with noted glass artist Ludwig Schaffrath and spent a year as a studio apprentice at Bleidorn and Maurer, a stained-glass firm in Speyer, Germany. Since 1983 she has worked in her own studio in a wide range of glass mediums including stained glass, *dalle de verre*, and glass etching. In 1999 Radoczy created the three-part sculpture *Earth*, *Wind*, and *Fire* in downtown Seattle (1.11).

Ramsay, Heather (b. 1953) Born in Oak Park, Illinois, Heather Ramsay is a self-taught artist who has lived in Seattle since 1974. She has been exhibiting sculpture here since 1979 and has worked in a variety of sculptural mediums, much of it on a miniature scale (past works have included diminutive furniture and buildings). In addition to nonfunctional sculpture, Ramsay creates sculptural jewelry, boxes, and artistic clocks at her Seattle company, Ramsay Studio. Her largest clock to date is *Pendulum Clock*, located on Fifth Avenue and Pine Street (6.23).

Rauschenberg, Robert (1925–2008) A native of Port Arthur, Texas, Robert Rauschenberg is considered by many to be one of the most, if not the most, important painters in the creation of pop art. His artistic education included study at the Kansas City Art Institute and School of Design (1946–47), Académie Julian in Paris (1947), Black Mountain College in North Carolina (with Joseph Albers) (1948–49), and the Art Students League of New York (1949–51). In 1955 Rauschenberg established himself as a major innovative artist by exhibiting what he called *combine paintings*, in which he combined painting and various objects affixed to the canvas. At first they were simple collage elements, such as photographs, newspaper clippings, or prints. He later began using such items as clocks, spoked wheels, and a functioning wireless set. The extreme example was his 1959 work *Monogram*, in which Rauschenberg attached to a painted collage base a stuffed ram encircled by a car tire. His only work in a Seattle public place is *Echo* at Benaroya Hall (sidebar following 6.10). *Star Quarters*, his 1975 serigraph on mirror-coated Plexiglass, hangs at Sea-Tac Airport.

Richards, Peter Peter Richards is an Oakland, California–based sculptor known for his site-specific public artworks in which he seeks to engage viewers with the sights and sounds around them and provide spaces to think. He is a graduate of Colorado College (BA, art, 1966) and the Rinehart School of Sculpture in Baltimore (MFA, 1969). For more than forty years, Richards has been involved in public art installations and projects throughout the United States and in Europe and has been included in group exhibitions in Washington, California, and New York, as well as in Australia and Switzerland. An example of his approach to people-related public art is *Blanche* in South Lake Union Park (9.28).

Rickey, George (1907–2002) George Rickey was a leading American kinetic sculptor who began his artistic career as a painter. He was born in South Bend, Indiana, and earned a history degree at Oxford University, England, and then studied art in Paris at Académie L'Hote and Académie Moderne. Before World War II he taught art at a number of schools in the United States and maintained a studio in New York. After serving in World War II, Rickey studied at New York University and the Institute of Design in Chicago and then taught at a number of American colleges. In the 1950s, he changed his focus from painting and became a prominent creator of non-mechanized kinetic sculptures. Rickey sculptures are included in the collections of major museums, and his sculptures can be seen in public places throughout North America, Europe, and Asia. (3.8, 4.9)

Robertson, Eric (b. 1959) Eric Robertson was born in Vancouver, British Columbia, and is affiliated with the Métis/Gitksan First Nations of Canada. He graduated with a degree in three-dimensional studies from Emily Carr College of Art and Design in 1988 and earned an MFA from Concordia University in Montréal, Québec, in 1992. Robertson began his career working in the conventional Northwest Coast Native style but soon turned to more contemporary approaches. He has created a number of well-received public art commissions including one at the Vancouver International Airport and *Evolving Wing and the*

Gravity of Presence at Seattle City Hall (5.13).

Rudolph, Glenn (b. 1946) Glenn Rudolph graduated from the University of Washington in 1968 with a BFA in painting, but photography has been his medium for over forty years. His work focuses on people and scenes in Washington, and he has been exhibiting his photographs in group and solo exhibits since 1976, primarily in Washington, Oregon, and British Columbia. Rudolph's photos are included in the collections of the Museum of Modern Art in New York, Fort Worth's Amon Carter Museum of American Art, the Museum of Contemporary Photography in Chicago, and the Seattle Art Museum. Three Glenn Rudolph photographs, on etched granite, can be seen in downtown Seattle (5.4). He lives in Roslyn, Washington.

Ruffner, Ginny (b. 1952) Born in Atlanta, Georgia, Ginny Ruffner is a longtime resident of Seattle who is known for her skillful and innovative use of the flame, or lampwork, glass technique that involves the heating and fusing together of multiple glass elements. Ruffner is a graduate of the University of Georgia, where she received both a BFA (1974) and an MFA (1975) in drawing and painting. In the early 1980s, she moved to Seattle and taught at the Pilchuck Glass School. Ruffner has been exhibiting her work frequently since 1984, and her imaginative creations have been included in solo and group exhibitions at many museums, including the Corning Museum of Glass; the Los Angeles County Museum of Art; the Museum of Fine Arts, Boston; and the Museum of Glass in Tacoma. Her work is in the permanent collections of more than thirty-five museums, including the Metropolitan Museum of Art and the Cooper Hewitt, Smithsonian Design Museum, in New York, and the National Museum of American Art in Washington, DC. Ruffner's talents are not limited to glass. Her two major pieces of art in Seattle's downtown public places are metal sculptures (3.9, 6.2).

Sato, Norie (b. 1949) Seattle-based artist Norie Sato was born in Sendai, Japan, and came to the United

States at the age of four. She earned a BFA in print-making from the University of Michigan in 1971 and then moved to Seattle the next year and earned her MFA in printmaking and video art from the University of Washington in 1974. Sato focuses on both sculpture and two-dimensional art and works in a wide variety of mediums. She has achieved considerable recognition for her work as a manager and designer of and contributor to public art projects around the country, including sites in San Diego, San Francisco, Portland, Fort Worth, and for Sound Transit Light Rail stations in Seattle. Sato's most recent work will be seen on Seattle's redesigned waterfront ("Six Artworks Scheduled for Installation," chapter 2). (5.11, 5.12, and 6.4)

Norie Sato has exhibited her work in galleries and museums in many locations around the country, and her creations are included in the collections of the Solomon R. Guggenheim Museum in New York, the Brooklyn Museum, the Philadelphia Museum of Art, and the Seattle Art Museum, to name a few.

Schneider, Victor (c. 1866–1930) Victor Schneider was responsible for crafting terra-cotta architectural decorations on Seattle buildings constructed in the early part of the twentieth century. He created the Indian heads on the upper façade of the Cobb Building in downtown Seattle and similar heads around town that once adorned the White-Henry-Stuart Building (6.9). Schneider was reportedly born in Austria, where he received his artistic training. He came to Seattle by way of Chicago and other locations where building construction required his talents. He is said to have worked on buildings at San Francisco's 1915 Panama-Pacific International Exposition, including the elaborately decorated Palace of Fine Arts, which still stands in the city's Marina District. His other Seattle works are said to include terra-cotta designs on the Smith Tower, the Arctic Building, and the Coliseum Theater (now the Banana Republic store at Fifth Avenue and Pike Street.

Schuler, Melvin (1924–2012) A native Californian, Melvin Schuler graduated from the California College of Arts and Crafts and in 1947 began a long teaching career at Humboldt State University, where he was an emeritus professor when he died. Schuler was known for his large sculptures using old-growth redwood carved into abstract forms and then covered in copper cladding fastened with bronze nails. A typical example stands across from Seattle's waterfront (2.4). Works by Melvin Schuler are in the collections of several museums, including the Hirshhorn Museum in Washington, DC, and Storm King Art Center in New Windsor, New York.

Schwartz, Martha (b. 1950) Landscape architect Martha Schwartz was born in Philadelphia and earned a BFA (1973) and then a master's degree in landscape architecture (1976) from the University of Michigan. In 1977 she studied landscape architecture at the Harvard University Graduate School of Design, where she is now a professor of landscape architecture. Schwartz is highly regarded for her creative combinations of landscape, art, and architecture, a fine example of which is *Jail House Garden* in downtown Seattle (5.9). Her designs have been featured widely in publications as well as in gallery exhibitions throughout the United States and internationally. In 1986 Schwartz founded Martha Schwartz Partners, a well-known international design firm that focuses on activating and regenerating urban sites and city centers.

Schwendinger, Leni For over twenty years New York–based lighting designer Leni Schwendinger has focused on light as an artistic medium in the urban environment. She studied film, narratives images, and storytelling at the London Film School from 1973 to 1975 before becoming a lighting artist and designer and founder of Leni Schwendinger Light Projects. She is now a creative director with Arup, a global engineering firm. Schwendinger leads that firm's lighting design network, which "aims to raise awareness of light, and shadow, for nighttime environments in cities worldwide, as well as to provide an overview of lighting theory to the general public and design professionals alike." Leni Schwendinger has worked on many significant projects in this country and internationally, including *Dreaming in Color* at the Seattle Center (8.29).

Scuri, Vicki (b. 1953) Born in Santa Rosa, California, Vicki Scuri is a Seattle artist who earned a BA from the University of California, Berkeley, in 1975. In 1977 she studied in Paris at the Atelier 17 under master printer S. W. Hayter, and in 1980 she earned an MFA in printmaking from the University of Wisconsin. She is widely recognized for her innovative creations that turn elements of urban infrastructure (such as building walls and highway overpasses) into artworks of cut metal or cast concrete, often supplemented with LED lighting. Early works by Vicki Scuri include her graphic designs for Metro's University and Westlake tunnel stations (6.11, 6.23). Her *Sail Light Armatures* and *DNA Wave Patterns* on the West Galer Street overpass at Elliott Way are later examples of her approach to public art.

Serra, Richard (b. 1938) A San Francisco native, Richard Serra studied art at the University of California, Santa Barbara (BA, 1961), and then studied painting in the MFA program at Yale University between 1961 and 1964. During his years in California he helped support himself by working in steel mills, thus creating experiences that would impact his future works. Although well regarded for the large-scale drawings he has created throughout this career, Serra is best known for the site-specific sculptures of welded weathered steel that he began creating in the 1970s. Those monumental works, which have been placed around the world, include *Wake*, a 2004 sculpture at Seattle's Olympic Sculpture Park (3.4). The *New York Times* has described Richard Serra as the "greatest living sculptor of Minimalist abstraction." His work has been exhibited in numerous solo exhibitions at major museums in the United States and Europe, and in 2007 he was the subject of a major retrospective exhibit at the Museum of Modern Art in New York.

Shaw, Benson (b. 1950) A native of Columbia, Missouri, Benson Shaw is a 1972 graduate of Colorado College in Colorado Springs, where he earned a degree in physics. In 1976 he earned an MA in fine art from the University of New Mexico in Albuquerque. Shaw has created many works in public places in Seattle, as well as in Washington State and Arizona. He has exhibited in the western United States and has works in collections in Denver, Colorado Springs, and Seattle. Shaw has created or co-created a number of artworks in Seattle's public places, including two in Seattle's downtown area (5.8, 7.1).

Shelton, Peter (b. 1951) Born in Troy, Ohio, Peter Shelton earned a BA in fine art from Pomona College in 1973. In 1974 he earned a trade certificate in welding from the Hobart School of Welding Technology in Troy, Ohio, and in 1979 he earned an MFA from the University of California, Los Angeles. Shelton is a postminimalist sculptor who works in a wide variety of sculptural mediums and textures that explore viewers' assumptions about their surroundings and experiences. He has exhibited extensively in the United States and in Europe and his artworks are included in major American museums, including New York's Museum of Modern Art, the Smithsonian's American Art Museum, the Getty Museum in Los Angeles, and the Walker Art Center in Minneapolis. Sculptures by Peter Shelton have been placed in several public places in the United States, including *ROCKshadow* in downtown Seattle (1.26) and *cloudsandclunkers* at Sea-Tac Airport. Shelton has lived and worked in Los Angeles since 1975.

Shimomura, Roger (b. 1939) Roger Shimomura was born in Seattle and holds a BA from the University of Washington (1961) and an MFA in painting from Syracuse University (1969). Shimomura is known for his combinations of pop art symbols, images from traditional Japanese ukiyo-e woodblock prints, and comic book characters that often focus on stereotyping and racism in America (6.23). His themes are often influenced by the fact that between the ages of two and five, he and his family lived at the Minidoka internment camp (in Idaho), when Japanese Americans were forced to relocate to prison camps during the United States' involvement in World War II. Since 1965 Shimomura has exhibited his paintings and prints in numerous individual and group exhibitions throughout the country, and his art is included in important museum collections throughout the United States. Roger Shimomura was a highly regarded professor of art at the University of Kansas from 1969 until his retirement in 2004. He continues to live and work in Lawrence, Kansas. (See also 1.10)

Sildar, William (1929–2006) William Sildar is a largely forgotten artist who spent a portion of his career in the Pacific Northwest. He was a sculptor whose principal mediums were wood and stone. In the 1960s the New York native was one of the many artists associated with a collection of avant-garde galleries in New York City's Lower East Side that were known as the Tenth Street Galleries. His work was shown at the Brata Gallery, which was cofounded by Ronald Bladen (8.3). Sildar was the City of Seattle's artist in residence 1975 when he created *Queue VI*, which can be seen inside the Center House at the Seattle Center (8.13).

Simpson, Lewis "Buster" (b. 1942) Buster Simpson was born in Saginaw, Michigan, and graduated from the University of Michigan, where he earned a BA in design (1963) and an MFA in sculpture (1969). A Seattle resident, he has been creating art in the Pacific Northwest since 1975 and has had works included in exhibitions throughout the country, as well as in Canada and England. Simpson has created public sculptures throughout the Pacific Northwest and in locations in California and Canada, to name a few. His varied career has also included working as a director, consultant, and designer for public art projects and workshops in the United States. Works by Buster Simpson are included in the collections of the Seattle and Tacoma Art Museums, the University of Washington's Henry Gallery, and the Corning Museum of Glass and have been placed in public places throughout downtown Seattle ("Six Artworks Scheduled for Installation," chapter 2 and 6.1, 6.17, 7.5, 7.6, 9.18).

Sindell, Laura (b. 1947) Seattle artist Laura Sindell has been exhibiting her art and creating public artworks, primarily in the Pacific Northwest, since the early 1980s. She has also had a long career teaching art throughout the region as well as in British Columbia and North Carolina. A native of Cleveland, Ohio, Sindell earned a BFA in ceramics from the Rhode Island School of Design in 1975. Her only work in a Seattle public place is *Sounding Wall* in the Pioneer Square Metro Station (1.1).

Skibska, Anna (b. 1959) A native of Wrocław, Poland, Anna Skibska has lived in Seattle since 1996. She initially trained as an architect and then in 1984 earned a degree in painting, glass design, and graphic arts from the Academy of Art in Wrocław, where she spent eleven years teaching fine arts and architecture. She has since taught at the Pratt Fine Arts Center and the Pilchuck Glass School. Skibska has spent over twenty years exhibiting her work and has been included in solo and group exhibitions in this country as well as in Poland, France, Italy, and Switzerland. Skibska was also the subject of a 2001 exhibit at the Seattle Art Museum (5.14).

Smith, Austin (b. 1977) Sculptor and painter Austin Smith grew up and lives in Ellensburg, Washington. He studied painting, sculpture, and music at Central Washington University (BFA 2003) and subsequently he spent fourteen months immersing himself in the self-study of art and music in Santa Fe, New Mexico. To date, the majority of his public work has been installed in Ellensburg, Washington, and environs. He has two sculptures in Seattle public places (3.27, 8.20).

Smith, Mara (b. 1945) Mara Smith is a native of Houston, Texas, and first came to in Seattle in 1984 to carve the brick murals on the CenturyLink building on Second Avenue and Lenora Street (7.2). She earned her BA in 1968 and her MFA in 1980 from Texas Women's University in Denton, Texas, and from 1969 to 1975 she was a crafts instructor at the University of Florida in Gainesville. Smith has been carving wet brick sculpture since 1977 and is one of the most widely known brick artists in the nation. She has created over 125 murals throughout the United States.

Smith, Tony (1912–80) Born in South Orange, New Jersey, Tony Smith was first educated as an architect. In the late 1930s he studied at the New Bauhaus in Chicago and then worked in various capacities on several Frank Lloyd Wright projects. After embarking on an artistic career, Smith became known in the art world as a teacher and intellectual rather than as a practicing artist. However, in 1960 he began devoting his time to sculpture and created his first metal sculpture two years later, when he was fifty. Smith soon became a leader (some critics say the leader) in minimal art, and he is considered one of America's major modern sculptors.

Sogabe, Aki (b. 1945) Aki Sogabe is a Bellevue, Washington, artist known both for her paper artworks and for her award-winning children's book illustrations. Born in Mishima, Japan, Sogabe studied design and illustration at the Japan Art Institute, a vocational school in Tokyo. In 1978 she began showing her works in the Japanese art of *kiri-e* paper cutting in which designs are created by means of a precise and delicate cutting technique. Sogabe's work at the Pike Place Market is a *kiri-e* design rendered in porcelain enamel (6.20). Her *Dragon Tower* in the International District is a rendition of the technique in metal sculpture (1.24). Works by Aki Sogabe are included in public and private collections throughout the region.

Sollod, Ellen (b. 1951) Seattle-based artist Ellen Sollod was born in Rockville Center, New York, and raised in South Carolina. She is a graduate of the University of North Carolina at Chapel Hill (BA, art history, 1972) and the University of Maryland's Institute for Urban Studies (MA, 1975). Sollod is an interdisciplinary artist and planner whose practice includes large-scale, site-specific public art, multimedia temporary installations, artist books, and photography. She has also been involved in a number of urban art programs, including terms with the Seattle Arts Commission and the Colorado Council of Arts as executive director. Her public artworks have been placed in the South Lake Union neighborhood (9.25, 9.26), as well as in Olympia, Bellingham, Portland, and San Jose.

Spafford, Michael C. (b. 1935) Michael Spafford was born in Palm Springs, California, and received his BA at Pomona College in 1959. He earned an MA in art history from Harvard University a year later. Spafford then spent three years painting and exhibiting in Mexico City. From 1965 to 1966 he studied under a Louis Comfort Tiffany Foundation grant, followed by two Prix de Rome Fellowships during the period of 1967 through 1969. The latter experiences intensified his interest in Greco-Roman mythology, which became the visual framework for his art, dealing mostly with themes of conflict, conquest, and origin. Spafford moved to Seattle in 1963 and taught painting and drawing at the University of Washington, where he is now professor emeritus. A noted painter and printmaker, Michael Spafford has exhibited widely throughout his career. His only work in a Seattle public place is his monumental *Tumbling Figure: Five Stages* (5.7).

Speidel, Julie (b. 1941) Julie Speidel was born in Seattle and is a graduate of the University of Washington (BA, 1959). She subsequently spent a year studying in Grenoble, France, (1961) and then at the Cornish School in Seattle (1963). She is largely a self-taught sculptor whose works are collected widely throughout the region, and she has exhibited principally in the western United States and in New York City. The forms of her abstract sculptures often arise from site-specific research and are influenced by prehistoric and early Chinese Buddhist works, Pacific Northwest Native American carvings, and sources from travels to many foreign locales. Although best known for her bronze sculptures, Speidel also works in marble, cast glass, and stone. A recent work in the South Lake Union neighborhood is stainless steel (7.10). (See also 5.17, 5.22, and 9.3.)

Sperry, Ann (1934–2008) Ann Sperry was a New York–based sculptor who was born in the Bronx, New York. She received a BA in 1955 from Sarah Lawrence College, where she studied with William Rubin and learned welding from abstract sculptor Theodore Roszak. Sperry exhibited her work in one-person and group exhibitions in New York, Seattle, and Paris, as well as in Israel and Italy. Her sculptures are included in the collections of the Storm King Art Center, the Skirball Culture Center in Los Angeles, the Rose Art Museum at Brandeis University, and the Tel Aviv Museum of Art, among others. *Seattle Garden* (6.19) is Sperry's only public work in the Northwest. Other large site-specific Sperry sculptures were installed throughout the United States, including at the University of Rhode Island, and in Boston and Aspen, Colorado.

Sperry, Robert (1927–98) Robert Sperry was born in Bushnell, Illinois, and received his art education at the Art Institute of Chicago (BFA, 1953) and the University of Washington (MFA, 1955). Sperry taught ceramics at the University of Washington and was chairman of its ceramics department from 1960 until his retirement in 1982. After retiring, Sperry devoted his time to his art, which has been included in exhibitions and collections throughout the United States and in Europe and Japan. Sperry was considered one of the region's most influential and respected ceramic artists, and his two works in downtown Seattle illustrate his unique, creative approach to that medium (5.3, 6.1, 6.3). In 1984 he was awarded the Gold Medal of the International Society of Ceramics.

Stahly, François (1911–2006) François Stahly was born in Constance, Germany, and began studying art during his youth in Switzerland. In 1931 he moved to France, where he spent the rest of his career. Stahly's first public sculpture was created for the 1937 World's Fair in Paris, six years after he had completed his studies with French sculptor Aristide Maillol. After lecturing at Harvard and teaching at the University of California, Berkeley,

Stahly came to Seattle in 1961 as a visiting professor at the University of Washington and then was an artist in residence at Stanford University (1964–65). Stahly's stay in Seattle reportedly had a great impact on him. As is evident in his sculpture at the Seattle Center (8.25), he was interested in vertically oriented works before his Seattle stay, and the totem poles he saw in the Pacific Northwest further inspired him to create other vertical sculptures in bronze and stone.

Steinbrueck, Victor (1911–85) Born in Mandan, North Dakota, in 1911, Victor Steinbrueck and his family came to Seattle two years later. He began college studies at the University of Washington when he was only sixteen and graduated with a degree in architecture. He subsequently had a successful career as an architect and a professor of architecture at the university, serving many years as chairman of the School of Architecture. In addition to teaching, Steinbrueck published numerous articles and sketchbooks, including popular books on the Pike Place Market and Seattle.

Fighting to save the Pike Place Market was one of many civic causes in which Steinbrueck was actively involved. He also had an influential role in promoting the renaissance of Pioneer Square and the creation of Gas Works Park. In addition to Steinbrueck Park near the Pike Place Market (6.21), he also designed Louisa Boren Viewpoint on Capitol Hill, Betty Bowen Memorial Viewpoint on Queen Anne Hill, and helped design Seattle's Space Needle.

Stumer, Mildred (1898–1997) Olympia native Mildred Stumer received her art education at the California School of Fine Arts and the Art Students League in New York. She came to Seattle in 1923 and opened a studio and exhibited her work, but she spent only a few years here before leaving to work and study in New York and Paris. In the 1930s, she returned to her roots in Olympia (her father, Henry Stumer, was an early Olympia resident and the original developer of the Alderbrook Inn on Hood Canal). Stumer continued sculpting and had a terra-cotta bust included in a 1934 Seattle Art Museum exhibit. Her only work in a Seattle public place is an architectural relief (4.1).

Sze, Sarah (b. 1969) Born in Boston and based in New York, artist Sarah Sze is known for her elaborate sculptures and installations that are composed of everyday objects. *An Equal and Opposite Reaction* at Seattle's McCaw Hall is a well-known example of her work (8.30). Sze earned a BA from Yale University in 1991 and an MFA from New York's School of Visual Arts in 1997. Six years later she was awarded a MacArthur Foundation Fellowship. She has exhibited in museums and group exhibitions worldwide, and her works are in the collections of many prominent museums, including the Museum of Modern Art, the Guggenheim Museum, and the Whitney Museum of American Art in New York; Chicago's Museum of Contemporary Art; and the Museum of Modern Art in Los Angeles. Her works in public places include those at Massachusetts Institute of Technology in Cambridge, the Walker Art Center in Minneapolis, and the High Line and Ninety-Sixth Street Station of the Second Avenue Subway Line in New York City.

Taglang, Hugo (1874–1944) Hugo Taglang was born in Vienna, Austria, and studied art in Hamburg, Germany, then at the Vienna K. K. Academy of Arts. He spent most of his life in Austria, and his three-dimensional sculptures and medallions can be seen throughout that country. Taglang's only work on display in Seattle is the medallion relief of D. E. Skinner in the Rainier Concourse (6.7).

Takamori, Akio (1950–2017) Akio Takamori was born in Nobeoka, Japan in 1950 and graduated from Tokyo's Musashino Art University in 1971. He then apprenticed to a master folk potter in the village of Koishiwara and worked in industrial pottery for a few years. He came to the United States in 1974 to study at the Kansas City Art Institute where he earned a BFA in 1976. In 1978 he earned an MFA from the New York State College of Ceramics at

Alfred University. Takamori moved to Seattle in 1993 to teach ceramics at the University of Washington and remained a member of the art faculty until retiring in 2014. He earned an international reputation as an innovative ceramic sculptor, and his work is included in the collections of many prominent museums, including the Victoria and Albert Museum in London, the Museum of Arts and Design in New York City, the Seattle Art Museum, the Nelson-Atkins Museum of Art in Kansas City, and the Los Angeles County Museum of Art (7.16).

Taylor, Doug (b. 1947) Sculptor Doug Taylor was born in Chilliwack, British Columbia. In 1981 he earned a BA in visual arts from the Emily Carr University of Art and Design in Vancouver. A resident of that city, Taylor specializes in large kinetic sculptures that include wind-, water-, and solar-powered features and often have whimsical folk art elements and figures from nature. Taylor has several commissioned public works in British Columbia. His only work in this country is *Birdsong Listening Station* at the Seattle Center (8.12).

Teeple, Robert (b. 1941) A Detroit native, Seattle artist Robert Teeple spent two years studying at the University of New Mexico and three years studying at the Museum Art School at the Portland Oregon Art Museum. During his career he has created and exhibited installations and sculptures, primarily in Seattle and Portland, and is best known for electronic animations in which thousands of LEDs create rapidly moving figures, schematics, and words, including random poetry. His *Electric Lascaux* in Seattle Metro's University Street station is a well-known example (6.11).

Tennis, Whiting (b. 1959) Seattle resident Whiting Tennis was born in Hampton, Virginia. He attended the College of William and Mary (1979–81) before attending the University of Washington where he earned a BFA in 1984. His UW experiences included independent study with Jacob Lawrence. Tennis is a well-regarded painter and sculptor whose work has been included in solo and group exhibits in Seattle and elsewhere on the West Coast, as well as in New York, Chicago, and Boston. His works are included in the Seattle, Tacoma, and Portland Art Museums. Seattle's downtown public places include both a Whiting Tennis painting (1.15) and a sculpture (9.16).

Tomkins, Margaret (1916–2002) Margaret Tomkins was born in Los Angeles and earned both a BA (1938) and an MFA (1939) from the University of Southern California. In 1939 she moved to Seattle to become an assistant professor of art at the University of Washington and soon joined the group of Northwest School artists, such as Mark Tobey, Morris Graves, Kenneth Callahan, and Guy Anderson, as they all developed their individual artistic styles. The first of her many solo exhibitions was held at the Seattle Art Museum in 1941, and her works were exhibited widely during her long career. Tomkins's paintings are included in the collections of both the Whitney Museum of American Art and the Metropolitan Museum of Art in New York and the Art Institute of Chicago.

Tsutakawa, George (1910–97) George Tsutakawa was born in Seattle and received much of his precollege education in Japan. He graduated from the University of Washington in 1937, where he earned a BA and an MFA. He was a member of the University of Washington art faculty from 1945 to 1980 and was subsequently an emeritus professor. A recognized sculptor and painter, Tsutakawa was an important member of the Pacific Northwest art community all of his adult life. He was the subject of numerous solo exhibitions, and his works were included in group exhibitions throughout the Pacific Northwest as well as in New York, Washington, DC, and Japan. He is best known for his commissioned fountain-sculptures in public places—eleven of which are in Seattle—throughout the United States and in Canada and Japan. He is one of the most widely represented artists in Seattle's public places. (1.21, 2.1, 3.26, 5.10, 5.19, 5.20, 5.23, 6.3)

Tsutakawa, Gerard (b. 1947) Seattle-born Gerard Tsutakawa is the son of George Tsutakawa. He watched his father work with bronze beginning in the late 1950s, became his assistant in 1970, and worked on all of George Tsutakawa's commissions from then on. Gerard Tsutakawa began his own sculpting in 1979 and exhibits regularly in Seattle. His abstract expressionist bronze sculptures can be seen throughout Seattle, the Northwest, and elsewhere in the United States. His best-known work may be *The Mitt* outside of Safeco Field. (1.27). (See also 1.22, 6.18, and 8.23)

Tuazon, Oscar (b. 1975) Oscar Tuazon is a Seattle-born, Los Angeles–based artist, who works in sculpture, architecture, and mixed media. He is a graduate of the Cooper Union (BFA, 1990). Tuazon first learned sculpture from Suquamish carvers Larry Ahvakana and Ed Carriere, but his professional career began in Italy at the studio of architect and artist Vito Acconci, after which he spent a number of years creating art in Paris. Oscar Tuazon's work has been shown in solo and museum exhibitions in this country as well as in Switzerland, France, Germany, and England. Tuazon is one of the artists commissioned to create sculpture for Seattle's redeveloped waterfront ("Six Artworks Scheduled for Installation," chapter 2).

Turner, Bart (b. 1968) Bart Turner is a Seattle-based blacksmith and artist who specializes in architectural glass and metal fabrication. Born in Fort Worth, Texas, he moved to Seattle in 1993, apprenticed for several years in a glass studio, and in 1999 founded Flying Anvil Studio. Turner has created a wide range of commercial and residential works and has shown his works in several local galleries and the Pratt Fine Arts Center. He has also collaborated with a number of artists and created public artworks in the Pacific Northwest. His only work in a Seattle downtown public place is *Old Time Jazz Scene* (7.9).

Turner, Richard (b. 1943) Artist and museum curator Richard Turner was born in Kansas City, Missouri, and holds a BFA from Antioch College (1968) and an

MFA in studio art from the University of Michigan (1970). Turner has spent most of his career teaching art history and studio art at Chapman University (where he is now an emeritus professor) and also served for many years as director and curator of the university's Guggenheim Gallery. Much of Turner's art, from stone sculptures to installations, is influenced by many years of studying and traveling throughout Asia and India. Since 1980 he has worked, both independently and as part of artist-architect collaborations, on a wide range of public art projects. He was a member of the team that created art for the Seattle Justice Center and the Municipal Court Building in downtown Seattle (5.11, 5.12).

Ushio, Keizo (b. 1951) Keizo Ushio was born in Fuku-saki, Japan, and is a 1976 graduate of the Kyoto City University of Arts. In 1979 his sculpture won first prize at a major Hakone Open-Air Museum exhibition, and he used that money to tour Europe and study sculpture. Ushio has received considerable recognition, including from the international mathematics community, for his unique stone sculptures that are manipulations of the Möbius band (2.7). The artist has exhibited around the world, and his work is included in public and private collections throughout Japan and Europe, as well as in the United States, Mexico, Israel, New Zealand, and Australia. Keizo Ushio lives and works in Himeji, Japan.

van Bruggen, Coosje (1942–2009) Coosje van Bruggen was born in Groningen in the Netherlands and studied art history at the University of Groningen. From 1967 to 1971, she was employed by the Stedelijk Museum in Amsterdam, where she worked with environmental artists and members of the Dutch avant-garde, and then taught at the Academy for Art and Industries in Enschede. In 1978 Van Bruggen moved with her husband, sculptor Claes Oldenburg, to New York and became an American citizen in 1993. The team of Oldenburg and Van Bruggen worked together for thirty years creating monumental sculptures, and Van Bruggen and her husband shared numerous awards for their work. One of their

sculptures, *Typewriter Eraser, Scale X*, stands at the Seattle Center (8.33). For many years Van Bruggen also worked as well-regarded critic and curator and wrote a number of books and essays on contemporary art and artists.

Venet, Bernar (b. 1941) Born in the Alpes-de-Haute-Provence, France, conceptual artist Bernar Venet is largely self-taught and has lived and worked in New York since 1966. He is best known for his *Indeterminate Lines* sculptures, which consist of straight lines, arcs, and angles that may be freestanding or may be jutting out of gallery walls. Venet sculptures have been exhibited and widely collected around the world and are included in the collections of many museums, including the Guggenheim Museum in New York; the Museum of Contemporary Art, Los Angeles; and the Musée National d'Art Moderne in Paris. Venet's only work in a Seattle public place is *11 Straight Lines* (3.31).

Vitiello, Stephen (b. 1964) Stephen Vitiello is a native of New York City and a graduate of the State University of New York at Purchase (BA, literature, 1986). He is an electronic musician (and former punk guitarist) and sound artist who began working with sound as an artistic medium around 1990. He has since created numerous sound art installations and has performed and exhibited throughout New York City, as well as in Paris, London, and Sydney. In 2013 Vitiello's work was featured in the exhibition *Sounding* at New York's Museum of Modern Art, which was the first survey of sound art at a major US museum. Sound will be a major component of the artist's commissioned artwork for Seattle's redeveloped waterfront ("Six Artworks Scheduled for Installation," chapter 2). Vitiello is currently a professor in the department of Kinetic Imaging at Virginia Commonwealth University.

Wagner, Catherine (b. 1953) California conceptual artist Catherine Wagner was born in San Francisco and holds both a BA (1975) and an MA from San Francisco State University. Wagner has created a number of large-scale, site-specific artworks using a variety of mediums, which often incorporate photographs or electronic imagery. In addition to *Atmospheric Flurry* in Seattle (9.24), Wagner has installed works throughout California as well as in Kyoto, Japan. She has been the subject of solo exhibits and group exhibitions throughout the United States and internationally. Museums that have her works in their collections include the Museum of Modern Art and the Whitney Museum of American Art in New York, the Los Angeles County Museum of Art, and the San Francisco Museum of Modern Art. Since 1979 Wagner has been a professor of studio art at Mills College, where she is now dean of the Fine Arts division.

Walker, Jamie (b. 1958) Jamie Walker was born in Houston and graduated from the University of Washington in 1981 with a BS in history and a BFA in ceramics. In 1983 he earned an MFA from the Rhode Island School of Design. Walker came to Seattle in 1989 to teach art at the University of Washington and has been there ever since, becoming director of its School of Art in 2014. Jamie Walker is predominantly a ceramic artist, and his art has been exhibited in numerous solo and group exhibitions throughout the United States and is included in the collections of many museums, including the Seattle Art Museum, UW's Henry Art Gallery, Tacoma's Museum of Glass, and the Racine Art Museum in Wisconsin. His best-known creations in Seattle are three outdoor sculptures in the South Lake Union neighborhood (9.21).

Warsinske, Norman (1929–2007) Born in Wichita, Kansas, Norman Warsinske was a well-known interior designer and sculptor in Seattle. He received a BA in interior design and sculpture at the University of Washington in 1958. Prior to that he received a BA in journalism at the University of Montana (1949) and studied jewelry design at the Kunstwerkschule in Darmstadt, Germany (1953). His only work in a Seattle public place is in the lobby of the IBM Building in downtown Seattle (5.24).

Washington, James W. Jr. (1909–2000) Born in Gloster, Mississippi, James W. Washington Jr. lived and worked in Seattle throughout his artistic career, which began in the mid-1940s as a painter when he studied locally with Mark Tobey, Glen Alps, and Harry I. Freund. In 1956 he began sculpting, influenced by an earlier trip to Mexico and exposure to primitive Mexican sculptures. Washington exhibited extensively throughout the United States and his stone sculptures—usually granite and replete with religious and personal symbolism—can be seen in several public places in Seattle, including three in downtown Seattle (5.19, 6.3, 8.27).

Webb, Dan (b. 1965) Dan Webb was born in East Lansing, Michigan, and raised in Alaska but is a longtime Seattle resident and graduate of the Cornish College of the Arts (BFA, 1991). Although his works at the Pike Place Market are metal (6.20) and he has worked with other sculptural mediums, Webb is best known as a master wood-carver who creates intricate, finely detailed sculptures. His artworks have been widely exhibited in Seattle and Portland, and the self-taught carver was the subject of a 2014 solo exhibition at the Bellevue Arts Museum.

Webber, Deloss (b. 1951) Kirkland resident Deloss Webber was born in Fort Dodge, Iowa. He is perhaps best known for his sculptures of stones that are partially encased in intricately wrapped weavings of cane, bamboo, and reed. He learned weaving techniques from his mother and was further influenced by forms of weaving through this country and the world, including his observations growing up in North Africa and Spain. Webber has also worked in a number of other sculpture mediums. His sculptures in the lobby of the 1700 Seventh Avenue Building are solid wooden spheres accentuated with inlaid bamboo strips (6.25).

Wehn, James (1883–1973) James Wehn was born in Indianapolis and came to Washington Territory in 1889. His formal art education was limited to part-time study at the Seattle Art League in the 1890s, an apprenticeship in Chicago with sculptor August

Hebert, and work at his father's foundry in Seattle. Wehn started his own studio at the turn of the century and spent the rest of his life focusing on sculpture. In 1919 he started the University of Washington's Sculpture Department and taught at the university until 1924. After that Wehn sculpted full-time from his Seattle studio. The artist is best known for his sculptures of Chief Seattle (1.3, 7.18), and he designed the City of Seattle seal, which includes a profile of Chief Seattle. Wehn also sculpted a number of bronze plaques of prominent people that can be seen in Seattle's public places (6.7).

Weiss, Dick (b. 1946) Dick Weiss is a native of Everett, Washington, whose career as a glass artist started in 1976, eight years after graduating from Yale University with a BA in psychology. While working as a railroad switchman in Everett, he took an evening class in stained glass art, and his interest soon blossomed into a full-time career. He has exhibited regularly in Seattle, where he now lives, and his works are included in many government and private art collections, including those of the Corning Museum of Glass in New York and the Victoria and Albert Museum in London. A large stained-glass mural by Dick Weiss can be seen at the Fifth Avenue parking garage across from the Seattle Center (8.32).

Wesselmann, Tom (1931–2004) New York artist Tom Wesselmann was born in Cincinnati, Ohio, and received his college education at Hiram College, in Hiram, Ohio, and at the University of Cincinnati, where he received a BA in psychology in 1956. He subsequently studied at the Art Academy of Cincinnati (1954–56) and the Cooper Union in New York City (1956–59). Wesselmann was a leading American pop artist and starting in 1961 exhibited extensively throughout the United States, Canada, and Europe in individual and group shows. His paintings are included in major museums and collections throughout the world. Although his place in art history is as a painter, Wesselmann created many sculptures. One of his largest is *Seattle Tulip*, a commissioned work in downtown Seattle (4.7).

Whipple, Bill (b. 1947) A native of Worcester, Massachusetts, Bill Whipple moved to Seattle in 1968 and earned a BFA in painting from the University of Washington in 1970. He has been exhibiting his whimsical, skillfully crafted sculptures in Seattle since 1975, including in group exhibits at the Henry Gallery. Collections containing his artwork include those of the City of Seattle, King County, Washington State, and the Seattle Art Museum. Bill Whipple has executed several commissioned works in the Pacific Northwest, including his *Question Mark Clock* at the corner of Fifth Avenue and Pine Street in downtown Seattle (6.23).

Whitesavage & Lyle Since 1991 Jean Whitesavage and Nick Lyle have been designing and fabricating steel sculpture and architectural ironwork, often in collaboration with one another, but also separately. Many examples of their site-specific work can be seen in Seattle public places, the largest of which graces the front of the King Street Center building (1.11). Jean Whitesavage was born in 1960 in Philadelphia. In 1982 she earned a BFA in painting from the Tyler School of Art in Philadelphia and in 1990 earned an MFA degree in sculpture from the New York State College of Ceramics at Alfred University. Nick Lyle was born in 1958 in New York City and is a 1981 graduate of Williams College (BA, history of ideas). He subsequently studied drawing, painting, and glassblowing and apprenticed with a stonemason, blacksmith, cabinetmaker, and sculptor. The artist duo lives and works on Whidbey Island, Washington.

Wickline, Pat (b.1964) Pat Wickline is a Bellingham-based sculptor who was born in Dallas, Texas, and came to the Pacific Northwest in 1978. He is a 1992 graduate of Western Washington University (MS, anthropology). Wickline creates wire artworks that are often portraits of people, but he has also created a number of three-dimensional sculptures of two of his favorite subjects, squid and octopuses. His only public artwork in the city is his massive *Seattle Squid*, at Pike Place Market (6.20).

Wiegman, Clark (b.1960) A native of Fort Dodge, Iowa, Clark Wiegman graduated from Macalester College in 1983 (BA, history and art). He has worked as an artist in Seattle since 1985 and has created art installations and temporary works that have been featured in many group shows throughout the United States. Wiegman has also created numerous site-specific artworks in a variety of mediums for public places throughout western Washington as well as locations in Oregon, Minnesota, Texas, and Washington, DC. *Tree of Life* is his most recent work in a Seattle public place (6.22).

Will, Bill (b. 1951) Portland-based sculptor Bill Will is a graduate of Washington State University (BA, fine arts, 1973) whose works can be seen in public places throughout Oregon and Washington and in several other locations in the United States. Since 1979 he has regularly exhibited his work in one person shows and group exhibitions, primarily in Portland, Oregon, and has completed numerous public art commissions. Will has also been a member of several artist-design team collaborations, primarily on the West Coast. He was a member of the faculty of the Oregon College of Art and Craft from 1996 until 2016. In 2001 Bill Will created *4 (Where shall I go ahead?)* in downtown Seattle (1.13).

Wu, Jason (Hai Ying) (b. 1962) Jason (Hai Ying) Wu was born in China and earned a degree in sculpture from the Sichuan Fine Arts Institute. Wu spent several years as the staff sculptor for the city of Chengdu, where he created a number of socialist realist sculptures. After participating in the 1989 Tiananmen Square protests, Wu emigrated to the United States and eventually enrolled in the University of Washington where he earned an MFA. His master's thesis was a sculpture (now located at Tacoma's Foss Waterway Seaport) that memorializes nineteenth-century Chinese workers who built American railroads. One of Jason Wu's best-known works is Seattle's *Fallen Firefighters Memorial* in Pioneer Square (1.6). Wu has since created other sculptures that honor firefighters in the United States as well as several other works in western Washington

and Oregon. Wu now lives in Everett, Washington, and Chengdu, China.

Yamamoto, Lynne (b. 1961) Born in Honolulu, Lynne Yamamoto is a graduate of the Evergreen State College (BA, art, 1983) and of New York University (MFA, 1991). She is currently an art professor at Smith College. Yamamoto's art has been included in solo and group exhibitions throughout the US, including at the Whitney Museum of American Art, as well as in Europe and Taiwan. Her works are included in the collections of numerous museums, including the Museum of Modern Art, Whitney Museum of American Art, and Los Angeles Museum of Contemporary Art. Lynne Yamamoto's only commissioned public artwork to date is her sculpture *Of Memory* at the Seattle Public Library (5.21).

Yung, Rene A native of Hong Kong, Rene Yung is a San Francisco–based artist, graphic designer, and writer who graduated from Stanford University in 1974 (BA, art). Since 1980 Yung has been the founding principal of Rene Yung Communications Design, Inc. She has been exhibiting her work in solo and group exhibitions, primarily in California, since 1987, and since 1993 she has been engaged in a number of interdisciplinary civil engagement and public art projects. *Wellspring*, her multipart creation at the International District branch library (1.23) is her only work in a Seattle public place. Yung is currently on the faculty of the Interdisciplinary Studies Department at City College in San Francisco.

Zach, Jan (1914–86) Born in Slany, Czechoslovakia, Jan Zach received his artistic education at the Superior School of Industrial Arts and the Academy of Fine Arts, both in Prague. He first came to the United States in 1938 to work at his country's pavilion at the New York World's Fair. After Germany's occupation of Czechoslovakia in 1939, Zach remained in New York. In 1941 he moved to Brazil, where he taught and sculpted for eleven years. He taught sculpture at the Banff School of Fine Arts in Alberta, Canada (1951–53), and then settled in Victoria, British Columbia, where he opened a school of painting and sculpture. In 1958 he became head of the Sculpture Department at the University of Oregon, where he remained until his retirement in 1980. Zach's works are included in public and private collections in the United States, Canada, and Brazil. (4.12)

Ziegler, Mel (b. 1956) Mel Ziegler was born in Campbelltown, Pennsylvania, and earned a BFA from the Kansas City Art Institute (1978) and an MFA from the California Institute of the Arts (1982). He attended both institutions with fellow artist Kate Ericson and worked and exhibited with her, primarily in New York, from 1980 until her death in 1995. Ziegler collaborated with Ericson on designs for Metro's Pioneer Square Station in downtown Seattle (1.1). Ziegler has placed a number of public artworks in the United States and has exhibited nationally and internationally. His work is included in many public and private collections, including those of the Whitney Museum of American Art in New York City, the Albright-Knox Art Gallery in Buffalo, the Los Angeles County Museum of Art, and the Museum of Fine Arts in Houston. Mel Ziegler now lives and works in Nashville, Tennessee, where he is an art professor at Vanderbilt University.

Zoccola, Susan (b. 1960) Seattle artist Susan Zoccola was born in Spokane, Washington, and attended the University of Washington from 1979 to 1982 and studied at the San Francisco Art Institute from 1986 to 1988. She has been a full-time studio and public works artist in Seattle for over twenty-five years. In 2003 Zoccola collaborated with John Fleming to create *Grass Blades* at the Seattle Center (8.34). She later created a number of public artworks in the region, including within Seattle and at Sea-Tac Airport. For many years Zoccola has exhibited her studio work in Seattle and elsewhere in the United States.

SOURCES AND SUGGESTED READING

Material for this book was compiled from far too many sources to list here. In addition to interviews with many artists and others involved in the arts and reviewing many websites related to the artists and their works, invaluable information was obtained from the files of the Seattle Office of Arts & Culture, 4Culture, the Washington State Arts Commission, the Seattle Art Museum, the Museum of History & Industry (MOHAI), the Seattle Public Library, the King County Library, and the University of Washington libraries. Articles from HistoryLink.org and the *Seattle Times*, the *Seattle Post-Intelligencer*, and the *New York Times* were additional important sources of information. Following is a collection of resources that readers may wish to consult for more detailed information about local history, artists, and art in Seattle public places.

WEBSITES

Seattle Office of Arts & Culture: www.seattle.gov/arts/
   permanently-sited
4Culture: https://www.4culture.org/public-art
Vulcan Real Estate: www.vulcanrealestate.com/stewardship
   .html#public-art

BOOKS

Ament, Deloris Tarzan. *Iridescent Light: The Emergence of Northwest Art*. Seattle: University of Washington Press, 2002.
———. 600 Moons: *Fifty Years of Philip McCracken's Art*. La Conner, WA: Museum of Northwest Art, 2004.
Arnason, H. H., and Elizabeth C. Mansfield. *History of Modern Art*, 7th ed. Englewood Cliffs, NJ: Prentice-Hall, 2012.
Averill, Lloyd J., and Daphne K. Morris. *Northwest Coast Native and Native-Style Art: A Guidebook for Western Washington*. Seattle: University of Washington Press, 1995.
Blonsten, Gary. *William Morris: Artifacts/Glass*. New York: Abbeville Press Publishers, 1996.
Calas, Nicholas, and Elena Calas. *Icons and Images of the Sixties*. New York: E. P. Dutton, 1971.

9.21 *Toto*, Jamie Walker

Campbell, R. M. *Stirring Up Seattle: Allied Arts in the Civic Landscape*. Seattle: University of Washington Press, 2014.

Celant, Germano. *Michael Heizer*. Milan: Fondazione Prado, 1997.

Cooke, Lynne, Michael Govan, and Mark Taylor. *Richard Serra: Torqued Ellipses*. New York: Dia Center for the Arts, 1997.

Corrin, Lisa G., Mimi Gardner Gates, Michael Manfredi, Chris Rogers, Marion Weiss. *Olympic Sculpture Park*. Seattle: Seattle Art Museum, 2007.

Etrog, Sorel. *Sorel Etrog: Recent Works*. Toronto: Marlborough Godard, 1976.

Farr, Sheila. *Fay Jones*. Seattle: Grover/Thurston Gallery and Laura Russo Gallery in association with the University of Washington Press, 2000.

Garfield, Viola E. *The Seattle Totem Pole*. Seattle: University of Washington Press, 1980.

Guenther, Bruce. *Fifty Northwest Artists*. San Francisco: Chronicle Books, 1983.

Herrera, Hayden. *Listening to Stone: The Art and Life of Isamu Noguchi*. New York: Farrar, Straus and Giroux, 2015.

Holm, Bill. *Spirit and Ancestor: A Century of Northwest Coast Indian Art at the Burke Museum*. Thomas Burke Memorial Washington State Museum Monograph no. 4. Seattle: University of Washington Press, 1987.

Hunter, Sam. *Tony Smith: Ten Elements and Throwback*. New York: Pace Gallery, 1979.

Johnson, Michael R. *Kenneth Callahan: Universal Voyage*. Seattle: University of Washington Press, 1973

Kingsbury, Martha. *George Tsutakawa*. Seattle: University of Washington Press, 1990.

Kraus, Rosalind. *Beverly Pepper: Sculpture in Place*. New York: Abbeville Press, 1986.

Lew, William W., *Minidoka Revisited: The Paintings of Roger Shimomura*. Clemson, SC: Lee Gallery, Clemson University, 2005

Mitchinson, David, ed. *Henry Moore Sculpture*. New York: Arthur A. Bartley, 1988.

Monte, James K., *Mark di Suvero*. New York: Whitney Museum of American Art, 1975.

Noguchi, Isamu. *A Sculptor's World*. New York: Harper and Row, 1968.

Paine, Roxy. *Roxy Paine: Bluff*. New York: Public Art Fund, 2002.

Poyner, Fred F., IV. *The First Sculptor of Seattle: The Life and Art of James A. Wehn*. North Charleston, SC: CreateSpace Independent Publishing Platform, 2014

———. *Seattle Public Sculptors: Twelve Makers of Monuments, Memorials, and Statuary, 1909–1962*. Jefferson, NC: McFarland, 2017

Reed, Gervais. *Art in Seattle's Public Places: Five Urban Walking Tours*. With Jo Nilsson. Seattle: Seattle Public Library, 1977.

Reynolds, Donald Martin. *Monuments and Masterpieces: Histories and Views of Public Sculpture in New York City*. New York: Thames and Hudson, 1988.

Riedy, James L., *Chicago Sculpture*. Urbana: University of Illinois Press, 1981.

Rosenthal, Mark, and Richard Marshall. *Jonathan Borofsky*. New York: Harry N. Abrams, 1984.

Sale, Roger. *Seattle, Past to Present*. Seattle: University of Washington Press, 1976.

Sander, Irving. *Antonakos*. New York: Hudson Hills Press, 1999.

Thrush, Coll. *Native Seattle: Histories from the Crossing Over Place*. 2nd ed. Seattle: University of Washington Press, 2017.

Wehr, Wesley. *The Eighth Lively Art*. Seattle: University of Washington Press, 2000.

Wheat, Ellen Harkins. *Jacob Lawrence, American Painter*. Seattle: Seattle Art Museum, 1986.

ARTICLES

Berkson, Bill, "Ronald Bladen: Sculpture and Where We Stand," *Art & Literature* 12 (Spring 1967).

Friedman, N. A., and C. H. Sequin. "Keizo Ushio's Sculptures, Split Tori and Möbius Bands." *Journal of Mathematics and the Arts* 1, no. 1 (March 2007): 47–57.

Gruen, John, "George Rickey, Choreography of Steel." *Architectural Digest*, June 1988.

Hackett, "James Washington: Secrets in Stone." *American Artist*, November 1977.

Hess, Thomas B. "Breakthrough with Tanks" (Alexander Liberman). *New York Magazine*, June 6, 1977, 70–72,

———. "Looking Back in Search of the Future: Some Thoughts on the Long Local History of Public Art." *PASSAGE* (Seattle and King County Arts Commissions), Spring/Summer 1987, 4–13.

Reed, Gervais. "George Tsutakawa: A Conversation on Life and Fountains." *Journal of Ethnic Studies* 4, no. 1 (1976): 1–36.

Rose, Barbara. "A Monumental Vision" (Beverly Pepper). *Vogue*, December 1987, 484–535.

Rose, Kenneth. "Booze and News in 1924: Prohibition in Seattle" (Mark A. Mathews). *PORTAGE* (Historical Society of Seattle and King County), Winter 1984, 16–22.

ACKNOWLEDGMENTS

OVER THE YEARS IT TOOK to create and publish this book, many individuals provided their thoughts, support, knowledge, and editing talents. There are too many to name here, but all can rest assured that their support and assistance were gratefully received and that without them the project would not have succeeded. Special thanks go to Mike Repass, an avid book fan whose generous grant made publication possible.

Leonard Garfield, Greg Kucera, Richard Andrews, and Dennis Anderson improved the "Historical Overview" and provided other helpful thoughts and edits. Over the years a number of people at Seattle's Office of Arts & Culture and King County's 4Culture have been enthusiastic and helpful. Those to whom I am grateful include Ruri Yampolski, Cath Brunner, Joan Peterson, Sandy Esene, Jason Huff, Esther Luttikhuisen, and Jordan Howland.

Miguel Edwards undertook the exhausting task of photographing more than 300 artworks, then culling his vast collection of shots to find the best ones. Travis Monroe, Jeremy Béliveau, Mike Skoptsov, and Rich Birmingham provided skillful assistance in the later stages of the photographic process.

Research, photographs, money, and advice will not by themselves create a good book. The best require skilled editors and designers, and special thanks go to many at the University of Washington Press, including Margaret Sullivan, Rebecca Brinbury, and Heidi Smets. I also want to recognize the work of Joeth Zucco, whose outstanding editing skills significantly improved the manuscript.

Many thanks to Arlene Van Woert, whose technical assistance at the outset allowed the project to proceed with some sense of order; to Betsy Fulwiler for her invaluable administrative support; and to Kimberly and Brendan Rupp for their help on many occasions in finding just the right word or phrase. And gone, but not forgotten for their influence and support, are John and Libby Rupp, Marshall and Helen Hatch, Anne Gould Hauberg, Maxine Cushing Gray, and Lee Soper.

Art in Seattle's Public Spaces is dedicated to Susan Rupp and Corinna Jill, but it is appropriate to express here the profound thanks, from the author and photographer, for the love and support of those two ever-patient spouses.

James M. Rupp
Seattle, Washington

6.20 *Short Cut 7* (part), Dan Webb

INDEX

Note: Artwork and artist entries include the relevant artwork numbers after the page numbers.

3.15 *Seattle Cloud Cover*, Teresita Fernández (Photo by Richard J. Birmingham)

4.11 *New Archetypes,* Anne and Patrick Poirier